Ethnic Diversity in Eastern Africa

Opportunities and Challenges

Edited by

Kimani Njogu
Kabiri Ngeta
Mary Wanjau

TWAWEZA
COMMUNICATIONS
"Working Towards a Better World"

Published in 2009 by:
Twaweza Communications Ltd.
P.O. Box 66872 - 00800 Westlands
Twaweza House, Parklands Road
Mpesi Lane, Nairobi Kenya
website: www.twawezacommunications.org
Tel: +(254) 020 375 2009
Fax: +(254) 020 375 3941

Design and Layout by Catherine Bosire
Cover design by Kolbe Press

With the support of The Rockefeller Foundation

ISBN: 9966-7244-8-6

Printed by Kolbe Press, P.O. Box 468 - 00217 Limuru, Kenya

Content

Acknowledgements

The discourses of solidarity, as encapsulated in nationalism and ethnicity, and their role in shaping events in Africa have continued to be of interest to scholars of politics and development. In most of Africa, the discursive energies harnessed during the struggle for independence have dissipated and the disillusionment with the performance of the state, seen as a venal predator, and declining economic circumstances in many countries have challenged national identity as a site of belonging. There is also the phenomenon of 'political ethnicity' (at times referred to as 'tribalism') which manifests itself most profoundly as citizens compete for power and resources. The genocidal tragedies of Burundi and Rwanda epitomize the devastating capability of ethnic polarization. But is there a way in which ethnic diversity can be harnessed to become a resource for political, economic, social, and cultural development? Through inter-ethnic solidarity and enhanced citizen participation in national affairs, accountable institutions of governance can be entrenched as society puts pressure on those who wield power. Furthermore, the accumulated knowledge on climate change and environmental protection within ethnic groups could be shared and made more sustainable. Creativity could be enhanced as communities come together and exchange learning and experiences.

This book is a collection of important and thought provoking papers presented at the *Ethnic Diversity in Eastern Africa: Opportunities and Challenges* conference which was held on 17th and 18th October 2009. The conference was organized by Africa Health and Development International (AHADI) with the support of Rockefeller Foundation. It brought together participants from academic and civil society institutions in Kenya, Tanzania, Uganda, Ghana, Burundi and Rwanda with the aim to create a space for candid discussions on ethnicity as an identity and ways in which diversity can be made a viable resource for political, economic and social well-being.

We are immensely grateful to the Managing Director, Dr. James Nyoro, and the staff of the Rockefeller Foundation Office of Eastern Africa for making it possible for AHADI to work with others to address ethnic diversity issues in Eastern Africa. Equally, we are thankful to the panelists and the participants who provided valuable input into the presentations by asking questions and suggesting pertinent solutions. We are also indebted to the thoughtful and committed contributors to this book. Their time and effort in conceptualizing and writing the papers presented in the book are invaluable. We hope that the issues raised can become points of reference in examining how ethnic diversity can be harnessed for the good of the region. The National Cohesion and Integration Commission took an interest in the Conference and invited us to share the proceedings with Commissioners. We are grateful for the opportunity to have an input into the thinking at NCIC and contributing in the valuable task of building inter-ethnic tolerance and learning.

The team at AHADI deserves gratitude for organizing the conference and coordinating various related activities prior, during and after the conference. We appreciate the input of Reynolds Ritcher (New York University) and Dr. Kabiri Ngeta for important comments and suggestions on the papers as well as Susan Bantu for assisting with the editorial work. Catherine Bosire deserves gratitude for typesetting the manuscript and designing it to completion. We thank you, the reader, for taking time to read this book. We hope that you will find some insights between these pages.

Last but not least, we want to thank the many people who in our respective organizations, networks and lives have enabled us to dedicate the time and energy to bring this book from vision to reality. We thank them for their encouragement and support.

AHADI

Nairobi

May 2010.

A Prologue to Ethnic Diversity in Eastern Africa

Kimani Njogu

The December 27th 2007 general elections in Kenya were the tenth since the country attained sovereign status in 1963. Between June 1963, when Kenya achieved self government, to December 2002, when the National Rainbow Coalition (NARC) won the elections, the country was ruled by the Kenya African National Union (KANU). For most of that period Kenya was either a *de facto* or a *de jure* one party state[1]. Disturbingly, since the reintroduction of multi-party political participation in 1991, Kenya has experienced violence with ethnic ramifications before, during and after elections The violence takes different forms such as disruptions of campaign rallies, eviction of citizens from their homes or constituencies, verbal threats and intimidation, looting, abductions, arson and destruction of property, torture, physical assault, obstruction of voting or nomination processes and death. It is preceded by ethnic hate speech, distribution of leaflets warning of dire consequences if targeted individuals and communities do not vacate their homes and extensive political mobilization based on ethnic identity. Around the 1992, 1997, 2002 (to a lesser degree), and 2007 elections. Kenyan citizens were internally displaced and injured or killed because of their ethnic backgrounds and due to their decision to vote for an 'alternative' candidate. Most violence is perpetrated by party supporters, political aspirants, organized groups and youth wingers.

Whereas between 1992 – 2002, most election related violence in Kenya occurred at the pre-election phase during the time of voter registration, party campaigns and nominations, the 2007 elections were characterized by excessive violence, and crimes against humanity especially after the declaration of Mwai Kibaki of the Party of National Unity (PNU) as president in the contested results. Four events would need to be considered in our efforts to understand the 2007/2008 post election violence. First, the two main presidential candidates (Mwai Kibaki and Raila Odinga) had combined forces in 2002 to remove Daniel Arap Moi from power. Apparently, a Memorandum of Understanding (MOU) was signed by the coalition partners but later ignored once Kibaki became President. Although the President was not legally bound to the MOU, the political ramifications of his action were mammoth and between 2003 and 2007 his government was under siege. Second, the 2005 Referendum on the Proposed Constitution had the effect of polarizing the country along ethnic lines; a situation that was replayed during the 2007 campaigns. Thirdly, the 1997 Inter Parties Parliamentary Group (IPPG) agreement required that political parties be consulted during the appointment of Commissioners to the Electoral Commission of Kenya (ECK). However, when the terms of some of the ECK Commissioners ended in 2007, the president made appointments without reference to the other political parties. Fourthly, is the lack of trust in institutions of governance such as the judiciary. According to the current Constitution, leaders of the opposition Orange Democratic Movement (ODM) party under Raila Odinga were supposed to go to court if they were dissatisfied with the results of the polls but they refused to do so. This was mainly because the judiciary has over the years been perceived as not a true arbiter in electoral grievances. This lack of confidence in institutions of governance has accumulated since the 1960s and exploded most violently in 2007/2008 after the hotly contested polls.

Notwithstanding claims to election rigging, the incumbent Mwai Kibaki was declared the winner by the Electoral Commission of Kenya (ECK) and sworn in by the Chief Justice. ODM argued that ECK had been compromised and election results tampered with. The Party did not concede defeat and called for mass action across the country. Mwai Kibaki moved on to consolidate his position by appointing a partial cabinet, bringing into government the third largest party—ODM-Kenya—and appointing its leader Kalonzo Musyoka, the Vice President. This initial coalition ensured that Kibaki had a significant following across the country and increased the number of Members of Parliament that would support his agenda. Meanwhile the country was on fire and hundred of thousands of citizens were displaced and subjected to grievous harm. The transport system was paralysed across the region and Kenya was on the brink of a devastating civil war as revenge attacks got underway. The country 'cooled down' after the African Union mandated Panel of Eminent African Personalities (PEAP) headed by former United Nations General Secretary Mr. Kofi Annan brokered a National Accord setting the stage for the formation of a Coalition Government, the establishment of the post of Prime Minister to be occupied by Hon. Raila Odinga, and bringing into government key actors in the post election violence. The Kenya National Dialogue and Reconciliation process also recommended the setting up of institutions that would deal with the root causes of the violence and ensure national cohesion and reconciliation. The country is still grapping with how to address ethnic nationalism and how to increase ethnic tolerance and co-existence. The National Commission on Integration and Cohesion is one of the institutions that is seeking to engage ethnic intolerance and to entrench the national identity.

As a response to these events, Africa Health and Development International (AHADI), with the support of the Rockefeller Foundation, organized a regional conference on the opportunities and challenges of ethnic diversity in eastern Africa which was held on 16th and 17th October 2009 in Nairobi. The conference brought together participants from academic and civil society institutions in Kenya, Tanzania, Uganda, Ghana, Burundi and Rwanda. The aim was to create a space for candid discussions on ethnicity as an identity and ways in which diversity can become a productive resource rather than a locus of animosity. The relationship between ethnicity and creativity, political mobilization, rural development, education, democracy, conflict and language were explored.

The Objectives of the Conference were to facilitate regional reflections on ethnic diversity as a resource for eastern Africa; to explore the opportunities and challenges that multiculturalism presents to African nations; to discuss ways in which a national identity can be cultivated and enhanced in a multi-ethnic situation. Participants reflected in plenary and group discussions on the following key questions:

- *What is the nature of ethnic identity in contemporary Africa?*
- *How is ethnicity in Africa a political and social construct?*
- *How can ethnic diversity be turned into a resource for political, economic and social development*
- *How can national and pan-African identities be strengthened and peaceful multi-ethnic nations built?*

The conference was significant in a number of ways. First, the eastern African region is home to close to two hundred ethnic groups and occasionally political and economic conflicts involving these communities manifest themselves ethnically as groups seek to protect their interests, acquire and maintain resources such as land or work in cohorts with the political and economic elite, in the pursuit of national power, to meet their local needs. The convergence of national and local interests contribute to the entrenchment of ethnic solidarity. Second, ethnic solidarity within the context of limited resources is rational and cannot be wished away because people tend to congregate around those with whom they have some form of affinity, be it linguistic or cultural, giving them a feeling of security and belonging. When communities feel excluded from centers of power and when resource allocation and maintenance are not addressed deliberately and aggressively through strategic reforms, conflicts are likely to occur and ethnic belonging solidified. Land has been at the centre of most local tensions not only because of rise in populations but also due to climate change. Significantly, when ethnic solidarity is activated in a context of political and economic needs it can be quickly strengthened and made volatile. But with accountability and transparency in governance, more equitable distribution of resources, cross-ethnic learnings and exchanges, urbanization, improved economic opportunities for the youth, gender equity, accommodative and responsible leadership, intermarriages and globalization, ethnic belonging as a strong form of identity is being challenged in fundamental ways. This suggests that strong ethnic affiliations can be interrogated because they are impermanent. Thirdly, ethnicity exists within a plethora of other solidarity relationships such as religion, class, gender and profession which may serve to reduce ethno-nationalism. These other identities are also subjected to ethnic tensions, suggesting the power of ancestral, linguistic and cultural affiliations over other identities. Because ethnicities cross national boundaries, such as in the case of Hutu and Tutsi in Rwanda and Burundi as well as Maasai and Kuria in Kenya, Tanzania and Uganda there is always the possibility of violence emanating from one country and spilling over to a neighboring country. Equally, moral ethnicity, viewed as a positive affiliation, may cross borders and contribute to stability of families and communities.

Negative ethnicity is nurtured through language, stereotyping and deliberate exclusion of members of society. But this can be reversed through cultural engineering, a process of deliberately engaging language, attitudes and cultural practices in order to change them. It will be recalled that before the 1970s, conversations on gender were not systematic and coordinated. However, over time gender perspectives have been incorporated in international and national affairs and there is greater consciousness of gender sensitive language. In the contemporary world, political and social life can no longer ignore gender matters because of the conscious conversations that have been held over the last few decades. In contrast, although ethnicity is an important defining factor of African political, economic, social and cultural life there has not been a rigorous conversation about it. Community sensitive language has not been crafted and ethnic stereotyping abounds in popular discourse and the media. Quite often, ethnic emotions are invoked to acquire and maintain power.

But we can learn lessons from Ghana, as Attafuah argues in his paper. Despite being a multiethnic state Ghana has not experienced ethnic rivalry of the level experienced in many parts of Africa and is realizing political, economic and social growth. How is that country managing ethnic diversity? Apparently, solidarities established through the educational system have reduced the poignancy of the ethnic group as a site of belonging. The same cannot be said with reference to Rwanda and Uganda which have in the past experienced ethnic driven violence and in the case of the former the 1994 genocide involving the Hutu and Tutsi. Although Rwanda is in the process of healing and reconstructing the wounds are deep and wide. In all eastern African countries, presidential and parliamentary elections have tended to be violent, albeit to varying degrees. Uganda has always had tensions between the North, South and West with successive governments being accused of favoring the President's region of origin in resource allocation and job opportunties. Although Tanzania has over the years attempted to build a sense of nationhood through Kiswahili and the philosophy of *ujamaa na kujitegemea* (socialism and self reliance), the country has recently manifested tensions between mainland and the Islands which are home to a predominately Muslim Swahili population. Many people in Pemba and Unguja feel excluded from political and economic activities because they are not from the mainland.

This conference opened up the possibility for deep non-disruptive debates and case studies about politically motivated violence, often seen in ethnic terms, and peaking during periods of elections. In most of Africa, there is evidence of politicized inter-ethnic rivalry and ethnic mobilization to acquire, maintain or monopolize power. Strong ethnic affiliation has also been viewed as a major barrier to human and economic development although ethnically bound welfare organizations do influence the economic and social life of citizens especially in the rural areas. In most of Africa, it is through ethnic identification that competition for influence in the state and in the allocation of resources becomes apparent. Occasionally, governments have sought to address this challenge through 'ethnic and regional balancing' in political appointments; a form of 'hegemonial exchange'. But the exchange does not always work and rebellion ensues as citizens feel marginalized from centres of power. In order to address ethnic rivalry at the political arena, it is important to have candid discussions about ethnicity and political representation, as we sought to do at the Conference. Claude Ake (1993: 4) has observed:

> *Conflicts arising from the construction of ethnicity to conceal exploitation by building solidarity across class lines, conflicts arising from appeal to ethnic support in the face of vanishing political legitimacy and from the manipulation*

of ethnicity to divide colonized people, are not ethnic problems but problems of particular political dynamics which just happens to be pinned on ethnicity. By the same token, solutions to these problems must address the political dynamics in question, not ethnicity.

In other words, conversations about ethnicity must of necessity explore political and economic needs of citizens. This is because ethnicity by itself is not a problem: it is the way it is used for political and economic survival and concealment of exploitative practices as well as its tendency to exclude. Used positively, it has functioned as a resource and engine of development in rural areas through mobilization of resources and maximization of opportunities within the nation-state or beyond.

In understanding the trajectories of conflicts in Africa it is also imperative that we reflect on the democracy and development project whose main goal was the state formation process. The process has included power structures devised by colonial regimes which relied on unified systems controlling a diversity of ethnicities and regions; the colonial power or another third party supporting certain positions in order to protect specific interests and competition for power and control of natural resources and territory. By its nature, state building generates competition, cooperation and conflict within the context of scarcity of resources and opportunities and the control of the state and its functions in the access, allocation and distribution of benefits and privileges to citizens. Despite the fact that common citizenship as enshrined in nationalism assumes that all citizens are equal in the eyes of the state, the state in most of Africa has tended to promote, protect or obstruct and frustrate ethnic interests through patronage. This has led to state weakness and decay because its legitimacy is often challenged by large sections of society and cannot provide for the satisfaction of basic needs - physical security, access to political, economic and social institutions. As a result, people revert to collective self-identification and organization. This explains to a certain degree why political parties in Africa are organized along ethnic lines instead of a shared ideology. State building should go hand in glove with nation building. Equally, economic and political development will be hard to realize without addressing nationhood alongside local and ethnic concerns.

With the emergence of political pluralism, various ethnic elites have exploited differences in ethnicity to add momentum to their struggle to maintain power or propel themselves to political leadership. The 1990s, sometimes referred to as the decade of democratization in Africa, saw the

"Third Wave of Democracy" sweep through many countries in Africa, enlarging the space for ethnic and other interest groups to demand larger inclusion in the running of the state. Ironically, as the democratic space became bigger, it raised the stakes for national stability as diverse voices demanded larger stakes in the national representation and access to resources. The struggle for power and resources entrenches ethnic solidarity and this occasionally leads to violent conflict. Yet inter-ethnic togetherness can lead to more accountable and transparent leadership because the various interest groups can exert pressure from below. Fundamentally, the rich ethnic and cultural diversity reflected in music, media, artifacts, language and traditions (as discussed by Mboya in this Volume) has often been blurred by the political differences which mainly exist along ethnic lines. Interestingly, in Tanzania where there are about 120 ethnic groups, language (Kiswahili) has been used to unify the different groups. Based on the policies of *ujamaa* (socialism), a principle closely associated with the late Tanzania's founding President Julius Nyerere, the country remains generally peaceful and stable. Evidently, leadership, a unifying popular ideology, and a value system encapsulated in a national language are key to the development of nationhood. Further, a number of African states are continuing to transform politically through adoption of democratic principles and practices; some (like Ghana) are de-emphasizing ethnicity as an identity and consciously promoting nationhood through extensive inter-ethnic interactions and civic education. The politics of inclusion and democratic practice are vital in diffusing ethnic nationalism although political organizing in most of Africa is almost always ethnically driven.

Participants at the Conference recognized that although efforts in the pursuit of democracy and good governance in some African countries are remarkable, there is more work to be done. The Conference came up with the following recommendations:

Political inclusion and minority rights

1. There is need to give voice to minorities through effective mechanisms such as affirmative action/positive discrimination. Minorities may include ethno- linguistic and religious groups, women, people with disabilities and youth among others.

2. It is imperative to implement proportional representation and party lists as the electoral system for the region to strengthen the basis of national level political parties.

3. It is important to undertake real and meaningful decentralization with clear checks and balances, to sanction the regime.

Interventions to empower youth economically

1. The government should increase the availability of funds allocated specifically for youth employment and development, targeting projects at the district and village level.

2. They should also create more jobs for the youth especially in the countryside. This can be done using the Constituency Development Fund (CDF), focusing on labour intensive projects such as road construction. It may also include skills development in agriculture and agro-business, anchoring of creative industries and investment in information technology.

3. They should also expand markets for agricultural products, targeting specific agricultural/livestock projects and products such as horticulture, fish and fruits among others.

Education

1. The selection and admission of students to secondary schools should be done through a digitalized blind system. This would ensure that students from different ethnic backgrounds learn together and establish national networks instead of the quota system;

2. The Teachers Service Commission should ensure that teachers and lecturers are posted to various learning institutions regardless of their ethnicity. Governors and leaders of academic institutions should be appointed on merit, without consideration for ethnic background. Communities should be sensitized to accept that institutions located in their neighbourhood are available to all learners irrespective of their ethnic origin;

3. All curricula – primary secondary, colleges and universities – should be revised so as to expunge any content that has connotations of ethnic stereotypes. More specifically, the history syllabus should seek to have a national outlook. Instructional, education and communication materials for all learning institutions should be geared towards promotion of unity and ethnic integration.

Competitive cultural shows such as schools' drama and music festivals should be maintained and enhanced at all levels of education. As much as possible the festivals should be held in different parts of the country and the local community should be involved.

4. Governance and leadership training at community levels needs to be carried out to encourage ethnic integration. This should target opinion leaders, leaders of academic institutions and cultural icons.

Nationhood, national cohesion and integration

1. The state should encourage people to recognize that they live in an artificial state and deliberately accept their commonness. Media can play a central role in entrenching inter-ethnic tolerance and trust. The Kenyan state should put in place mechanisms to promote Kiswahili as a national language and the 'lingua franca' of the region.

2. The establishment of a social movement is crucial to mobilize the people cutting across communities and other identities, to demand for economic development, legal and other changes towards the artificial statehood. To be spearheaded by civil society organisations, the social movement ought to involve the gatekeepers and opinion leaders to ensure community ownership.

3. There is a need by civil society to design and implement programmes that empower communities. This will ensure equitable distribution of resources and access to opportunities by all communities. The government should adopt strategies and policies that ensure redistribution of resources.

4. Establishing basic principles and values on how a society is managed is needful. These principles should be agreed upon and written down in a National Political Charter.

Interventions in the land sector

1. *Policy implementation level*

Recognizing that the recently adopted land policy is largely considered progressive,

a) Create community awareness in order to put pressure on relevant state organs to act on the policy.

b) Translate the policy into law by establishing a legal regime to charter implementation of the policy.

c) Establish an institutional framework through capacity building for policy implementation and develop relevant institutions representative of all stakeholders, including civil society.

d) Establish a monitoring and evaluation framework, with appropriate milestones/indicators to ensure that policy and legal commitments are followed through.

2. Documentation of best practices and learning processes

a) At national level research the land practices of different communities;

b) At regional and continental level, determine lessons learnt and best practices which can enrich the region;

c) Facilitate the sharing experiences nationally, regionally and continentally;

d) Pilot land administration/customary systems based on findings of a-c above.

3. Land, historical injustices and ethnicity

a) Following the enactment of land policy, research and concretize claims related to this phenomenon across the country.

b) Establish a forum for discussion on this phenomenon (include outside experience to give the exercise a trans-national outlook), for example by supporting a joint state-civil society project.

c) Design a program on how to move forward, in line with the provisions of the land policy, for example on how to engage the relevant regional and national institutions including the National Cohesion and Integration Commission as well as the Truth Justice and Reconciliation Commission.

These recommendations can be picked and worked on from a number of angles depending on national and local needs.

The chapters in this book show that ethnicity, as a form of identity, is potentially 'innocent' and 'resourceful'. However, within the context of poor governance, competition for resources, corruption, and uncaring leadership it can be used to harm others. Equally, ethnic diversity can be marshalled to entrench democratic ideals, increase accountability in governance, facilitate economic wellbeing and socio-cultural innovations.

PART 1 of the book seeks to conceptualize ethnicity and how it functions as an identity whereas PART 2 examines how it plays out in politics. The Epilogue highlights some of the emerging issues from the various papers.

Notes

[1] Although there was always a national urge for multiparty political participation, Kenya was a *de facto* one party state in the following years: 1964-1966; 1969-1982. Between 1966 and 1969 the Kenya People's Union was the opposition party. It became a *de jure* one party state in June 1982 when Section 2(A) was inserted in the Constitution. The amendment was made to deny opposition leaders Oginga Odinga and George Anyona from registering a political party: the Kenya African Socialist Alliance (KASA). Due to internal and external pressure *Section 2* Constitution of Kenya (Amendment) Act No.2 of 1991 was put in place, re-inscribing multi party political participation. By repealing Section 2(A) the opportunity for vibrant multi party political engagement was ensured. Furthermore, Section 9(1) and (2) were also introduced, restricting the president to two five terms.

Conceptualizing Ethnicity

Ethnic Pluralism and National Governance in Africa: A Survey

Michael Chege

Introduction

At the height of the post-conflict violence in Kenya early in 2008, the noted *New York Times* columnist Nicholas Kristof visited Kenya and described (in the Times issue of February 21, 2008) the most gruesome human butchery in what he referred to as savage "primeval tribal tensions that threaten Kenya's future". Like many others before him, he concluded that tribalism is the curse of Africa. Prior to that, the *Los Angeles Times* in its issue of 2nd January, 2008 had reported "savage tribal killings" in Kenya, while in the *New York Times* issue of December 31, 2008, its Nairobi correspondent, in an article that provoked an outrage in Africa, the US and Europe, wrote that the killings in Kenya had "tapped into an atavistic vein of tribal tensions that always lay beneath the surface…but until now had not produced widespread mayhem". With few exceptions, western press coverage of the Kenyan crisis took similar lines. All of this cruel, gratuitous violence was taking place in Kenya, the readers were informed, in a country which was previously considered one of the most stable and promising countries in Africa. Reading this soon after the human disasters in once-promising Zimbabwe and Cote d'Ivoire, even Western readers who would be normally well-disposed to Africa would have been inclined to think that the banner heading of *The Economist* magazine's issue of 20th May 2000 proclaiming Africa "The Hopeless Continent" may not have been wrong altogether.

And it is not just western readers and journalists who may have been inclined to feel that way. For the record, I have heard and read many times the same sentiments conveyed by many educated Africans in their lament on violence and political instability in Africa. Almost in unison, African political leaders and intellectuals denounce "tribalism" in Africa (or what some in this volume refer to as "negative ethnicity") as the root source of Africa's political problems. Invested with this negative connotation, what is commonly called "tribalism" is viewed as an introverted moral corruption on the part of a social group (or its leaders) and failure to rise up to the higher standards of nationalism and ethnic impartiality in making important political decisions. Logically then, the solution to the problem becomes a wholesale moral regeneration of a nation's communities to transcend tribalism, which is why African political leaders literally "preach" against tribalism. Abolishing tribalism, overcoming ethnic parochialism with an all-embracing nationalism is seen as the overriding nation-building test, in which so many African countries have failed.

In this chapter, we take a different perspective. We take ethnic (or what is derisively called tribal) identity in Africa as a universal phenomenon under which political mobilization is done using primary human characteristics like region of one's origin, skin colour, mother tongue, culture, and—above all—putative ancestral origins. It bears most if not all the traits that are conventionally associated with nationalism. Furthermore, we seek to demonstrate that the first step towards dealing with conflict based on ethnic identities is not national uniformity, rather it is found in toleration and respect of cultural differences (see, Schipper, this volume), combined with placement of national interests above the parochial. It is largely a matter of peaceful coexistence of many diverse interests, combined with great deference to shared national values and institutions by all of them, rather than an elimination of any group's ambitions. In addition there are now tested political and institutional arrangements that African countries should adopt in order to remove the negative sting associated with ethnic identity without losing some of the benefits that come along with cultural diversity (see Kimonye, this volume). In fact, some of best suited institutional arrangements are those commonly abjured by simplistic moral analysis and prescriptions of the kind mentioned above.

Global resurgence of ethnic claims

Contrary to the racist claims from the international press (and elsewhere) that attribute African political conflicts and mass murder to the unique African psychological attachment to "tribalism", the problem of conflicting ethnic claims is a universal one, a resurgence of which we have seen particularly after the collapse of global communism in 1989. What varies most is its intensity from country to country over time, and the local capacity to devise lasting governance institutions to manage it in the interests of the common good. In one of the most celebrated analysis on the resurgence of ethnic conflicts after 1989, the late US Senator Daniel P. Moynihan characterized ethnic-based conflict world-wide as a pandemonium. "The world", wrote Moynihan, "was entering a period of ethnic conflict following the relative stability of the Cold War... As formal structures broke up, and ideology lost its hold, people revert to more primal identities".[1] As evidence in support of his argument, Moynihan cited the bloody implosion of Yugoslavia, problems facing the Russian diaspora in the former Soviet states, conflict in Caucasia and wars in the Middle East, the Persian Gulf, South Asia, and of course Africa where the problem looms especially large. No region, it seems, was spared the problem of political conflict demarcated along ethnic lines.

This of course is not the first time that the world has witnessed a global upsurge in identity-based political conflict. The period following the Second World War and the emergence of post-colonial states in Africa and Asia saw considerable inter-ethnic conflict in the new states and extended debate on the role of ethnic, cultural and religious diversity in the construction of the post-independence era. Like at present, experts on the subject and most national leaders saw a solution to the problem in the submerging old ethnic and cultural identities under the rubric of a new national consciousness and an unwavering allegiance to new state institutions and values.

This is particularly true of Africa after independence in the 1960s. Under Pan-African leadership of Kwame Nkrumah and Gamal Abdel Nasser, Pan-African nationalists abhorred ethnic-based sub-nationalism in Buganda, Ashanti, Katanga, Barotseland (Zambia) and the "majimbo" (regionalism) policies of the Kenya African Democratic Union (KADU) in Kenya. Creative writers and social scientists went along with this. The best example of this remains the exponents of "national integration" (in political science) as one of the major "crises" that the new states needed to resolve, as advocated in the discipline of "modernization" by the Comparative Politics Committee of the US Social Science Research Council.[2] Other scholars, notably anthropologists with tested field experience like Clifford Geertz were less sanguine. They stressed the enduring nature of communal and particularistic attachments to local languages, culture symbols and ethnic identity, arguing that it was preferable to find ways of accommodating rather than repressing or replacing these seemingly "backward-looking" political sentiments as portrayed by nationalist leaders and intellectuals.[3] Geertz left open to political experimentation and deliberation the form which such governance institutions would take. But he was sure they would not be the same in every state.

Misunderstanding ethnic reality in Africa and the solution for it

Apart from a select number of Africanists who saw merit in Geertz's proposal and thinking close to it, the overwhelming perspective on the most appropriate political treatment of ethnic and cultural diversity in Africa has continued to be the nationalistic pipe dream of the "triumph of nation over tribe" on the road to modernization. At independence, for example, FRELIMO (in Mozambique) pledged "to kill the tribe to build the nation." FRELIMO grounded its doctrine on the class struggle, and being essentially Marxist, it considered any assertions of cultural identity as a false consciousness that obscured conflicts based on the mode of production. Marxist institutional solutions to ethnic parochialism therefore, differed less from those of "modernization" than one would think at first blush. This failure to accept the enduring nature of ethnic identity as both a positive and negative force in African political life, depending on how it is used, has been a major contributing factor to the unceasing tragedy, bloodletting and poor governance in Africa. After all, wisdom in the use of all human inventions — from fire to the atom — depends on how well it is applied to advance human welfare rather than to damage it, since the invention can serve both purposes.

And it is not just the unilateral espousal of the unitary nationalist identity that is the problem. With few notable exceptions, the conventional wisdom in Africa about what passes for knowledge on "tribes and tribalism" has been remarkably superficial conceptually, factually inaccurate and politically self-serving, whether one is speaking of political leaders, journalists, pamphleteers, or intellectuals. We must therefore begin with a brief survey of the classical literature on the formation of ethnic identities in Africa, juxtaposed to some of the most recent literature and statements on the subject. We then proceed to examine some of the most appropriate institutional solutions to the problems associated with ethnic conflicts, not just in Africa but elsewhere. With an estimated 2000-plus languages and cultural groupings, Africa is far and away the most ethnically-diverse region in the world and there is now almost a knee-jerk attribution of this violence to age-old ethnic rivalries. It has also been the most violence-ridden region of the globe since 1989 that is often attributed to "age-old ethnic rivalries". This is reason all the more to probe the nature of ethnic identity in Africa and its links to violent conflict.

In a survey of violent conflict and its casualties around the world between 1990 and 2000, Virgil Hawkins found that about 88 percent of the deaths reported from such conflicts could be traced to Africa. Of the 56-odd Sub-Saharan states, 28 had experienced internal warfare since 1980.[4] Simultaneously, African countries — save exceptions like Botswana, Mauritius, South Africa, Seychelles and Cape Verde — have experienced the most lackluster economic growth rates of any developing region in the world since the 1980s. Per capita growth rates in Sub-Saharan Africa fell by 0.6 percent between 1975 and 2004, and barely rose (by a mere 0.3 percent) between 1990 and 2004, as compared to a growth of 2.4 and 3.0 percent in the respective periods for all the developing countries.[5]

Western economists seeking to explain the cause of Africa's dismal performance compared to other regions—and particularly to the flourishing East Asian countries—soon latched on to what they claimed was a link between ethnic diversity and poor development performance, claiming that Africa's high "ethno-linguistic" diversity as the driving factor behind the region's economic regress. So began the second academic phase of inquiry into the nature of ethnic diversity in Africa and its relationship to national governance and economic prosperity. "Ethno-linguistic" diversity was now blamed for recurrent conflict, corruption, low investment, negative interest rates and poor investment decisions.[6] In short, it was blamed for practically everything that has gone wrong in Africa.

Paul Collier and his acolytes went further. They attributed African civil wars to ethno-linguistic diversity *per se*. "Among developing countries", Collier wrote, "Africa is more ethnically diverse than other regions and it has the highest incidences of civil war, a phenomenon often interpreted as post-colonial re-emergence of ancient ethnic hatreds."[7] In a burgeoning sub-set of this literature, Collier and his associates have attempted to prove, via econometric treatment and African case studies, that while ethnic fractionalization renders countries prone to civil war, democratic governance tends to minimize its occurrence while ethnic-domination does the opposite. More importantly, in Collier's case, African civil wars are not about ethnic grievance; they are prompted by greed for "lootable resources" like the alluvial diamonds in Angola and Sierra Leone. All this has proved most controversial, but this has not stopped Collier from stating further that competitive democratic elections (like those held in Kenya in 2007) in what he calls "the bottom billion" of humanity—the poor, small, unstable states on the fringes of the world—have become a predictable trigger of irrational ethnic violence that could destabilize poor countries and ultimately the wealthy industrial states as well. To prevent that, Collier concludes, Western governments should hold African states (and dictators) to the principles of democracy, no corruption, and accountability—failing which Western powers should intervene militarily to pre-empt disaster or, alternatively, allow military coups against African despots to succeed.[8]

None of this is convincing. Against the backdrop of the most informed literature on the genesis of the evolution of "tribes" and "tribalism" in Africa— derived primarily from social anthropology—the burgeoning literature on

African "ethno-linguistic fragmentation" and its baleful political consequences seems deeply flawed conceptually and dead wrong on many points of fact. Granted, some economists using econometric techniques have made some empirical contribution to the recent wave of knowledge on the genesis and consequences of ethnicity in Africa. However their contribution to our *substantive* understanding of ethnic problems in Africa pales in comparison with the classic post-war studies on the subject from anthropologists and political scientists who used first-hand field data. The discipline of economics in Africa has gone astray in this case, by invading other social sciences (like anthropology, sociology and politics) without understanding the substantive concepts being quantified and by asserting spurious causal relationships between variables associated with ethnicity (like language) and secular variables like communal-based warfare, economic growth rates, and political competition.

One of the most erudite and evidence-based sources on the origins of "tribe" and "tribalism" in Africa has to be the studies produced by the Rhodes-Livingstone Institute in Lusaka (now the Institute of African Studies at the University of Zambia) in the 1940s and 1950s. Under the leadership of the noted South African social anthropologist, Max Gluckman, these essentially empirical studies were to change the way serious scholars understood "tribes" and "tribalism" in Africa. The wisdom they contained has resonance outside Africa, and their contribution on the substantive content of ethnicity in Africa is unsurpassed.

At the very onset of this intellectual movement, F. S. Furnivall, an economist working on pre-war Indonesia and Burma, observed the segmentation of the region's major peoples—Malay-speakers, Chinese, Indians and expatriate Europeans—in social life.[9] However, this did not stop them from interacting with mutual profit in the market-place: "Each group holds to its own religion, its own culture and languages, its own ideas and ways. As individuals, they meet but only in the market-place in buying and selling." Put differently, they mix but do not combine. These, however, were not dysfunctional societies. They resolved conflicts reasonably well all the same. This led to the evolution (in anthropology) of the theory of cultural or "ethnic pluralism", (as M. G. Smith called it) which is the title of this paper. This approach recognized the value of a functional society based on social and cultural segmentation, but incorporated in a state—the only territorial organization in the overall picture.

Empirical studies from the Rhodes-Livingstone Institute confirmed this formulation indirectly. Their everlasting contribution lay in recognizing firstly that, what colonial authorities thought were genuine pre-colonial "tribes" were in fact new aggregates of related peoples united by a loyalty to new regions and districts whose boundaries (in this case) had been delimited by the British authorities. In case after case, and far from being traditional, the ethnic groups were founded in the urban areas by elites and workers who shared related languages (or cognate areas of origin) compared to their rivals or competitors. The "Kalela Dance" observed by J. Clyde-Mitchell in the Zambian Copperbelt in 1956 is, in this author's estimation, the most engaging and illuminating example of this.[10] This dance, which mining administrators had considered a traditional one, turned out to be an elaborate discourse on and mockery of the western ethnic pecking order in the mines, as well as a re-affirmation of the desire for the material comforts procured by mining wages. The Kalela Dance, in effect, was a working-class commentary on life in the Zambian Copperbelt.

Secondly, the Rhodes-Livingstone research brought out the fact that far from being attached to one identity—the traditional "tribal" one—Africans exhibited *different* kinds of identities in the rural areas as well as the cities. Evidence showed that "rural" tribalism was different from "urban" tribalism. Finally, and this was an observation brought out by A. L. Epstein in *Politics in an African Urban Community*, while urban Africans were segmented (and competed) on the basis of new urban ethnic identities, they always unified in opposition to policies they did not like, fronted by mining authorities or the "urban tribal chiefs" who represented colonial authorities in the Copperbelt. Thus, while Bemba, Nyanja, Lozi, Tumbuka and Tonga were operative social categories in the Copperbelt, when it came to industrial action, they united as "Africans" and as "employees" of the mines; here class replaced tribe.[11] The similarity between this and Furnivall's account in the then—East Indies is clear. Gluckman for one thought this interplay between ethnicity and class a universal one, applicable even to Britain.

But in many cases even the names of the so-called "tribes" of modern Africa their languages and solidarity were self-invented social artifacts created by the vortex of forces unleashed by the competition for power, economic advancement and social prestige under colonial rule. Such "invention of tribe", as Leroy Vail and his associates called it, has been cited among Yoruba, Ibo and Acholi in Nigeria, and among Luhya, Kalenjin, and Mijikenda in Kenya.

In that connection, I can think of no better example of what some have called "artificial ethnicity" in the invention mode than the Bangala of the

Democratic Republic of the Congo as narrated by Crawford Young in his classic book on Congolese nationalism, *Politics in the Congo*[12] As Young writes, "The most striking example of an urban ethnic group which is a pure specimen of ' super-tribalism' is the Leopoldville 'Bangala'. The most recent ethnological study of the region of Equateur which was believed to be their home states: 'We believe for a long time in the existence of a people called Bangala, speaking Lingala and possessing very definite ethnic and cultural characteristics... We know today with certainty that, in all of Belgian Congo, there exists no ethnic group bearing this name'.

"The origins of the myth are not entirely clear. Stanley, the first foreign visitor to the region, first used the name. He drew attention to the Bangala, whom he termed the 'Ashanti of the Congo', unquestionably a very superior tribe, in the same breath, he remarked that they only amounted to the string of villages extending ten miles along the Congo river banks, near what is now Nouvelle Anvers. His attraction to this small cluster led him to deposit Coquilhat amongst them with the task of establishing a station in 1883. Coquilhat gave a great impetus to the myth, in lending credence to the tales spun by Mata Buike, a village chief at his station; 'If these reports are true, Mata Buike governs one of the most vast states in equatorial Congo'. That he did not take him seriously is indicated by his estimate that there were 110,000 Bangala. He was more than a little disconcerted, however when one day Mata Buike told him that he was not a Bangala after all, but this name referred to the peoples downstream".

"This would never have been more than a historical anecdote were it not for Coquilhat's success in persuading a large number of the area surrounding his Equateur station to enter the service of the state. "They formed an important part of the *Force Publique* rank and file in the early years and also the bulk of the crews for the river streamers. The recruitment extended rapidly along the river banks and with it the boundaries of the "Bangala" tribe began to grow". An early officer, Lothaire, observed "Take a contingent of workers engaged aboard the steamers, or workers in the state posts along the Congo River, choose them from all the tribes of all the area; they all become Bangala...Even if they belong to hostile groups, while out of their areas they will unite'.

"The myth of Bangala was given archeological sanction when a volume dedicated to them was included " the important ethnological survey of the Congo...An ethnic map was published which indicated that the "tribe" covered an enormous area, extending from Coquilhatville 400 miles upstream and running inland some 100 miles on each side of the river. An immediate caveat, however, was entered by the first Protestant missionary to establish a post in the area… 'in a work published in Brussels the term Bangala is made to cover a vast area…This includes a dozen or more different tribes talking as many distinct languages…among whom there is nothing in common except their black skins. The natives themselves, he said, never used the name 'Bangala'.

"The legend was consolidated by the adoption of Lingala as a language for the army and communicating with the population. This river language was influenced by Lobobangi but it also included infusions from Swahili, Kikongo and other more local dialects. It is widely believed that this synthetic "lingua franca" was the Bangala language as its name implies".

"In later years in Leopoldville, all 'gens du Haut' or immigrants arriving from up the river were referred to as Bangala. The Bakongo in particular referred to all non-Bakongo as Bangala and the term has been accepted by all but the Kasaiens, Mongo and Kwango-Kwiluites. As Young concludes: "An ethnic federation, the Liboke-Lya-Bangala was organized…Both Europeans and African tended to analyze Leopoldville society in terms of a Bakongo-Bangala duality, and the 1957 urban elections were generally described in these terms. "

Nor does one want to limit the invention of African ethnic identities to such unusual but clear cases as the Bangala. As John Londsdale has stated at one point, "the British insisted on tribes and Africans found tribes to belong to." Even the way pre-colonial kingdoms like the Bakongo, Baganda, Mossi, Ashanti, Amhara, and others defined their relationships with their neighbours in respect to the opportunities and obstacles encountered under colonial rule. That also applies to groups whose origin lies between pre-colonial kingdoms (like Buganda) and newly-minted identities (like the Bangala). These include Kikuyu, Kamba, Luo, and others in Kenya. As Elizabeth Colson memorably remarked, "At least in Africa, tribes and tribalism as we know them today are recent creations reflecting the influences of the colonial era when large-scale political and economic organization set the scene for the mobilization of ethnic groups based upon linguistic and cultural similarities which had formerly been irrelevant in effecting alliances."[13]

However, many educated Africans continue to defend their "tribes" as ancient communities marked by common traditions, novel cultures, languages, home territories and distinct values. Like the promoters of ethnic nationalism elsewhere in the world, they defend with ferocity what Aidan

Southall called the "illusion of tribe." In fact considering the invidious and racist connotations that "tribe" comes with—best illustrated by the foreign newspaper quotations in this paper—"tribe" and "tribalism" are terms we could do without altogether. "Nations" or "communities" would be infinitely more accurate substitutes. Post-independence African states are therefore more accurately described as "multinational states" or better still "ethnically plural societies" as discussed earlier in this paper.

Three important factors are worth pointing out in closing this section of the chapter. Firstly, ethnic identity is a shifting and elusive phenomenon that could be activated at an infinite layer of levels, e.g. colour of skin, mother tongue, culture, region of origin linguistic dialect, ancestry, region, etc. It all depends on what the political issues at stake are. As experts in the field say, "ethnicity is always situational". Ethnic identity that applies in one context (the city for instance) differs from one that applies in the rural homelands. Identities that apply within one country mutate into new ones when people travel to other states.

Secondly, although Africans use the term "tribe" to describe their ethnic affiliation, they do not use it to imply attachment to primeval crudity in manners, mental simplicity and savagery in the form Western papers have continued to use it. Rather, Africans attach a sense of belonging and cultural pride in the institution so designated. It would be advisable to construct African governance systems with that in mind. Thirdly, ethnic identity in and of itself is a neutral factor just like nationalism. Ethnic-based mobilization can be used for good or ill, largely depending on the goals, promises, and objectives of the ethnic elites and entrepreneurs who employ it. It can be applied to advance a community's development, or mobilized to murder perceived enemies. The late Tom Mboya wrote of positive and negative "tribalism". Put differently, ethnic mobilization for political, or economic purposes is clearly a dependent variable, a function of deliberate strategy by political actors, and intellectuals in particular. And so, contrary to those economists who conceive politics and economics in Africa as dependent on the extent of ethno-linguistic fragmentation, the exact opposite is what we have established here: ethnic identities are mobilized by elites (including scholars) to gain power and economic control by means fair or foul.

Under these circumstances, governance policies and a legal framework ought to be designed that limit the very real dangers posed by baleful ethnic mobilization and conflict, but without destroying the benefits of pluralism, competition and individual choice. National governance structures can therefore be tailored, to corrupt Rousseau, to suit African societies as they are, rather than as they might be. This is the subject we next turn to.

National governance under conditions of ethnic pluralism in Africa

Despite the declared pursuit of elusive national unity, love of the fatherland, and the subjugation of ethnic and other particularistic affiliation to the new nation, the experience of Africa (and Eastern Africa especially) should now be cited as evidence of failure to achieve these naively idealistic goals. In a split second following the 2007 general elections, Kenya came as close to the calamity of state collapse as have Democratic Republic of Congo, Somalia, Cote d'Ivoire, Liberia and Sierra Leone in the past. Kenya, supposedly the most economically-sophisticated and socially advanced country in the region, faced imminent rupture. But for international intervention and the genius of Kofi Annan, Kenya was ripe for violent ethnic fragmentation. Some of its politicians said then that this was what they desired.

Kenya was also saved by some last-minute compromise and graciousness by its top leaders (Mwai Kibaki and Raila Odinga) who ignored the extremists in their ranks. The best testimony of what actually happened over that period is the shocking gallery of photographs, *Kenya Burning,* assembled by Joy Mboya (and her associates at The Go-Down), which anyone interested in the future of Kenya must read. Still, it is an illusion to assume that Kenya has definitively pulled back from the brink. Some progress, however, has been made toward crafting state institutions that respond to Kenya's ethnically-charged politics. These governance measures — grand coalition, power-sharing, ethnic inclusiveness and wider representation — correspond to the "consociational model" of governance. Unpopular as they are in Kenya after 2008, the institutional measures adopted in February 2008 helped to restore the uneasy calm that Kenya now enjoys. They represent *some,* but not all, of the most authoritatively — recommended measures for stable national governance in conflicted ethnically-pluralistic societies, including Kenya and practically all its neighbours.

These governance policies include the following:

(i) grand coalition governments as a permanent form of rule;

(ii) political inclusion in government of all the major ethnic segments of society;

(iii) minority set-asides for groups too weak to obtain full electoral representation;

(iv) local autonomy and federalism that does not penalize economically-advanced regions;

(v) parliamentary government;

(vi) proportional representation (based on multi-member constituencies and party lists) as opposed to the US and British "winner-take all" first-past-the-post electoral system;

(vii) judicial autonomy and scrupulous observation of individual rights and security of property rights; and

(viii) a fair representation of all groups in the executive arm of government.

How much the proposed new constitution will adhere to this, remains to be seen. But if it is to really address Kenya's core ethnic political problems, it should not shy away from adopting them. Already, many political commentators in Kenya disparage some of these reforms, thinking them inferior to the ideal of two competitive parties, and (taking refuge in naïve moralizing yet again) of the need to inculcate a new national culture starting with the younger generations after putting aside the old guard which is blamed for "tribalism" and so much of the misery the country has gone through since independence. Some (wrongly) describe Tanzania as success worth emulating, ignoring its problems (as in Zanzibar) and the large extent in which it has ignored political competition in favour of consensus. As in the past, the naïve idealism will fail yet again if we do not think harder than this.

What is true for Kenya ought to be even truer for Uganda, Zanzibar, Ethiopia, Somalia, Democratic Republic of Congo, Rwanda, Burundi and Sudan especially. But the illusion of the good national government and one-dimensional national identity based on one language still overwhelms academics, NGOs, activists and many well-meaning political reformers in our region. What they really ought to do is look at how close the repertoire of solutions cited above is to many countries in the short list of the best-governed African societies such as Mauritius, Botswana, and above all, South Africa after apartheid. India, Switzerland, Belgium, the Netherlands, and Austria represent successful examples outside Africa.

The system of consensus government proposed here is called "consociational democracy" for a good reason—it represents consensus between ethnic segments of society. It is associated with ethnically-segmented states like Switzerland, Austria, Netherlands, and Belgium as Arend Lijphart has demonstrated. But it is also true of India, Mauritius, South Africa, and

Lebanon (before its collapse in 1972). Neither is it a new set of recommendations for Africa. Writing at the height of the emergence of one-party rule in West Africa, W. Arthur Lewis (like Furnivall, also an economist) advocated what amounts to the consociational model, avoiding the British and French two-party systems which he thought was the bane of African societies. The reason he said was because "Britain and France are class societies and their institutions and their conventions are designed to cope with this fact. West Africa is not a class society; its problem is that of a plural society. What is good for a class society is bad for a plural society. Hence to create good political institutions in West Africa, one has to think of their problems from the foundation up." These words were written in 1965 before the first round of the African military coups in 1966 and outbreak of the Nigerian Civil War in 1967. They are as relevant today as they were then.

Conclusion

Before concluding remarks of this paper, two important qualifications should be made to qualify the support the paper gives to the most appropriate institutional mechanism to handle ethnic pluralism in countries like Kenya. First, in dealing with the complex issue of income and asset distribution, there is a danger creeping in based on archaic economic reasoning that African ethnic groups are mobilized to capture power on the basis of the fact that "it's their turn to eat." That position is gaining popularity now. It is also deadly mistaken. African politics according to this theory, best reflected in Michela Wrong's book on Kenya *It is Our Turn to Eat*, is depicted as a struggle over consumption by tribes without any reference to the production and investment that produces what is consumed. Empirically, as Kimuli Kasara, a young African political scientist at Columbia University has shown, in a detailed survey of 50 country-crop combinations that the eating ethnic-group theory is a farce: groups identified with government and the head of state faced *higher*, not lower taxes compared to the rest. This does not mean that the eating-theory of African politics is entirely contrived. It is widely believed and propagated by misguided African propagandists, journalists, intellectuals and their external mentors. But popularity does not necessarily amount to the truth. After all, most people in the world once believed the sun goes round the earth.

Secondly, nations and states are not forever. The OAU 1963 convention on the sanctity of African boundaries must now be revised. It has actually been ignored already in Eritrea and Ethiopia, Somaliland and Somalia, and could be violated yet again in Sudan as following the 2011 referendum. The truth is that some countries like Cote d'Ivoire, Chad and Central African Republic have *de facto* two or more governments within them. In the long run, states come and go. Fission and fusion of states is a historical inevitability. Separation in the last instance could be a solution to Africa's chronic ethnic problems, contrary to what the OAU and many African nationalists in the past and at present believed. The maps of Europe and more recently South Asia attest to the fact that boundary change over time has been an instrument of state construction. States in those regions have come and gone and Africa will not be an exception to this rule. But a solution can also be found in the opposite direction by bringing diverse small states under grand federation common markets, and by community arrangements like those of the EU or the US. Bringing many rival ethnic groups under a broad supra-national government is yet another way of removing the sting of ethnic animosity over power and resources within narrow national governments.

Two over-arching problems characterize the intellectual discourse on ethnic pluralism and governance in Africa: one is a fundamental misunderstanding of what "tribalism" really is, and a second (issuing from that) is a flawed theory of the institutional governance frameworks that are congruent with the character of ethnic politics in the region. Since one can never experiment with real states, the most instructive manner to verify the propositions advanced in this paper on both counts is to examine in detail what has worked in states with problems similar to those in Africa. Within the continent and outside it, what has worked has been largely at variance with the received nostrums on African "tribalism" propagated by the international press, as we saw in the beginning, and by some Africa journalists, columnists, and academics. It's now time to change all this and move the debate into a new and more productive dimension along the lines presented here, if a solution for successful government under ethnic pluralism in Africa is to be found. It is time to think outside the box.

Notes

[1] Daniel P.Moynihan, *Pandemonium: Ethnicity and International Politics.* (Oxford: Oxford University Press, 1993), p.xiii.

[2] Leonard Binder, et.al, *Crises and Sequences in Political Development.* (Princeton, NJ: Princeton University Press, 1971).

[3] Clifford Geertz, "The Integrative Revolution", in Geertz, *The Interpretation of Cultures.* (New York: Basic Books, 1973) pp.255-310.

[4] Virgil Hawkins, Stealth, *Conflict: How the World's Worst Violence is Ignored*. (London: Ashgate Publishers, 2008).

[5] UNDP, Human Development Reports Database (www.undp.org/hdr).

[6] The defining article of the movement was William B. Easterly and Ross Levine, "Africa's Growth Tragedy: Policies and Ethnic Divisions", *Quarterly Journal of Economics*, 1997.

[7] Paul Collier, "Implications of Ethnic Diversity", Economic Policy, Vol. 16, 32, 2001) p.129; and Paul Collier and Anke Hoeffler, "On the Economic Causes of Civil War", Oxford Economic Papers, Vol. 50, No.4, 1988.

[8] Paul Collier, *Wars, Guns and Votes*. (London: Bodley Head, 2008).

[9] J.S. Furnival, *Colonial Practice and Policy*. (Cambridge: Cambridge University Press, 1956).

[10] J. Clyde Mitchell, *The Kalela Dance*. Manchester: Manchester University Press, 1956).

[11] A. L. Epstein, *Politics in an African Urban Community*. Manchester: Manchester University Press, 1958); See also Max Gluckman, "Tribalism in Modern British Central Africa," Cahiers d'Etudes Africaines (January, 1960).

[12] Crawford Young, *Politics in the Congo: Decolonization and Independence*. (Princeton, NJ: Princeton University Press, 1965).

[13] Elizabeth Colson, in June Helm (ed.,) *Essays on the Problem of Tribe*. (Seattle: Washington University Press, 1968), pp. 201-202.

What Do We Share?

From the Local to the Global, and Back Again

Mineke Schipper

Us and them

Throughout the centuries, human beings have created binaries, devising images of themselves as against those of others. They have embedded each other's images in their thoughts, their stories, songs, and other forms of artistic expression. The nature of these images has varied according to the interests of those involved and the contexts in which they lived. Over the past years I have been doing research about those human imaginings in proverbs and myths, two genres which exist globally.

In this chapter I want to argue that there are not only differences between people, cultures, ethnic groups, nations, the sexes, and so forth, but also quite striking similarities, even in the ways in which people tend to emphasize their differences.

All over the world, peoples and cultures have their own oral traditions in the form of proverbs, poetry, myths, epics, and all kinds of narratives. One of the main tasks of my field, comparative literature, is to study the how and the why of similarities and differences in both historically related and historically unrelated cultural tradi-tions, literary themes, genres and so forth. If myths are mainly concerned with establishing a human order of hierarchy in various ways, proverbs are mainly struggling with a precarious balance of power in society.

Studying people's proverbs in different cultures, I found amazingly similar messages. Many reminded men to behave responsibly, using the same formula "a wife is not" or "a woman is not like", followed by all sorts of metaphors: food such as cassava or maize, musical instruments such as a guitar or a violin, garments such as a shawl or a shirt, and so forth, thus producing comparable messages that not only resemble each other in content but also in form, in spite of their widely different areas and cultures of origin. Here are a few examples:

> A woman is not cassava to be valued by roasting and tasting. (Baule, Ivory Coast)
> A woman is not a boot; you cannot kick her off. (Russian)

A woman is not a fiddle you can hang on the wall after playing. (German/Finnish)
A wife is not a shirt you can change according to your needs. (Ladino, Morocco)
A wife is not a bedcover. [One cannot simply change her after a while.] (Creole, Haiti)

This is just a simple example, but it illustrates that across cultural diversities other commonalities exist. Moreover, such similarities in ideas about each other exist everywhere and certainly not only thanks to globalization, but also without any cultural contact at all. How is this possible? Our common patterns as human beings have to do with the shape and functions of the human body and its basic needs, such as food, shelter, safety and procreation. And with emotions such as fear, longing, joy and sorrow that we all experience as human beings living on planet earth.

I always tell my students: if you look for differences, you'll only find differences, and if you look for similarities, they are right there. However, instead of looking for what we share as human beings, we seem to be more inclined to blow up the differences—differences of race, gender, class, ethnicity, and so forth.

Looking into the worldwide harvest of cultural legacies in all their differences and similarities may help us put our own local differences into a more global perspective, whereas limiting the world to locally fixed Self-and-Other images gets in the way of the awareness of a wider picture. Awareness is always a first crucial step towards questioning our established views of each other.

Crocodiles and tree trunks

"However long the tree trunk lies in water, it never becomes a crocodile," goes the West African Mandinka proverb, referring to the others, those who are different from us, the outsiders, those who will never really belong here, even though they try their utmost.

Indeed, the world seems to "naturally" consist of us and them, of crocodiles and tree trunks, and "them" are not allowed to become part of "our" community. From the insiders' crocodile perspective, they will stay tree trunks, however much they twist and turn. Us and them, Self and Other, the drawing of demarcation lines of culture and ethnicity have separated us as human beings in an ongoing history of inclusion and exclusion, often with devastating consequences.

Cultural differences have rarely been acknowledged as self-evident and the definition of what is human often extends no further than the borders of one's own ethnic group, country, religion, race or sex—the borders of one's own language, township, village, nation, culture. The barbarians are always the others. Thus the ancient Greeks viewed Romans as barbarians. Romans did the same with the peoples they subjugated. Aryans looked down on Jews and Jews on Palestinians. Europeans felt they were more civilized than Indians and Africans, but did not realize that from the perspectives of these peoples, Western savagery had become proverbial. In China, the Wall was the dividing line between culture and barbarism. The philosopher Shao Yong (1011-1077) expressed his ethnocentric mentality quite clearly when he stated: "I am happy because I am a human being and not an animal, a man and not a woman, a Chinese and not a barbarian, and because I live in Loyang, the most beautiful city in the world" (quoted in Sinclair 1977: 20). The tendency to judge others as being inferior to one's own group is widespread, for the truthfulness of world views is often less valued than the extent to which they serve prevailing interests.

Non-compatible input?

People are inclined to create demarcation lines by marking differences with other groups. There is always a difference between how people view themselves and their group, and how they see others. In fact it is as simple as that. However, the interest in the ideas of others has never been quite intense. Usually we are significantly silent about the question of how Self and Other are described from the perspectives of other ethnicities, cultures, classes, or the other sex. Usually marginalised groups have only been allowed the position of Other, not Self; of object, not subject. Still, beliefs and convictions are not fixed forever and new perspectives can make people modify earlier assumptions. Boundaries between "us" and "them" can be redefined according to the interests of those concerned, and our own and other people's narratives can be compared, questioned and discussed. The point is that, in daily life, our own self-evident background thinking is so much taken for granted that deviant views are easily discarded as *non-compatible input*. It first needs awareness of the mechanism and then creative efforts to take that unwelcome input into account.

Identities

To those willing to listen, global history is ready to tell more than one version of past events. Identity is related to the question of the difference between us and others: a difference in culture, social class, caste, sex, religion, age, nationality, living area etc. From these separate (or mixed) identities, views are developed on Self and Other. As soon as people feel threatened as a group, they attach great importance to their identity. Collective identity highlights a common group's point of view.

- It is experienced subjectively and confirmed by members of a group

- It is derived from the consciousness of belonging to the group

- It is determined by boundaries excluding the Other in general, and marking out differences with certain groups in particular

- Its boundaries and differences are based on a system of relatively intuitive images (of the Self as well as of the Other), determined by a set of negative (avoidable) aspects and a set of positive ones.

- The positive aspects form the group's ideal model, inspired by a defensive ethnocentrism, resulting in chauvinism, nationalism, patriotism etc.

Thus a relatively coherent ideology can be established on the basis of these characteristics and attitudes. This ideology can be studied in the discourse of the group, as expressed in all kinds of texts.[1]

The cultural interpretations of one's own identity and its surrounding world merge from childhood; they are experienced as natural. Ideally, we should be able to consider ourselves against the background of others, in just the same way as we put others against our own background. But usually it does not work that way. It takes serious efforts to switch one's perspective.

Since the second half of the twentieth century a dramatic contradiction has been developing, and we have seen it happen all over the world. On the one hand there is the technological advancement which covers our planet as a levelling cosmopolitism, and on the other, a continuous protest going against this levelling by all kinds of groups—in the name of nationalism, race, ethnicity, culture, religion and other forms of collective identity. The other side of the globalization coin has been a growing preoccupation with ethnic belonging.[2]

This deep-rooted human feature of creating demarcation lines by marking differences is so much easier to detect in others than in oneself. It can be defined as: a group attitude in which a self-evident central position is given to one's own cultural group amidst other groups, and in which one's own group characteristics are valued positively and those of others negatively. Ethnocentrism and racism and other forms of exclusive attention paid to human differences obscure the image of those who belong to the out-groups as a result of the value judgement of the in-group. Those so-called differences promote a hierarchical order in economic, poli-tical and cultural relations and, consciously or subconsciously, people's origin stories have sometimes contributed to opposing in-groups and out-groups.

Origin stories and hierarchies

> No people on the face of the earth is so great and noble as we, the people of Tonga. Other nations may be richer, and perhaps even stronger than we; but we are the greatest, and we alone. (Tonga)[3]

Does our own origin myth make us feel prestigious and lucky in life or does it have the opposite effect on us? What if one set of first ancestors gets all the favoured goods the creator has in store, whereas the ancestors of others are excluded or seem to be doomed, because they happen to be less blessed in the beginning?

The Polynesian kingdom of Tonga lies south of Samoa. Like the Samoans, the Tongans believe that in the beginning a god descended in the form of a bird and there are many stories about it. The quotation at the beginning of this section comes from a Tonga version of the myth telling about runaway gods who settled on the earth in the land of the Tongans, and who had no slaves yet.

> One day a sandpiper was seeking food and scratched at the ground in a muddy place. The worms that crept out were so slimy and smelly that the sandpiper couldn't eat them. He spurned them, and with his feet scattered them all over the surface of the mud. The sun shone upon them for many days, and gradually they grew into men. The first Tonga ancestors appropriated them as their slaves. These slaves have no souls: at the end of their days, they die, and that's the end of them. This is also how it is with the white men. We know that for sure, since we have asked them about it, and this is what they told us: there are sandpipers in their land too. This is why we, the people of Tonga, are the noblest among the nations. All the other people are children of the earth; but we are children of the gods. (Tonga)[4]

Being the first physical children of their divine ancestors, the Tongans were exceptionally lucky. They received souls which allowed them to live eternally, whereas all other peoples were doomed to live soulless and disappear forever. Still, the Tongans are not unique in this respect.

As mentioned in the book of Exodus in the Bible, the Hebrew people are God's chosen people, and from them the Messiah shall come, the redeemer of the human race. Christians associating themselves with Israel as God's own children, may also believe to be *the* chosen people, and Muslims may lay similar superiority claims for their own religious community. And other groups of believers may have similar reactions.

People apply their own cultural models to the world around them, a world divided according to religion, ethnicity, caste, class, race and gender, endowing themselves and certain people with superior qualities and others with inferior ones. Origin stories, accordingly, justify people's place as higher or lower in the order of things. In this respect narratives about the beginning reflect and confirm society's most stubborn beliefs about hierarchy.

The Tutsi in Rwanda also had a special position amongst other peoples, likewise traced back to their creation myth in which originally people lived in heaven with their god Imana. In the story, things went wrong when a mother who drank too much beer went against Imana's will by revealing to her sister the secret origin of her miraculous pregnancies. As a punishment her three children were dramatically expelled from the heavenly residence: sitting on a mat they sank down to the earth. Helplessly the lamenting mother stayed behind in heaven and ultimately Imana pitied her, granting the wishes she uttered on behalf of her children. He even promised her that one day her children would return to the sky. (Tutsi, Rwanda).

In their own origin myth the Tutsi themselves play the most prominent and privileged role, whereas the other peoples of the same country, the Hutu and Batwa, had to be humbly grateful to the Tutsi who called themselves the blessed children of Imana. Their oral tradition emphasised that without their help the Hutu and the Batwa would not have been able to survive: "They had been driven from the sky before us and Imana has refused to forgive them. It is we who obtained for them the little well-being that they are enjoining today. The King and the Tutsi are the heart of the country. If the Hutu should drive us out, they would lose all their possessions and Imana would punish them."[5] Prolonged echoes of old myths keep resounding over the generations, even though nobody can prove a direct link between the message of the traditional Tutsi myth and the extremist Hutu violence.

Throughout history people have made war with neighbours who looked exactly like themselves as well as with people who looked differently. And myths may be dangerously involved: "One culture's cleansing ritual, based on myth, can become another culture's holocaust", as in Germany's Third Reich, when Hitler justified the concept of the Aryan master race using

Germanic myths as popularised by Wagner in his operas.[6] Origin myths tend to privilege one group over the other by creating hierarchies and differences expressed in terms of "us" and "them", terms often based on physical appearance.

Different colours, different races

What was the skin colour of the first humans? DNA studies suggest that all humans today descend from a small group whose posterity is living in Southern Africa today: the San. Around 600,000 years ago their early ancestors migrated and spread all over the earth, as can be seen from the genetic markers they left behind in the various peoples living today. This indicates that people are genetically far more connected than they ever thought. Like some present-day DNA specialists, many myths argue that all people living on the earth originate from the same first ancestral couple. The well-known and widespread story of Adam and Eve is a case in point. It still has an impact in many places blaming women for having spoiled paradise "for all of us".

Origin stories not only wonder about the origin of men and women, but also about why there are different races in the world.[7] In many myths the origin of people with different skin colours is explained *en passant* in the context of other events without further reference to superiority or inferiority.

The Wa who live in the border area of Myanmar and China have an origin myth in which the "sixty races" of humankind all emerged from one and the same gourd, and that's all there is to be said about the matter.[8] The differences among them do not really come into the picture. Other stories explain the different skin colours by suggesting that in different parts of the world the available material used for the fashioning of people was variable, from white sand to red soil, black earth or yellow clay, and as a result people look different, as in the following example from Shilluk, Sudan:

> Jwok fashioned the different shades of the various races with the different coloured clays out of which they were moulded, and while he was doing his work of creation he wandered about the world. In the land of the whites he found a pure white earth or sand, out of which he shaped white men. Then he came to the land of Egypt and out of the mud of the Nile he made red or brown men. Finally, he came to the land of the Shilluk, where he found black earth out of which he created black men.[9]

Myths about the origin of different skin colour shades exist in many varieties in Asian, African and Amerindian stories. The differences are not much of an issue here and there are more such cases. There are also myths in which people who are marked as different for one reason or another have to leave simply because "they are not like us". This happens, for example, in an Amerindian Pima myth in which the Maker's first effort to make people resulted in dogs, because the trickster Coyote had interfered. The Maker decided to try once again and put freshly formed clay figures into the oven.

> After a while Coyote, still around, insisted that they were done, and the Creator took them out of the oven but too early: they were not brown enough. The Maker brought them to life, but could not use them here, because they belonged someplace across the water. Once again on the advice of Coyote, the next set remained too long in the oven. They were "overdone", "burned too dark" and that is why they didn't belong here either: they too had to go across the water. Finally the Maker no longer allowed Coyote to interfere, and the clay images turned out exactly right: neither underdone nor overdone. And the creator was happy. Yes, indeed, these perfect human beings belonged here: they were really beautiful. And that's us, the Pueblo Indians.[10]

Several other Amerindian groups have stories with similar proud conclusions, confirming that "we" are the most attractive kind. The first Indians were made from balls of red earth, the Okanagon Indians in Canada explain, and this is why their colour is reddish. Other races were made from soil in different colours. Afterwards some of these different races met and mingled, and thus intermediate shades of colour evolved. Since red earth is more related to gold and copper than other kinds of earth, they argue, the Indians are nearer to gold, and finer than other races.[11]

In this case of slight self praise, "them", the others, cannot help being less beautiful than "us", the ideal copper coloured ones. Still, in the stories concerned, the narrators do not blame the other peoples for having received the "wrong" colour. They cannot help it and cannot change it. It is rather a matter of fate.

No less than in Amerindian cultures, there are oven stories in Africa. Congolese students told me several versions of the story, in one of which all the clay people were put into the oven at the same time. The white people couldn't stand the heat of the fire and immediately ran out of the oven. That's why they have such a sickly white skin. Others tolerated the heat a bit longer, but after a short while they also ran out and those turned out red. Only the Africans were able to bear with the heat of the fire until the very moment the creator had decided that it was time for them to come out. That is why Africans are tough enough to bear with the sorrows of life. In Africa there are strikingly many myths broaching the topic of the origin of black and white people.

The origin of black and white people in Africa

> My brothers, you see, the white man is very bad, very ugly, no good. You want to know how this kind of men has come to the world? Well, I'm going to tell you. Adam and Eve, people of colour, were very beautiful. They lived in a beautiful garden. There they had all sorts of good things: plantains, yams, sweet potatoes, fufu, palm wine, too much of it! They had two children, Cain and Abel. Cain did not like to palaver with Abel. One day he killed him. Then God was angry and said: "Cain!" Cain went to hide himself. He believed himself very clever. Hey, hey... Again God said: "Cain, do you think I don't see you, you bush nigger, hey? Then Cain came forward and said: "Yes Lord, here I am, what is the matter, my Lord?" Then, out of fear, Cain turned white all over: the first white man. (Pidgin, Sierra Leone).[12]

Even though inequality is not always brought into the picture, in the practice of storytelling people's different looks are frequently associated with difference in status. To many African peoples, the power of the white people was felt as so stark in contrast with the poverty of most Africans that they invented myths to unravel this intriguing mystery.

Some African origin stories about colour and race resemble the myths from Asia or the Americas that we came across earlier: skin colour as a pure coincidence, depending on the available soil in a particular place. Or as a freak of nature: just as there is a varied world of plants and animals—for example, sheep and cows in different colours—the existence of differently coloured people is an enrichment of the species.

The main themes are however: colour as a fatality of destiny, a committed error or mistake, or two brothers put to the test with a different outcome for both. There are also myths about the wrong choice people made in the beginning. There is, for example, an Ewe myth from Ghana and Togo about two baskets which Mawu, the High God, sent down to the earth to be shared by a black and white couple. The black couple quickly and greedily claimed the biggest basket. It contained a hoe to till the earth, some cotton to spin, some bows and arrows for hunting, and gold dust for trading. The basket left for the white people only contained a small book which taught them all that was worth knowing.[13]

In such myths usually the African is the first to be born with the European as the younger brother who ultimately turns "white" and gets the better position. The whites and their offspring are always better off—as in the colonial reality of everyday life that the myth needed to explain. And the whites then usually have to leave Africa, as in a Bashi myth from Democratic Republic of Congo:

> The first creature the creator Nyamuzinda fashioned was a hen. It laid forty eggs from which forty human beings were hatched to serve the creator. One of them, Mushema, had to go down to Cape Mwanda close by Lake Kivu and he became the first ancestor of all the earthlings. With his wife Mwabunyoko Mushema had more than a hundred children who were the ancestors of all the kings and all the people. Nyamuzinda decided that they must disperse and settle across the globe. However, Mushema was poor and Nyamuzinda came to his aid, providing his progeny with an inheritance.

What happened? Nobody knows. One thing, however, is for sure: at the break of day, all children held a gift from God in their hand. One had a cow, another had an ox, a third had a goat, and so on. Chihanya, the forefather of the Bashi, woke up with a pot of milk in his hand. That is the reason why the Bashi like milk and cows so much. However, the people found that Nyamuzinda had endowed them unequally. Envy sparked quarrel among the children of Mushema. The forefather of the Europeans, whose name has been lost, could hardly recognize himself when he woke up. Not only had he received a special gift from Nyamuzinda—stationery and firearms—but also his skin, black, like his brothers', had turned white, so that he looked like a European. When his brothers saw this, they said: "You are not a human child like we are. Our mother Mwabunyoko did not give birth to you and who can understand the things you hold in your hand?"

They decided to slaughter a young chicken and to read the meaning of all this in her intestine. It became obvious that Nyamuzinda himself had changed him thus and revealed the secret of those gifts to this white creature only. He left for a distant country, named Bulayi (Europe), but it is not known which way he took. Did he die first, then arise from the grave to be taken to his country invisibly? Was he carried by the clouds or did he follow the path of the rain? Mystery. One thing is for sure: he took his godly gifts with him. And that is why his offspring, the Europeans, are still in possession of the stationery and the fire arms.[14]

In the story all children share the same first father and first mother, but the unequally distributed gifts cause the trouble in the first place, and then there was the favoured son's colour change. He became a stranger to his brothers, because to them white was the colour of death, and the presumed forefather of the Europeans had to leave the family.

The explanation for the racial inequality people experienced in reality had to be couched in mythical stories in which the European had to be the outsider, the one sent far away at the dawn of time, the stranger belonging to an unknown world, an under water world, a faraway country overseas, or the ghostly kingdom of the dead.

Among African myths about the origin of black and white people the Sierra Leonean story this section began with is rather exceptional.[15] The conclusion is almost always that God privileged the Europeans. They received the knowledge, the binoculars, the books, the stationery, the guns, the machines and the money.

In the colonial context, the skin colour, as the most striking contrasting feature, was associated with economic, military, political, social, cultural issues, and with difference in power, knowledge and technology. "The only thing that Europeans are still wanting for is immortality," people in Congo used to say.

When I was teaching in Congo, my students split their sides laughing when I told them that in Europe white skinned men labour on the land, sell fruits or fish in the market and collect garbage, that white women peel potatoes and cook meals, clean their own or other people's homes, and that some people are so poor that they sit on the pavement begging for money because they are hungry. The students found the idea hilarious and refused to believe me. Thanks to glossy magazines and American B-films they had a totally different picture of Europeans in mind, a picture that made them stick to the more familiar mythical message that white people are rich people.

The echoes of a long colonial history have left strong marks in African myths about the origin of the races. After all, myths are meant to explain how things have come to be the way they are. However, in origin myths the question of differences is not limited to ethnic and racial issues. The unfairness of fate results in all sorts of inescapable bearings on everyday life, in need of explanation through myth and narrative. For example: why do we have to sweat for our hard earned daily bread, and why do some of us have to sweat a lot more than others? This question reaches far beyond mythical ethnicity or race perspectives. It touches upon humanity at large.

The rich and the poor

One of the most puzzling questions in life is why there are such striking differences in material well-being between people living together in the same village, clan or country. What lies at the origin of the worldwide existing inequality that is so strikingly visible around us everywhere until this very day? People have invented myths to explain (and often tend to justify in the meantime) the good luck of the rich and the bad luck of the poor. They do so in different ways, even though in the end the message works out much the same.

Among the Chinese Han people, one of the most popular goddesses is Nüwa the creator of the first human beings. Having moulded a number of them from the yellow earth, with her own hands, the work began to drain so much of her strength that she decided to proceed differently: she took a cord, pulled it through the mud, lifted and shook it. The sludge falling down from the cord also became men and women: the people carefully handmade by Nüwa became the rich and noble ones whereas those made by her dragging the cord through the mud were hardly formed and therefore became poor and lowly ones. That is why people are different in life.[16] Riches and noblesse are connected in this Chinese story, and so are poverty and lowness: material wealth is directly associated with nobility and a superior position on the social ladder.

Hierarchies are established in a large variety of ways. In the Hindu Vedic "Hymn of Man" (*Purusha sukta*) the human race comes into being in a primeval sacrifice along with a given social order.[17] One famous passage quoted earlier (p.000) wonders how the body of Purusha was divided, into how many parts, and what became of those various parts, the mouth, the arms, the thighs and the feet. The answer equates the body with the caste system: there are "higher" and "lower" parts. Purusha's mouth or head became the Brahmin, that is the priests and philosophers involved in religious activities; his arms and hands were made into the kings, noblemen, and warriors dealing with matters of defense and administration; his thighs and groin became the common people, such as farmers, herdsmen and traders who are economically active; and from his feet the labourers and servants were born.[18]

Over time India developed an unchangeable caste (*varna*) system which divided and subdivided itself more and more. Many local Indian origin stories tell how and why the gods began to work on human fate ever since life on earth began. Some stories tell that a goddess marked people's hands with an iron needle fixing people's destinies for life with wealth, greatness, barrenness, or poverty, as we are told this myth in more or less detail.

They made the eldest brother a Raja, the second brother a Brahmin to worship the gods, the third a Dhakad to fight for the Raja, the fourth a Rawat to care for his cattle, the fifth a Muria to carry his loads, the sixth a Kuruk to catch his fish and the seventh a Maria to see to his hunting. These were the seven castes of Bastar. From seven they have grown, to thirty-six. (Raja Muria, India)[19]

Such narratives are meant to impose an unchangeable ideology for the members of society to function according to their respective positions and duties in society. Since this hierarchy was divinely ordained, those who refused to agree with this ideology were considered as barbarians and must be chased away. Moreover, this message of unchangeable positions and duties refers to men only. Irrespective of their caste, for women there was in this system no position at all. Theirs was only a position of obedience to man.[20]

A Tahitian origin myth also institutionalized a class system of its own, presented as fixed right from the first human beginnings:

When Ti'i, the first man, and Hina, the first woman, begat children they became the high royal family as the descendents of the gods from darkness. The people that they conjured into being became the common people, the plebians of the world. Through their marriage with the common people the royal family begat the gentry of the world, and through their marriage with the gentry the royal family begat the nobility of the world. The long capes became the inheritance of royalty and nobility, because that is where the great temples of the land stood. The deep bays were declared to be the inheritance of the gentry. As the land became thickly populated, the people spread everywhere, but on the seashore and inland the plebeians' lands bordered on the lands of the great. (Tahitian)[21]

Myths often serve to justify the dividing of the land according to clans and classes, and the marginalising of "lower people" thus seems to become a matter of logical consequence. Or they insist that the first ancestors crept up from the inside of the earth at this particular place, and therefore we are still entitled to occupy the land here. The usual argument is that no one can change the mythical "facts". Such myths may result in bloody conflicts with others who lay similar claims.

However, the *Popol Vuh*, Book of the Ancient Maya, presents an encouraging exception to such reasoning which often favours the more wealthy ones. After some failed efforts, the four gods succeeded in creating a man out of gold. However, the man who was lying there on the earth, remained lifeless and cold. Finally the creators successfully used bits of their own flesh in making real human beings. The kind presence of those humans warmed the heart of the man of gold, so much so that he came to life. The man of gold and his descendants became the rich, whereas the men of flesh were the poor. In this story we are told that "no rich man can enter heaven unless he is brought there by a poor man." (Maya, Guatemala)[22] At his death, the rich man will be judged on the basis of how he cared for the poor. The gods themselves ordained that the rich must look after the poor, and the story reminds the audience of their tradition of communal living and co-operative work. Such a command is strictly lacking in the African stories about the races.

When Portuguese explorers arrived in Brazil in the 1500s, lots of new local myths about the rich and the poor came into being, and the superior (gun) power of the non-Indian settlers. The stories strongly remind of the earlier discussed African stories explaining the origin of the dominant position of the white settlers. A Paressí myth, for example, tells about how in the beginning the Supreme Being generously offered cattle, guns, bows and arrows to the ancestors of both the whites and the Paressí. However, the Paressí found the guns too heavy and also refused the cattle because the animals would soil the beautiful plazas of their villages. They preferred the bows and arrows and went off to the forest. The Ufaina have a very similar message about the origin of the difference in power. In their myth the first ancestors of the whites and those of the Ufaina were both hatched from eggs. However, at the request of God, one of the four immortals took care of the whites, while the jaguar was invited to take care of the Ufaina, and "that's why the whites know so much and can make things."[23]

The conclusion is again and again that nothing much can be done about one's being rich or poor. One is lucky only because one's first ancestors were lucky, made the right choice, avoided errors, or received the right knowledge. As in the African myths about the races it is most likely that by laughing at one's predicament the presentation of a presumed fatalistic self-image also functioned as a kind of "sardonic humour", resulting in a psychological advantage over those in power.[24]

The children of Eve

When I was recently in Cairo, a taxi driver told me that Adam and Eve had lived in Saudi-Arabia, he was sure about it. I told him that according to scientific research the first people were supposed to come from Africa. He looked puzzled and after a long silence he said: "You know, what I think? It became so unbearably hot in Saudi-Arabia that they decided to move southward."

Given the numerous unorthodox invented variants of the biblical Adam and Eve story told or written down over the centuries, the characters must surely have been extremely popular. One of the puzzling questions was how to explain social inequality: if we are all children of Adam and Eve, how then to justify society's social class structure?

Wondering about their own unequal destinies, people fantasised about what had happened to the children of Adam and Eve. The story exists all over Europe, there are Christian and Muslim versions in Africa and Asia, and South American variants inspired by Spanish versions. The events take place after Adam and Eve had been expelled from Paradise. Adam and Eve had many more children than the Bible accounts for, and in some versions Eve does not even remember how many she has got. The main storyline is that since God had told them how to beget children, they begat so many that Eve believes the number of children would mirror her unbridled lust, at least in the eyes of the Lord.

In one version God came for a visit to find out how Adam and Eve were coping on earth, and mother Eve called in the clean and neat children, and those were blessed by God: their descendants would be kings, emperors, princes, aristocrats, knights, bishops, or learned and remarkable men. As soon as she heard God giving out those blessings, Eve became so alarmed that she quickly called for the sniffing and dirty children, and God blessed those too, saying that they would be peasants, fishermen, shoemakers, tailors, farmers, etc. And this is how the social ranks came into being, justified as indispensable for the well-being of the world.

When Eve began to protest against the unequally distributed gifts, God calmly justified his policy as right and necessary: "Eve, you do not understand. It is right and necessary that your children should supply the entire world; if they were all princes and lords, who would grow corn, thresh it, grind and bake it? Who would be blacksmiths, weavers, carpenters, masons, labourers, tailors? Everyone shall have his own place, so that one shall support the other, and all shall be fed like the limbs of one body." And Eve humbly submitted: "Oh, Lord, forgive me. I was too quick in speaking to thee. Have thy divine will with my children."[25]

Various versions provide different details. One interesting variant tells that Eve had twenty-four children, twelve of each sex. When God wanted to see all her children, Eve, protective of the girls, only showed the boys, and the lads were promised good fortune and happiness in life. Eve quickly started looking for the girls to show to God, but no blessing was left for them. In a version from Argentina, there is an explicit question from the audience about what then happened to those poor girls, and the narrator argues that before they are being born, "God can give them beauty, charm, and sometimes, he even gives them talent, but as soon as they are in the world man is their only hope. To him they owe everything." In spite of all his power the Lord cannot give women anything anymore after their birth.[26]

People experience inequality as an unfair fact of human life. In origin myths ethnicity, race and gender differences go back to humanity's early days. If we all descend from the same pair of ancestors, why then came the difference? Existing wealth, power, skills, qualities and privileges must be due to the distinctive origins, good luck or bad luck, or a first ancestor's misbehaviour, or to the very way in which we have originated. Strikingly then, the irresponsible behaviour of the first people or the gods' distribution of destiny have led to positions perpetuated in society. Even though all first people are referred to as human beings, some have become more equal than others and "ever since" things are as they are.

To what extent, one wonders, do the messages of origin myths mark the now living descendants of the clan, caste, class, race or sex concerned? We don't know, of course, but if stories repeat certain ideas often enough, people are inclined to believe them subconsciously. Familiarity with each other's cultural contexts and myths puts our own culture and ethnicity and origin stories in a new and wider frame of reference, reaching across the borders of our own ethnic or religious group, our own ideology, race or sex. Exchanging and listening to each other's arguments from a compassionate open perspective is more urgent than ever for our hopelessly divided human community. It makes us more aware that globally speaking there is only one humanity to which we all belong.

A world in need of a future

As it looks now, in a decade or two, or even sooner, there will not be enough water for all of us to drink or even enough fresh air for all of us to breathe, if we stick to being divided against each other. Today, we need to unite our local energies and we need to be globally united for our planet to survive. How can we be helpful as individuals and as communities?

Since living memory, ethnicity and religion have ordered the social structures of society. And origin myths have contributed to that order. For most people ethics depend on religion. More than ever before in history, our ability of living together cross-culturally depends on what we are able to share in our ethics across the various beliefs in our global and local human society.

It means that we have to learn to see others as human beings like ourselves and not in terms of suspicion, automatically opposing 'us' and 'them'. Each of us can create a bit more order instead of more chaos in the place where we live, and each of us can promote understanding where suspicion and hostility set the tone.

In Confucius' (551 BC-479 BC) words: "Don't do to others what you don't want others to do to you." This saying, known since the eighteenth century as the "Golden Rule," the rule of empathy and respect, can be found in many cultures and religions. In the Bible it has been formulated as: "Do to others as you would have them do to you." In reality this message has "naturally" been restricted, to those who belong to "our own group." Instead of despising or suspecting each other, respect for each other as human beings has become an urgent matter of survival, not only locally but globally. [27] The emphasis on difference will always get in the way of integration.

Though the human species is between four million and two-hundred thousand years old (depending on the view of what a human is), culturally speaking we are not much older than about five-thousand years. Still, we have developed spectacularly since our early beginnings. In the future, if things go well, we can build structures for human society never seen before, thoughts never thought before, music never heard before." [28]

So, what do we share? If things go well, we will share a future; if things go wrong, there will be no future. Today, humanity looks like a huge animal walking around on the earth with innumerable legs and brains, with contradictory minds, ideas, beliefs, emotions and narratives. Those various parts can go against each other and devour each other, or enrich and stimulate each other, so that it can move forward in harmony and peace. In order for this animal to survive at all, it has to strive for integration at all levels, it has to learn how to adapt and live more in agreement with the planet it inhabits. It needs to take care of its contradictory body parts with compassion, in order to prepare humanity for a safe and prosperous future.

Notes

[1] Cf. Michaud 1978:112.

[2] As Peter Geschiere observed in his book *The Perils of Belonging: Autochthony, Citizenship, and Exclusion in Africa and Europe*. Chicago: The University of Chicago Press 2009.

[3] Lorimer Fison. *Tales from Old Fiji*. London: Alexandre Moring 1907: 135.

[4] Fison, ibid. 135, 161

[5] Père Loupias. Tradition et légende des Batutsi sur la creation du monde et leur établissement au Rwanda. In: Anthropos, III, 1908: 2-13. The Hutu living in the same country have a very different more egalitarian genesis myth: according to them, in the beginning Imana created on earth a boy and a girl who became the ancestors of all people. They married each other and got three children, the first one was Gatutsi, the father of the Tutsi; the second one was Gahutu, the father of the Hutu; the third, Gatwa, became the father of the Batwa.

[6] Cf. Leeming p.5.

[7] See my forthcoming book *In the beginning. The first people in creation myths from around the world.*(2010)

[8] The Wa live in former Indo-Chine. *The Mythology of All Races*, vol. xii *Egyptian and Indo-Chinese*. Cambridge Mass: The University Press 1918: 290-291.

[9] Shilluk: Translated and abridged from W. Hofmayr, 'Die Religion der Schilluk,' Anthropos, VI (1906), pp. 128 ff. See also Veronika Görög Karady 264.

[10] The Amerindian Pima story goes back to fragments recorded in the 1880s which have been re-used in: Bierlein 1994: 63-66 and Erdoes & Ortiz. 1984: 46.

[11] Retold from Franz Boaz, James Alexander Teit, Livingston Farrand, Marian K. Gould, Herbert Joseph Spinden. *Folk-Tales of Salishan and Sahaptin Tribes*. New York: Kraus Reprint Co., 1969: 84.

[12] The original Pidgin text from Sierra Leone can be found in: W.W. Reade. *Savage Africa*. London: Smith & Co 1864: 24.

[13] Baumann (1936) 1961: 332-333 ; Ellis 1887 Tshi 340. Ellis suggests that this storytelling tradition be of European invention: "At all events it must be of a comparatively recent date, and have been invented after the advent of Europeans." I don't think those stories have been invented by Europeans. I found many versions of the myth in Congo and have discussed its origin with a number of people. They all repeated and confirmed that this was "a real Congolese story" which had no European roots.

[14] P.W. van Hoef 1911: 321-325

[15] Görög-Karady 1976: ch. 5. In African novels a very different portrait of the white people and the Western world is being depicted. See also my books *Imagining Insiders* and *Le Blanc vu d'Afrique*

[16] Lihui Yang a.o. 68. n other variants the cord is a piece of vine or rattan from the mountainside which she dips into her damp yellow soil. Yuan Ke, *Dragons and Dynasties. An Introduction to Chinese Mythology*. London: Penguin and Beijing: Foreign Languages Press 1993:4.

[17] According to Wendy Doniger this is possibly the "most explicitly hierarchical hymn in the whole of the *Rig Veda*." See her *Hindu Myth*. London: Penguin 1975: 27; Dedutt Pattanaik, *Indian Mythology. Tales, Symbols, and Rituals from the Heart of the Subcontinent*. Rochester Vermont: 2003.

[18] The four classes *(varòas)* of ancient Indian society were the priests *(brahmins)*, nobles or warriors *(kºatriyas)*, the "all" - i.e. the general populace *(viœ* or *vaiœyas)*, and the servants *(úûdras)*. Cf. Pattanaik, o.c. 2003: 122-123.

[19] See Verrier Elwin, *Tribal Myths of Orissa*. London: Oxford University Press, 1954: 456-457. Summarized from Verrier Elwin. *Myths of Middle India*. Madras etc.: Oxford University Press, 1949: 47-48

[20] Pattainak o.c.: 174-175.

[21] Teuira Henry 403.

[22] Bierlein o.c.: 69.

[23] J.F. Bierlein. *Parallel Myths*. New York: Ballantine Books, 1994: 69; Kay Almere Read and Jason González. *Mesoamenican Mythology*. Santa Barbara/Denver/Oxford: 2000: 67; John Bierhorst, 2002: 39.

[24] As D.L. Ashliman suggests in an interesting comment on this topic. See his contribution to Jane Garry and Hasan El-Shamy (eds), o.c.: 53

[25] Jakob Ludwig Karl Grimm and Wilhelm Karl Grimm. *Kinder- und Hausmärchen. 20e Auflage*. Berlin1885: 624-625 (my translation).

[26] Vicente Blasco Ibañez 1929 qtd in Geddes o.c.: 166.

[27] Matth 7: 12; Luke 6: 30- 33. I am summarizing some of Karen Armstrong's ideas here from her work and interviews.

[28] See Lewis Thomas, Seven Wonders. In: *The Oxford Book of Modern Science Writing* (Richard Dawkins ed.). Oxford: Oxford University Press, 2008.

References

Ashliman, D.L. (2005). Origins of Inequality. In: Jane Garry and Hasan El-Shamy (Eds). *Archetypes and Motifs In Folklore and Literature. A handbook.* Armonk/New York/London: M.E. Sharpe pp. 50-51.

Baumann, H. (1936). *Schöpfung und Urzeit der Afrikanischen Völker.* Berlin: Dietrich Reimer Verlag.

Boaz, F., J.A. Teit, L. Farrand, Marian K. Gould, H. J. Spinden. (1969). *Folk-Tales of Salishan and Sahaptin Tribes.* New York: Kraus Reprint.

Bierlein J.F. (1994). *Parallel Myths.* New York: Ballantine Books.

Ellis, A.B. (1887). *The Tshi-speaking Peoples of the Gold Coast of West Africa. Their Religion, Manners, Customs, Laws, Language, etc.* London: Chapman and Hall.

Doniger, W. (1975). *Hindu Myth.* London: Penguin.

Elwin, V. (1954). *Tribal Myths of Orissa.* London: Oxford University Press.

Elwin, V. (1949). *Myths of Middle India.* Madras etc.: Oxford University Press.

Erdoes, R. & A. Ortiz. (1984). *American Indian Myths and Legends.* New York: Pantheon Books.

Fison, L. (1907). *Tales from Old Fiji.* London: Alexandre Moring.

Geddes, V. (1986). *"Various Children of Eve" (AT 758). Cultural Variants and Antifeminine Images.* (Etnolore 5). Uppsala: Uppsala Universitet Etnologiska Institutionen.

Geschiere, P. (2009). *The Perils of Belonging: Autochthony, Citizenship, and Exclusion in Africa and Europe.* Chicago: The University of Chicago Press.

Görög-Karady, Veronika. (1976). *Noirs et Blancs. Leur image dans la littératue orale africaine.* Paris: SELAF.

Grimm, J. Ludwig Karl and Wilhelm Karl Grimm. (1885). *Kinder- und Hausmärchen.* 20e Auflage. (n.p.) Berlin.

Hoef, P.W. van. De oorsprong van het menschelijk geslacht. In: *Missiën der Witte Paters* 1911: 321-325.

Hofmayr, Die Religion der Schilluk. *Anthropos*, VI (1906)p. 128.

Leeming, D. A. (1990). *The World of Myth. An Anthology.* Oxford: Oxford University Press.

Lihui, Y. & Deming An, with Jessica Anderson Turner. (2005). Handbook of Chinese Mythology. Santa Barbara/Denver/Oxford: ABC-CLIO.

Loupias, R.P. (1978). Tradition et légende des Batutsi sur la creation du monde et leur établissement au Rwanda. In: Anthropos, III, 1908: 2-13. Michaud, Guy et al. *Identités collectives et relations interculturelles.* Paris: Editions Complexe.

Pattanaik, D. (2003). *Indian Mythology. Tales, Symbols, and Rituals from the Heart of the Subcontinent.* Rochester Vermont.

Reade, W.W. (1864). *Savage Africa.* London: Smith & Co.

Read, Kay A. and J. González. (2000). *Mesoamenican Mythology.* Santa Barbara/ Denver/Oxford.

Sinclair, A. (1977). *The Savage. A History of Misunderstanding.* London: Weidenfeld & Nicolson.

Schipper, M. (1973). *Le Blanc vu d'Afrique.* Assen: Van Gorcum/ Yaoundé: Editions CLE

Schipper, M. (1999). *Imagining Insiders. Africa and the Question of Belonging.* London and New York: Continuum.

Teuira, H. (1928). *Ancient Tahiti. Based on Material recorded by J.M. Orsmond.* Museum Bulletin Series 48. Honolulu: Bernice P. Bishop Museum.

Thomas, L. (2008). Seven Wonders. In: *The Oxford Book of Modern Science Writing* (Richard Dawkins ed.). Oxford: Oxford University Press.

Yuan, K. (1993). *Dragons and Dynasties. An Introduction to Chinese Mythology.* London: Penguin and Beijing: Foreign Languages Press.

Production of Ethnic Identity in Kenya

Karega-Munene

Introduction

Human beings have, through space and time, used numerous markers of identity to distinguish themselves from the next person or group. These markers include one's name, which is given at birth, a few days after birth or through rituals like baptism; the sex and age of a person both of which are biologically determined although one can cross-dress, undergo sex-change or plastic surgery or even dye their hair in an attempt to conceal their age; plus gender which is socially ascribed. Other important markers of identity include family, lineage, age set, clan, ethnic, racial or religious affiliation as well as cultural, social, economic, political, national and continental markers. All these markers are learned from older members of society (especially kin, friends and leaders), educational institutions, the media and one's circumstances and experiences.

One's title,[1] position in society, occupation, educational attainment, demeanour, plus manner of dress, presenting the self and addressing others also serve as markers of identities. Visibility of the manner of dress, for instance, renders dress a 'loud' marker of identity for Kenyan pupils, high school students, the police, military personnel and medical professionals because they all wear prescribed dress (i.e., uniform). Such 'loudness' is also evident among communities like the Maasai and the Turkana who live in southern and north-western Kenya, respectively. That is because they have maintained their 'traditional' ways of life, including distinctive modes of dress. Similarly, members of religious groups like the Muslims, the Sikhs and the Akorino[2] are identifiable from their manner of dressing.

In response to a question on identity in an ongoing research on heritage management and memorialisation in Kenya[3] Maasai female respondents have identified dress as a marker of Maasai identity together with walking style, body type and economic lifestyle. Thus, to the informants, language, culture, political organisation and occupation of a defined territory, which are generally agreed on as markers of ethnic identity (e.g. Eriksen 2002) are unimportant. That is probably because these attributes are shared with people who are not Maasai.[4]

Ethnic identity and ethnicity

Of all the markers of identity named above, the most pronounced and also the most divisive in Kenya and elsewhere has been ethnic identity. That is because it can and is often is manipulated by sections of the elite, largely for selfish political and economic gains. Where this happens it leads to polarisation in society between groups, hence the 'us' versus 'them' phenomenon. Indeed, just as "Colonial states deliberately kept the colonized peoples in perpetual tension through the well-known imperial tradition of *divide and rule*" (wa Thiong'o 2009: 20), the 'othering' of those who are deemed not to belong to a given ethnic group creates or aggravates inter-communal tension often leading to destruction of human life, livelihoods and property as well as displacement of citizens from their homes. In the eastern African region, for instance, this is evidenced by the 1994 Rwandan genocide (Cook 2006; Melvern 2004) and by occurrences of pre- and post-election violence in Kenya (Republic of Kenya 1999, 2008).

The divisive nature of ethnic identity has been most evident in Kenya during a few months before and after general elections since the re-introduction of multi-party politics in the early 1990s (Republic of Kenya 1999, 2008). Multi-party politics is competitive and, therefore, requires mobilisation and consolidation of fairly solid voting blocks in order to capture power. That Kenya's political parties are devoid of ideologies, politicians find it easier to organise their voting blocks along ethnic lines. Consequently, people who are generally reasonable beings and exercise the ability to think individually acquiesce to the wishes of the politicians concerned and suddenly seem to acquire the capacity to think and behave uniformly as members of a given ethnic group!

This apparent powerfulness of ethnic identity begs understanding of how ethnic identity, which is not biological, comes into existence. Two ethnic groups in Kenya – the Kalenjin and the Luhya – provide us with outstanding examples of social-political production of group identities within the last sixty or so years. Although the two are among the five largest ethnic groups in the country today, during the sunset years of British colonialism they regarded themselves as minority groups, hence their membership of Kenya African Democratic Union (KADU) (Blundell 1994; Goldsworthy 1982). While this situation may appear ironical, it provides us with a clear illustration of how malleable ethnic identities are and, can be depending on group interests. Constraints of time and space, however, do not permit us to explore the evolution of ethnic identities of the two groups. Instead, we shall address ourselves to the production of the Kalenjin identity, but first we turn to definitions of the terms *ethnic* and *ethnicity*.

The term *ethnic* is derived from the Greek word *ethnos*, which originally meant *heathen* or *pagan*. In time, however, usage of the term *ethnic* was expanded to refer to 'racial' groups that were considered inferior to descendants of the British stock, namely, Jews, Italians and Irish in the USA. It is from these concepts that the words *ethnic* and *ethnicity* have evolved into their modern meanings (Eriksen 2002:4). According to *The American Heritage College Dictionary* the word *ethnic* now refers to "groups of people with a common, distinctive racial, national, religious, linguistic, or cultural heritage" or "a people [who are] not Christian or Jewish". Thus, the concept of 'race' in this definition explains why in the USA, for instance, minority groups like African Americans with disparate geographical and cultural heritage are categorised as one ethnic group. The definition may also explain why minority groups like the Muslims of the former Yugoslavia, who are ethnically Serbian or Croat, are identified as a distinct ethnic group (Eriksen 2002; Goldstein 1999; Shrader 2003). In any case, they are neither Christian nor Jewish!

Today, the phrase *ethnic group* is generally used to refer to a group of people who have a shared history (through a common myth of origin), cultural heritage, economic circumstances, language, territory and political organising. Interestingly, unlike in Europe, the phrase is used interchangeably with *tribe*, a pejorative word connotations of "the primitive and the premodern" in Africa (wa Thiong'o 2009:17). Similarly, the term *ethnicity* which generally refers to "relationships between groups whose members consider themselves [culturally] distinctive" (Eriksen 2002: 7) mutates when used with reference to Africa into the pejorative *tribalism*, which connotes a state of primordial barbarism in the Western world (wa Thiong'o 2009). In this essay we shall use the words *ethnic* and *ethnicity* instead of the pejorative ones.

Evolution of the Kalenjin ethnic identity

The word *kalenjin* (plural *kalenjok*) means 'I tell you' (Kipkorir 1973: xvii) or 'am telling you'.[5] The word was reportedly first used as a form of identity during the Second World War by John arap Chemallan, a Nandi radio announcer. The servicemen from what was then described as 'Nandi-speaking tribes' picked the cue from Chamallan and refered to themselves as *kalenjin*. Subsequently, a group of 14 students at Alliance High School who came from the 'Nandi-speaking tribes' also picked the cue from Chamallan and formed a 'Kalenjin' Club. Taita arap Towett, who was then a student at the school –

and went on to become a Member of Parliament and Minister in Independent Kenya – led the students in choosing the name 'Kalenjin' for the club (Gulliver 1969; Kipkorir 1973). In so doing, he and the other students gave themselves a useful group identity in a school whose majority students were from the communities living around Mount Kenya (Kipkorir 2009; Ndegwa 2006).

In the political world the word 'kalenjin' was first used in 1948 with the formation of the Kalenjin Union in Eldoret by a group of politicians who had acquired basic literacy. Additional usage of the word in a political context happened through the publication of a monthly paper by the name *Kalenjin* in the early 1950s (Kipkorir 1973). The publication was supported by the colonial administration because it served as an anti-Mau Mau propaganda tool, thus helping to demonise the Mau Mau. This, in turn, helped to further the colonial administration's divide and rule policy by delaying politicisation of the Kalenjin through the agitation for independence then spearheaded by Gikuyu and Luo leaders (Lynch 2008).

Interestingly, although the *Kalenjin* monthly paper was quite popular, the word 'Kalenjin' only served as a form of ethnic identity among the nascent academic and political elite (Kipkorir 1973). The ordinary folk identified themselves as Keiyo, Kipsigis, Marakwet, Nandi, Pokot, Sabaot, Terik or Tugen. Some of them like the Marakwet even employed a lower level of group identity such as the Almo, Sengwer, or Endo (Kipkorir 1973).[6] However, from the mid-1950s through the early 1960s the political elite who included Taita arap Towett and Daniel arap Moi ardently promoted use of the Kalenjin ethnonym. That was because it gave them a potentially wider political base than would have the Keiyo, Kipsigis, Marakwet, Nandi, Pokot, Sabaot, Terik or Tugen alone.

In their construction of the Kalenjin ethnic identity, the emerging elite emphasised on the shared attributes among the eight groups. The attributes – common linguistic roots, cultural practices, historical and economic circumstances, plus occupation of contiguous territory – served as unifiers. They helped to nurture a sense of cultural and political unity among members of the eight groups, thus consolidating the groups' political support. All this served the politicians very well by aiding the subsequent crystallization of the political aspirations of the eight groups and the Kalenjin ethnic identity. The efforts paid off handsomely in 1957 when Moi was elected to the newly created Rift Valley African seat in the Legislative Council by "his Kalenjin ethnic group" (Throup and Hornsby 1998: 8). This achievement served as the first clear signal that the Kalenjin ethnic identity was taking shape.

Besides Moi's election to the Legislative Council, the socio-political efforts of constructing the Kalenjin ethnic identity culminated in the application of the 'Kalenjin' ethnonym to the political party Kalenjin Political Alliance, a party whose name "suggested…[its] essentially defensive rationale" (Goldsworthy 1982: 146). The Alliance was founded in 1961 by among others, Towett and Moi, and was among the political parties that dissolved themselves to form KADU (Goldsworthy 1982). Like other sub-national or district parties of the time, the purpose of the Alliance was to further the interests of an ethnic constituency, which in this case was the emerging Kalenjin ethnic group.

It is noteworthy that since Moi's election to the Legislative Council in 1957, the Kalenjin have voted as a block for the party chosen by their popular political leader(s) in every general election. In 1963, for instance, they voted for KADU in which Moi ranked as leader alongside Ronald Ngala and Masinde Muliro. Upon dissolution of KADU in 1964, the Kalenjin crossed over with Moi to Kenya African National Union (KANU), a party they voted for as a block in subsequently general elections under the Jomo Kenyatta's presidency. Kalenjin loyalty to KANU flourished even further from 1978 when Moi became president and, in particular, in the 1992, 1997 and 2002 general elections. In the 2002 elections their loyalty enabled the political neophyte Uhuru Kenyatta to garner about the same number of votes that ensured Moi's win in 1992 and 1997 against a divided opposition. In the 2007 general elections, they voted *en masse* for the Orange Democratic Party (ODM) which was led by, among others, William Ruto (Lynch 2008), a rising Kalenjin political star.

There is no doubt that Moi's presidency facilitated the general acceptance and popularisation of the Kalenjin ethnonym. Indeed, when Moi succeeded Kenyatta in 1978 the media, academicians, politicians and religious leaders described him as a member of a small ethnic group, the Tugen, not as a Kalenjin. The Tugen label was neither disputed by Moi nor by any of his associates.[7] By the time Moi left office twenty-four years later, the eight groups had coalescence into the Kalenjin ethnic group and Moi had metamorphosed from a Tugen into a Kalenjin. This metamorphosis literally transformed the Kalenjin from their earlier classification as one of "the smaller less-developed people of Kenya who feared domination by a potential Gikuyu-Luo axis" (Blundell 1994: 107) to one of the large ethnic groups. Today, the group enjoys remarkable political clout and visibility, as witnessed during the December 2007 general elections.

Besides the role played by politics, the metamorphosis was aided by the popularisation of the Kalenjin ethnonym by academicians like Kipkorir (1973:

59) who "rationalised the various 'tribal' people's traditions and customs [of the eight groups] into ethnic 'Kalenjin' ones"; the academicians also popularised the "new ethnic consciousness" among what are now known as the Kalenjin sub-groups (Kipkorir 1973: 59).

Discussion

It is evident from the foregoing that from the outset the word Kalenjin was used as a form of group identity with the express aim of bringing together a small group of Alliance High School students from what were then considered disparate Nandi-speaking groups in colonial Kenya. Subsequently, the students' idea of group identity was seized upon by the nascent political leaders who included Taita arap Towett and Daniel arap Moi for purposes of producing the Kalenjin ethnic identity. In this exercise, the politicians whose concern was building a large political base were encouraged by the British colonial administration which even funded the publication of an anti-Mau Mau propaganda paper bearing the name *Kalenjin*.

Thus, the Kalenjin ethnonym, which has been adopted by all the 'Nandi-speaking groups', "is not only of *recent coinage*, [but] it is *unpretentiously artificial* and *political* in its origins' (Kipkorir 1973: 57; emphasis added). That the politicians concerned successfully constructed a single ethnic identity from groups that are far from being homogeneous, but have political divisions within them (Kipkorir 1973) and speak languages that have "varying degrees of mutual intelligibility" (Kurgat 2009:92), is a clear indication of their determination and focus in executing their socio-political project. The success of the political engineering is evidenced by the fact that since Moi's election to the Legislative Council in 1957, the Kalenjin generally have spoken in one political voice, hence voting *en masse* for their preferred political party.

This may explain Moi's angry reaction to what he characterised as "fragmenting [of] the Kalenjin in the…[2009 national] census."[8] The said fragmentation arose from the fact that for the Kalenjin the Kenya National Bureau of Statistics' data collection sheets allowed respondents to name their ethnic group as either Kalenjin, Kipsigis, Marakwet, Sabaot, Keiyo, Nandi, Terik, Sengwer, Cherangany, or Tugen. To Moi, the provision of alternative ethnic identities "was disappointing [as] the [Kalenjin] community was being divided into sub-groups."[9] Interestingly, Moi did not speak for ethnic groups like the Luhya of Western Kenya who have similar historical circumstances. Yet, for the larger Luhya ethnic group the data sheets provided for identification with either the larger Luhya ethnic group, or with the smaller

Banyore, Bukusu, Isukha and Maragoli ethnic identities, to mention a few. Further, for the Mijikenda of the coastal region, provision was made for identification with the larger Mijikenda ethnic group or with smaller ethnic identities like the Digo, Duruma, Giriama and Ribe, to mention a few. Undoubtedly, Moi's concern was political: the larger Kalenjin ethnic group not only provides a platform to further the idea of a common political destiny among the groups concerned, but also a sizeable vote and, by extension, political visibility and voice at the national level.

It must be pointed out here that there is nothing wrong with the socio-political construction and perpetuation of the Kalenjin ethnic identity for, history is replete with such productions (e.g., Fearon and Laitin 2000; Kolossov 1999; Nagel 1994). Indeed, as the Kalenjin experience illustrates, ethnic identity is perceived, defined and created by people through the processes of their social, cultural, economic and political life. Granted community interests are not static, ethnic identity is generally not fixed or stable. Rather, it is fluid and malleable and, therefore, negotiable, contestable, destructible and re-constructible. In the recent past, the malleability of ethnic identity in Kenya has been evidenced by the deconstruction of the Embu and Meru ethnic groups leading to the emergence of the smaller Mbeere and Tharaka ethnic groups for political purposes, respectively.

It is hardly surprising, therefore, that the Sengwer, for instance, who are part of the larger Kalenjin ethnic group (Kipkorir 2009: 407) have in the recent past sought a separate and distinct identity.[10] Another Kalenjin group, the Nandi, "sometimes... regard themselves as unique from the larger Kalenjin group because they had a different immediate pre-colonial experience, namely, ten years (1895-1905) of armed resistance to colonial invasion" (Kurgat 2009: 92).[11] Other factors that the Nandi use to differentiate themselves from the other Kalenjin groups include rituals, occupation of a contiguous territory in the Rift Valley (in particular Nandi and Uasin Gushu Districts), socio-political organisation and socio-cultural outlook (Kurgat 2009).

Thus, construction and deconstruction of ethnic identities did not end with colonialism. Indeed, as recently as the late 1980s and early 1990s a section of politicians from the Rift Valley Province attempted to create a larger group identity for the Kalenjin, Maasai, Turkana and Samburu, namely, KaMaTuSa. The underlying assumption in the attempts was that these groups shared a common heritage (i.e., indigenousness in the Province), economic circumstance (i.e., attachment to livestock) and political destiny (i.e., desire to avoid domination by 'larger' ethnic groups). This happened at a time when

Moi's presidency appeared threatened by the re-introduction of multi-party politics that saw large ethnic groups like the Luo, Luhya and Gikuyu working together in the opposition. Although the political project ensured Moi's victory in the Province and nationally, the creation of a larger group identity did not succeed. That was probably because competing interests among the political leaders from the ethnic groups concerned were not in favour of the larger group identity as it would have drowned their voices and ambitions.

In the 1970s attempts to create a large, but loose, group identity for the Embu, Gikuyu and Meru who share common linguistic roots, cultural practices, historical and economic circumstances and territory was somewhat realised with the formation of Gikuyu, Embu and Meru Association (GEMA) in 1971. In the words of the Association's longest-serving Chairman, the Association "was seen by many as a tribal alliance that gave the Mount Kenya communities leverage to dominate other tribes and, by extension, the whole of Kenya" (Karume 2009: 156). The Association also faced critical reception by other Kenyans because of its leaders' involvement in the campaign for constitutional amendment to bar Moi, then Vice-President, from automatically succeeding Kenyatta (Karume 2009). It is hardly surprising, therefore, that Moi proscribed GEMA shortly after he succeeded Kenyatta.

There is hardly any doubt that the history of the 'defunct' Association together with the population size (read number of votes for general elections), plus the economic and intellectual muscle of the Gikuyu, Embu and Meru may explain why attempts to construct a larger group identity for the communities faced, and continues to face, stiff resistance, especially from the political class. Equally significant is internal divisions and competition for power, especially among the three ethnic groups' economic, political and intellectual elite, which did not, and still do not, allow for construction of a larger group identity. Further, unlike the elite from the Luhya, Luo and Kalenjin, to mention three ethnic groups, who will push ethnic agendas without being labeled 'tribalists', Mount Kenya communities appear to be too sensitive to charges of 'tribalism' by others. Yet to non-Kenyan scholars (e.g. Anderson 2005:5), the Meru and Embu are basically Gikuyu-speakers.

One is wont to hypothesise that the interests of the more than 40 ethnic groups in Kenya are more divisive than would be the case if the country had fewer ethnic groups. Could this explain why political organising in the country is not based on important issues or ideologies? Could it also explain why virtually every politician desirous of occupying a prime position in government deliberately builds a strong ethnic base first? Could this parochialism explain why it is difficult for the interests of the numerous ethnic groups to overlap in a manner that fosters *Kenyanhood*?

Two suggestions come to mind. Firstly, that deliberate and purposeful construction of fewer ethnic groups may be the way to go. Ideally, the larger or supra ethnic identities so-constructed could bring together smaller groups sharing similar economic interests and worldview. Such a phenomenon could reduce ethnic group identities to a smaller number, besides infusing issues- or ideology-based political organising. It could also lead to meaningful economic competition, which the country needs if it is to create adequate employment for the burgeoning youth population. In light of what we have learned above, such a project is not infeasible. In any case, ethnic identities are, as we have noted, malleable and ethnic boundaries tend to shift with socio-economic and political fortunes.

Secondly, that deconstructing all the existing large ethnic groups into smaller groups, as the 2009 national census data collection sheets did in certain instances may be the way to go. This could lead to the peopling of the country by minority ethnic groups only. Hopefully, this could help minimise fears of domination of smaller groups by larger ones in the *short-term*. The reason why we have qualified this latter suggestion by use of 'short-term' is that experience involving the construction of the Kalenjin identity, for instance, informs such deconstruction could also lead to formation of alliances by some of the smaller groups thus forming larger ethnic identities in the long-term. This rounding of the circle suggests the first option may be a more viable option.

Conclusion

An assumption is made in Kenya that deliberate discontinuation of ethnic identities is *sine quanon* to attainment of *Kenyanhood*. This thinking informed debate on the question of ethnic identity in the 2009 national census and continues to inform debates about *Kenyanhood*. The question to ask is: if human beings all over the world have multiple identities, including ethnic identity, why should we expect Kenyans to be different? Tanzania is often cited by some Kenyans as an example of a country where citizens have suppressed their ethnic identity for their *Tanzanianhood*. But nothing could be further from the truth. Tanzanians also bear ethnic identities. The main difference from the Kenya experience is that in Tanzania one is Chagga and Tanzanian at the same time, just as one can be English, Welsh or Scotch and British at the same time in the United Kingdom.

It must be pointed out here that ethnic loyalty is not always a bad thing. Indeed, it "can also lead people to do good things for fellow members of their...[group], even when this is not at the expense of others" (Appiah and Gates 2005: 571). Indeed, this has been happening in some parts of Kenya for many years. For example, schools, churches and health facilities have been built and young men and women educated overseas through fund raising efforts appealing to ethnic groups' need to advance themselves.

Thus, the problem in Kenya is not ethnic affiliation *per se*, but the coupling of ethnic identity with land, a finite resource, political power and access to public resources. This is what makes the elite to zealously advance "internal [ethnic] solidarity, guard mutual boundaries, organize competition against rival...[ethnic groups] for public goods and [to] reduce contemporary politics to...[ethnic] conflict" (Berman and Lonsdale 1992:267). Tropes of marginalisation and dispossession of ancestral lands have since the early 1990s in particular served this purpose extremely well (Republic of Kenya 1999, 2008).

However, granted ethnic identity is a fact of life all over the world, Kenyans cannot be expected to run away from their ethnic identity, just as they cannot run away from their names. Therefore, there is a need for outright acknowledgement that multiplicity of ethnicities is a good thing for Kenya's cultural, linguistic and historical diversity. There is also a need to make deliberate efforts to move away from balkanising the country by overemphasising cultural differentiation for the political gain of a few. The country's leadership must of necessity decouple political rights from land rights and access to public resources by distributing public revenues through programmes like the extant Constituencies Development Fund[12] and other mechanisms of devolution. Judicious utilisation of such devolved funds, plus infusion of sobriety especially among the political elite, would help ensure ethnic identity ceases to be the curse it appears to be today.

Equally important is the need for soundly reasoned identification and/or creation as well as utilisation of sites and monuments that can serve as places of collective remembrance for Kenyans regardless of one's ethnic affiliation. The existence of national monuments and war museums[13] in Europe and the USA, for instance, has and continues to aid patriotism and evocation of feelings of nationhood. The war museums and monuments celebrating military victories serve as permanent reminders of existence of a common external enemy in a country's history (e.g. Udovicki and Ridgeway 2000; Ziblatt 2006), thus promoting feelings of nationalism.

Granted Kenya lacks a war museum for the simple reason that she has not been at war with any of her neighbours, efforts should be made to use extant national monuments like the bomb blast monument and the Kimathi statue (both in Nairobi), plus the mausoleums scattered around the country as rallying points in building *Kenyanhood*. Additional monuments can be purposely developed for the same reasons.

Kenyan athletes' victories in international competitions can also be creatively employed in fostering nationhood granted Kenyans do not regard the athletes concerned as members of given ethnic groups, but as Kenyans. By so doing, all ethnic groups would celebrate *Kenyan* victories together. Similarly, adversities like the bombing of the US embassy in Nairobi on 7th August 1998 and the 2007–2008 post-election violence can serve as rallying points for *Kenyanhood*. As a matter of fact, victims of these adversities are generally acknowledged as Kenyans, not as members of given ethnic groups. Statistics of how many Gusii, Luo, Meru, Kalenjin, Somali, or Rendille died in either case have not been bandied about. The only time ethnic statistics are of concern, especially to sections of the elite, is during peace time, when public officers' ethnic identities are deemed to be more important than their qualifications, ability and suitability for the office.

Notes

[1] The importance of titles as markers of identity was first brought to my attention by an incident at a Texan bank when I was a Visiting Research Scientist at Texas A&M University, College Station, in 1996. In filling forms to open a bank account, I omitted the title 'Dr' from my name. On noticing the omission, my host and friend who had accompanied me to the bank, advised me to insert the title in order to avoid inordinate delays at the service counters as my transactions were likely to be closely scrutinised (read discrimination due to colour/ethnic profiling). I followed his advice and, as a result, I received what I still consider to have been service reserved for cousins of royal families! Back home, the title 'Dr' or 'Prof' has opened some doors for me where otherwise I would have been turned away by a bossy receptionist or secretary. The love for titles as identifiers in Kenya is also borne out by the adoption of honorary degrees as titles, professional training in engineering as the title 'Eng.' (for engineer), and announcements in the obituary pages of local newspapers like *Daily Nation* and *Standard* where holders of first degrees in Quantity Surveying are known by the title 'QS'.

[2] The Akorino are African Christian pacifists. The men wear turbans and the women head-dresses and flowing ankle-length dresses.

[3] This research is being conducted in different parts of Kenya by Dr. Lotte Hughes of Open University, Prof. Annie Coombes of Birkbeck College, University of London, and me. The research is supported by the UK Arts and Humanities Research Council.

[4] Considerable emphasis is placed on the manner of dressing at the national level, largely for economic and political purposes. In 2003-2004, for example, Kenya witnessed the expenditure of fifty million Kenya Shillings on a well-orchestrated competition for designing a national dress that was sponsored by Unilever Kenya Limited. Unilever, a private company, cleverly seized the opportunity provided by the installation of a new government when Kenyans were yearning to reassert their 'national' identity after twenty-four years' of Daniel arap Moi's dictatorship to successfully launch their new 'Sunlight Washing Powder' product. In 2005 an Assistant Minister in the Office of the President appeared in Parliament sporting the 'national dress' only to be ordered out of the House by the Speaker for wearing what one Member described as 'pyjamas'. In expelling the Assistant Minister, the Speaker ruled: "It is the opinion of the Chair that if that be our national dress, then the Ministry [of Gender, Sports, Culture and Social Services] needs to go back and think very hard." To the Speaker, the Assistant Minister's 'national dress' did not show any seriousness at all for, he added: "I think whatever you people do, you should at least come to the House with something that shows *seriousness*" (Faris 2004: 23, added emphasis).

[5] Dr. Kurgat, P.K., personal communication, October 2009.

[6] Kipkorir (1973: 57) also includes the Ndorobo (i.e. Ogiek) in the larger Kalenjin group. In another publication (Kipkorir 2009: 392) he also includes the Bongom (Terik?).

[7] I remember when growing up in a cosmopolitan village at Spring Valley in Subukia, Nakuru District, in the 1960s that members of the eight Kalenjin groups in the village identified themselves as distinctly Tugen, Nandi or Kipsigis, but not as Kalenjin. Moreover, a member of a community like the Tugen took offence when called a Nandi.

[8] *Standard*, 26 August 2009.

[9] *Ibid.*

[10] *http://membres.multimania.fr/sengwer/* and *http://www.iapad.org/applications/ich/sengwer2.htm*, accessed 22 February 2010.

[11] Newspaper reports of the Nandi hero Orkoiyot Koitalel arap Samoei who led the resistance do not mention the Kalenjin ethnonym. In the reports, Koitalel is Nandi, not Kalenjin. See the *Standard* online, 'Freedom hero immortalized' and 'Pray... how did Kenyan artefacts end up in UK?' *http://www.standardmedia.co.ke/InsidePage.php?id=2000007379&cid=4&story=Freedom%20hero%20immortalised* and *http://www.standardmedia.co.ke/InsidePage.php?id=2000009599&cid=4&*, respectively, accessed 16 May 2010.

[12] Constituencies Development Fund is a mechanism through which 2.5% of all the government ordinary revenue collected annually has been distributed to all the constituencies since 2004. The money is for financing development projects identified locally (Republic of Kenya (2003).

[13] See *http://www.warmuseums.nl/index.html* (accessed 7 March 2010) for details of War Museums in Europe.

References

Anderson, D. (2005). *Histories of the Hanged: Britain's dirty war in Kenya and the end of empire*. London: Phoenix.

Appiah, K.A. and Gates, Jr., H.L. (2005). *Africana: the encyclopedia of the African and African American Experience*, Vol. 2. Oxford: Oxford University Press.

Berman, B. and Lonsdale, J.M. (1992). *Unhappy Valley: conflict in Kenya and Africa: Book Two: violence and ethnicity*. London: James Currey.

Blundell, M. (1994). *A Love Affair with the Sun: a memoir of seventy years in Kenya*. Nairobi: Kenway Publications.

Cook, S.E. (ed.) (2006). *Genocide in Cambodia and Rwanda: new perspectives*. New Brunswick, NJ: Transaction Publishers.

Eriksen, T.H. (2002). *Ethnicity and Nationalism*, 2nd edition. London: Pluto Press.

Faris, S. (2004). Dress to Impress: Kenya is trying to launch a new national costume. But some see it as the emperor's clothes. *Time,* December 20, 2004, p. 23.

Fearon, J.D. and Laitin, D.D. (2000). Violence and the Social Construction of Ethnic Identity. *International Organization* **54** (4): 845-877.

Goldstein, I. (1999). *Croatia: A History*. London: C. Hurst & Co. Publishers.

Goldsworthy, D. (1982). *Tom Mboya: the man Kenya wanted to forget*. Nairobi: Heinemann.

Gulliver, P.H. (1969)l *Tradition and Transition in East Africa*. Berkeley and Los Angeles: University of California Press.

Karume, N. (with Mutu wa Gethoi) (2009). *Beyond Expectations: from charcoal to gold*. Nairobi: Kenway Publications.

Kipkorir, B.E. (1973 [re-issued 2008]). *The Marakwet of Kenya: a preliminary study*. Nairobi: East African Educational Publishers.

Kipkorir, B.E. (2009). *Descent from Cherang'any Hills: memoirs of a reluctant academic*. Nairobi: Macmillan.

Kolossov, V. (1999). Ethnic and political identities and territorialities in the post-Soviet space. *GeoJournal* **48**: 71–81.

Kurgat, P.K. (2009). The Dynamics of Ethnicity in a Multicultural Society. *Journal of Language, Technology and Entrepreneurship in Africa* **1**(2): 90-98.

Lynch, G. (2008). Courting the Kalenjin: The failure of Dynamism and the strength of the ODM wave in Kenya's Rift Valley Province. *African Affairs* **107** (4290; 541-568.

Melvern, L. (2004). *Conspiracy to Murder: Rwandan genocide*. London: Verso.

Nagel, J. (1994). Constructing Ethnicity: Creating and Recreating Ethnic Ientity and Culture. *Social Problems* **41** (1): 152-176.

Ndegwa, D. (2006). *Walking in Kenyatta Struggles: my story*. Nairobi: Kenya Leadership Institute.

Republic of Kenya (1999). *Report of the Judicial Commission Appointed to Inquire into Tribal Clashes in Kenya*. Nairobi: Government Printer.

Republic of Kenya (2003). *The Constituencies Development Fund Act*. Nairobi: Government Printer.

Republic of Kenya (2008). *Report of the Commission of Inquiry into Post Election Violence (CIPEV)*. Nairobi: Government Printer.

Shrader, C.R. (2003). *The Muslim-Croat Civil War in Central Bosnia: a military history, 1992-1994*. College Station: Texas A&M University Press.

Throup, D. and Hornsby, C. (1998). *Multi-party Politics in Kenya: the Kenyatta and Moi states and the triumph of the system in the 1992 election*. Oxford: James Currey.

Udovicki, J. and Ridgeway, J. (eds.) (2000). *Burn This House: the making and unmaking of Yugoslavia*. Durham, NC: Duke University Press.

wa Thiong'o, N. (2009). The Myth of *Tribe* in African Politics. *Transition: An International Review* **101**:16-23.

Ziblatt, D. (2006) *Structuring the State: the formation of Italy and Germany and the puzzle of federalism*. Princeton, NJ: Princeton University Press.

Links Between African Proverbs and Sayings and Ethnic Diversity

Joseph G. Healey

A proverb (and other forms of African oral literature) has been described as "a window into the African worldview." Many African proverbs and sayings were sprinkled throughout the presentations, discussions and informal conversations at our conference on "Ethnic Diversity in Eastern Africa: Opportunities and Challenges." These proverbs and sayings revealed both the positive and negative aspects of ethnic diversity. In the context of the challenges of the present tribalism and ethnicity in Africa today there is a mutual enrichment of the values of unity and diversity, that is, both/and approach rather than an either/or approach. Unity is an important value in African society. *Unity is strength; division is weakness* (Swahili, Eastern African Proverb). *One finger cannot kill a louse* (many African languages). *When spiders unite, they can tie up a lion* (Amharic, Ethiopian Proverb). *Let us pull together* (Swahili, Eastern African Saying).

Diversity is an important value in the rich cultural heritage of the African people that is reflected in their many languages, customs and traditions. *Wisdom is like a baobab tree; no one individual can embrace it* (*Akan* and *Ewe*, Benin, Ghana and Togo Proverb). *God is color blind* (universal proverb) The Akan, Ghana symbol of unity in diversity is the two headed crocodile with one stomach seen in the proverb: *Many mouths, one stomach.* Two distinct, but related themes emerged during the conference:

1. African proverbs and sayings that describe and analyze the present reality in Africa today

When elephants fight the grass gets hurt. In Africa and worldwide this is the most commonly used Swahili proverb (translated into English). In the past two years in Kenya it has been often used to describe the period after the postelection crisis and the uneasy alliance between President Mwai Kibaki and Prime Minister Raila Odinga, their respective political parties (including different ethnic groups and languages) and the difficult repercussions for ordinary people. On the difficulties of power sharing a popular proverb is *Two bulls can't stay in the same kraal* (*Tswana*, Botswana Proverb) and *Two bulls don't live in the same cow shed* (Swahili, Eastern Africa Proverb).

If you provoke a snake, you must be prepared to be bitten by it (Gikuyu, Kenya Proverb). Its most famous use was by the Kenyan Minister of National Security and Provincial Administration when justifying his decision to raid the Standard Group's Kenya Television Network (KTN) and *The Standard* newspaper offices and printing press respectively in Nairobi, Kenya at dawn on 2nd March 2006. Kenyan newspapers took the proverb to mean that the minister was comparing the government to a snake that bites at the slightest provocation. But the proverb in the original Gikuyu language was used by the minister (himself a native speaker of the language) as he clarified: People who start a quarrel should be ready for a fight. Among its many uses the proverb also describes situations that can lead to the disruption of harmony and peace in society

A further example regarding Christianity. Recent research shows that there has been is a lot of tribalism and negative ethnicity in the Christian Churches in Kenya and other African countries. One would have hoped that the deeper Gospel values could overcome these ethnic divisions, but this has not always been the case. Our research found that in certain churches, the well known African proverb can sadly be rewritten to say: *The blood of tribalism is thicker than the water of baptism.*

2. African proverbs and sayings and stories that promote peacebuilding and reconciliation in Africa today

After the national elections in Kenya on 27th December, 2007 there was a lot of discontent and accusations of widespread vote rigging. This led to riots, violence, killings, burning of homes and shops and displacement of people throughout the country. By the end of February, 2008 over 1,000 people had been killed and over 500,000 people made homeless. In the midst of these political and ethnic group (tribalism) crises various peace campaigns emerged with appropriate messages, sayings and slogans. This shows the influence of oral culture in our contemporary African society. While African youth know fewer and fewer traditional proverbs, the use of popular sayings and slogans is increasing especially in cities. The youth are now using these sayings and slogans to promote harmony and reconciliation among different ethnic groups in Kenya. They are involved more and more in peacemaking and reconciliation activities in Kenya through using their street language of Sheng and other slogans.

Our research in Nairobi, Kenya during the months of January and February, 2008 uncovered 40 sayings and slogans of the youth on justice, peace, peacemaking and reconciliation These messages are listed in English in alphabetical order together with the Sheng and Swahili translations where used and available:

> Choose Peace for Kenya (*Chagua Amani Kenya*)
> Choose Peace, Prevent Bad Situations (*Chagua Amani, Zuia Noma*).
> Drive peace my colleagues (*Dere amani manzee*).
> Extend an olive branch to your neighbour, symbol of peace.
> Help save Kenya.
> I am a Christian first, a Kenyan second and a Kikuyu third.
> I am KENYAN. I want PEACE. Let's WALK the TALK.
> If Annan can't resolve our political crisis, we should be prepared for anything.
> I'm 4 peace.
> I spit out bad things, I welcome peace (*Noma naitema, amani naikaribish*a).
> I support Peace in Kenya
> Justice 4 Kenya.
> Keep peace.
> Kenya — Our Unity Is Our Pride.
> Lay down your pangas, arrows, rungus, guns.
> Leave bad things, talk peace (*Wacha noma, bonga amani*).
> Let peace fill our heart, our world, our universe.
> Let peace prevail.
> Let's emphasize peace, let's satisfy God (*Tuzingatie amani, tumridhishe Mungu*).
> Let's unite.
> Make Me an Instrument of Peace in Kenya.
> May peace rule over Kenya. And this peace should begin with me
>   (*Amani itawale Kenya. Na amani hiyo ianzie kwangu*).
> Mothers, Daughters, Sisters, Wives: Help to Stop the Violence.
> Promote Peace Through Forgiveness and Reconciliation.
> One people. One nation. Choose peace.
> Our beloved country. Let Kenya be for ALL.
> Peace. Love. Unity. Now's the time.
> Peace — Wanted Alive.
> People for Peace in Kenya. Promote Change Through Active Non-Violence.
> Resettle ALL IDPs.
> Say NO to Corruption.
> Say "No" to Violence. Say "Yes" to Peace.
> Stand Up for Safer Neighbourhoods.
> Support peace. Cool down. (*Weka amani. Poa*).

Through young people a march to freedom has started. It is a march without violence.
Use your freedom to express yourself in a non-violent way.
We are for peace.
We are Kenyans. Why fight
We Kenyans have the terrible disease of tribalism.
We Want Our Country Back

The *2009 African Proverbs Calendar* on our African Proverbs, Sayings and Stories Website (www.afriprov.org) had the overall theme of "Reconciliation, Justice and Peace." There was a theme for each month (i.e. "Talk Peace, Make Peace," "Foster Dialogue, "Suffer for Justice") that corresponded to a previous "African Proverb of that Month" already posted on our website along with African-themed photographs. The United Nations designated 2009 as the "World Year of Reconciliation." The theme of the Second African Synod of the Catholic Church that took place in Rome, Italy from 4-25 October, 2009 was "The Church in Africa in Service to Reconciliation, Justice and Peace." A special effort was made to choose proverbs that help in peacemaking and reconciliation in such countries as Kenya, Sudan and Zimbabwe.

This 2009 calendar included a selection of 12 African Proverbs from 11 different African countries: Benin, Ghana, Kenya, Libya, Nigeria, South Africa, Swaziland, Tanzania, Togo, Uganda and Zambia. The full explanation of the proverb includes its "Contemporary Use and Religious Application." Some examples:

1. *Leave bad things, talk peace* and *Drive peace my colleagues* (Sheng, Kenya Sayings).
2. *Great fires erupt from tiny sparks* (Arabic, Libya Proverb)
3. *Only a wise person can solve a difficult problem* (Akan, Ghana Proverb).
4. *Suffering is prior to attaining success or perfection* (Chagga, Tanzania Proverb).

Other examples of relevant proverbs: *Peace with justice is everything* (Swahili, Eastern African Proverb). *Don't celebrate war, cry for peace* (Swahili, Eastern African Proverb). *Where there is dialogue and an agreement there is God* (Burundi Proverb). Sometimes the opposite meaning and a negative wording teaches a positive value. *War has no eyes* (Swahili, Eastern African Proverb).

Peace and reconciliation flow into the wholeness of our life and the integrity of creation. There is a Kikuyu, Kenyan Saying that goes: *You must treat the earth well. It was not given to you by your parents. It was loaned to you by your children.* Those who strongly support peace and reconciliation, but wonder what difference we can really make may find solace in the South African Proverb that says: *If you think you are too small to make a difference, try sleeping in a closed room with a mosquito.*

3. Telling our African stories of forgiveness, justice, reconciliation and peacemaking

It is also important to tell our African stories of forgiveness, justice, reconciliation and peacemaking. After the post December 2007 election crisis and violence in Kenya there **were** many inspiring, uplifting and positive witness/testimony stories. To be valuable these stories must be **real,** that is, having a sacrifice/struggle/vulnerability/overcoming adversity and odds "reality edge" to them ("hali halisi" in Swahili stories).

Many African Stories related to ethnic diversity and *related topics* can be found on the African Proverbs, Sayings and Stories Website: http://www.afriprov.org. *Searching in the* online, searchable *"African Story Database"* (http://www.afriprov.org/index.php/africanstories-database.htm) *by theme and sub-theme one finds* the *following number of stories:* Healing (37); Peace/Peacemaking (36); Reconciliation (14); Forgiveness/Mercy (13); and Justice (13). *There are 95 stories with the locale in Kenya alone. Some positive examples from the continent of Africa:*

1. "I Am a Christian First" (Story No. 173 in the online African Story Database).

   > After the post-December, 2007 election crisis and the resulting tribalism-related violence in Kenya in early 2008, a *Catholic* woman in a St. Paul Chaplaincy Center Prayer Group in Nairobi said: "I am a Christian first, a Kenyan second and a Kikuyu third."

2. "Pray for Me to Forgive President Mwai Kibaki" (Story No. 327 in the online African Story Database).

   > During a meeting of the St. Jude South Small Christian Community (SCC) near the main highway going to Uganda in Yala Parish in Kisumu Archdiocese, Kenya in March, 2008 the members reflected on the Gospel passage from John 20:23: "If you forgive the sins of any, they are forgiven them; if you retain the sins of any, they are retained." Speaking from the heart one Luo man emotionally asked the SCC members to pray for him. He said: "Pray for me to forgive

President Mwai Kibaki." During the post election crisis period in Kenya he said that every time he saw the president on TV he got upset and angry and so he needed healing. The other SCCs members were deeply touched and feelingly prayed for him. He said that he felt peaceful again.

3. "The Merciful Rwandan Wife" (Story No. 433 in the online African Story Database).

> In a particular section of Kigali, Rwanda of mixed Hutu and Tutsi Ethnic Groups, the genocidal war broke out with a bloody vengeance. Neighbors attacked neighbors. In one area a Hutu man murdered his Tutsi neighbor. Later after the Rwandan Patriotic Front won the war and took over the government, local investigations of the atrocities started. The wife of the dead Tutsi man was asked to identify her husband's murderer. She refused knowing that the Hutu man would be arrested, imprisoned and perhaps killed in return. The woman said that she preferred to remain silent to save another life. She said: "This is enough. This killing has to stop somewhere. One murder does not justify another killing. We have to break the cycle of violence and end this genocide." So she chose to forgive.

Three African Proverbs describe the ongoing importance of using African Proverbs, Sayings and Stories to promote reconciliation and peacebuilding in Africa today. A Ganda (Uganda) Proverb says: *One who sees something good must narrate it.* A Sukuma (Tanzania) Proverb says: *That which is good is never finished.* An Igbo (Nigeria) proverb says: *When a road is good you walk on it twice.* African proverbs and sayings can be part of our good road to peace in Africa.

(Over)riding the Rainbow

Ethnic Diversity and the Kenyan Creative Economy

Joy Mboya

The term 'rainbow', to denote advantages attained by bringing together multiple and diverse ethnicities, has been popularized in Kenya via politics. This chapter, using the word 'rainbow' in a similar sense, examines how interventions, purposeful or circumstantial, in Kenyan creative domains, have metaphorically taken hold of the rainbow of ethnic and cultural diversity, de-constructed it, contemporized it, and innovated it, thereby contributing towards the evolution of a potentially exciting, forward-looking Creative Kenya. The chapter will also consider benefits and challenges in conserving ethno-cultural art forms and art practices for their intrinsic and heritage value.

The rainbow, that ephemeral but beautiful natural phenomenon that sits arched in the sky, has captured human imagination in folklore and mythology across all cultures. In Australian Aborigine legends, the rainbow is a powerful multi-colored snake, *Thugine*, commanding respect as the guardian of rivers and seas, which are the source of life. In Western folklore, the rainbow is a promise of prosperity –it is said that at the end of it there is a pot of gold. Closer to home, in the beliefs of my own Luo community, the rainbow called *ndanya* is seen to be a good omen -in times of severe flooding, the appearance of the rainbow was understood to signify that the worst was over. The term 'rainbow' referring to ethnic, or racial, or cultural diversity in social and political parlance today has positive connotations.

Today of course, the cultural myths about the rainbow have been overtaken by scientific knowledge - we know that a rainbow is the result of refraction, where a seemingly singular structure of light deflected through water particles in the atmosphere, is split and revealed to comprise multiple wonderful colors, arched beside each other in a single band. The challenge for peoples and societies today is to broaden the metaphorical meaning of rainbow to embrace not only all within the clan, or all within the ethnic group, or even all within the nation, but also all within the world. Historical and present-day events, it seems, are pushing humanity towards a unification of its diverse elements. In the political and economic realms, regions are consolidating into common unified blocs such as the European Union, the East African Community and SADEC. Nations today struggle to contain the potential clashes of cultures within their borders – in Kenya, for example, *Najivunia kuwa Mkenya* is a slogan that attempts to rally the populace to embrace 'Kenyan-ness' as the higher glue that can bond 42-odd ethnic communities together, who in 2008 unleashed long-suppressed violence against each other after a contested presidential election. And if one were to take the long view of history, might one not discern a fitful but nonetheless progressive movement towards a more unified humanity, from the nuclear family and clan groupings, to the tribe, the city-state, the nation state and now regional and global structures? Perhaps the principle of biodiversity in plant and animal life, that holds diversity as a complex but sure foundation for the survival of the planet, also applies to human societies? That for our human survival, not only as a biological species, but also as social organized systems, we must not fail to embrace, appreciate and utilize human diversity. This chapter examines how practitioners in the creative economy have risen beyond one level of distinction – the ethnic identity – to find a higher yet all-embracing distinction – Kenyan-ness, as a marker for their creativity. But the merit and viability of ethno-cultural activities for the creative economy is also considered. The latter is discussed as 'riding the rainbow', while the former is seen as 'overriding the rainbow'.

Part One: Overriding the rainbow

Progression towards a Kenyan creative economy

We find ourselves, as Kenyans, (and this is true of most African states), at an interesting transition point in relation to our indigenous arts, and also in relation to the new paradigm of creative or cultural economies, where debates rage about the polarities between the intrinsic and instrumental values of arts and culture. Discussions frequently also take place about how market economies, with profit-making as their primary objective, are in fact antithetical to the values of culture and the arts, which have aesthetic, intellectual, social and even spiritual values. The 'dark side' encountered by the arts when they enter into the market economy, includes 'tough competition, risks, and inadequate or non-existent guarantees of the right to work and earn.'(Razlogov2008). Razlogov's view is a commentary on the situation prevailing in his home country Russia, and other Eastern bloc countries after the end of socialism/communism.But there is resonance with the Kenyan situation, although, of course, the Russian transition has a different genesis. In the Kenyan case, not only are we are transitioning from a colony state but also from discrete traditional worldviews, values and social formations. Shifting from traditional communities and colonialism, the biggest change for Kenya's communities with regard to creative economies, is the cessation of that integral relationship that the arts had with everyday life. In other words, art fitted, in an almost- for-granted way, within the economic, social and spiritual life of the community. In that past, (according to researchers of African art like Laure Meyer), traditional craftsmen and artists 'worked within the context of customs observed by everyone else. In turn, their imagination was nourished by myths, artistic traditions, and specific history of the culture and world in which they lived.'

The situation today is radically different and raises several issues for African nations as they participate in a globalizing world: How to develop their arts and creative economies? How to mitigate the effects of a market economy on creative/cultural products? Whether it is desirable to resist the instrumentalization of the arts and of culture –that is the use of arts and culture as tools for educational, health and other development agendas? How to receive and respond to the current focus on culture and creative pursuits as potential drivers of the economy capable of generating wealth and creating jobs? What role and impact might cultural diversity have on the creative economy?

But before going further, let us try to quickly understand how the creative and cultural economies are currently being defined. Concepts and understandings around the creative and cultural industries abound. Perhaps a Wikipedia definition will suffice for the purposes of this chapter:

> The phrase creative industries (or sometimes creative economy) refers to a set of interlocking industry sectors, and are often cited as being a growing part of the global economy. The creative industries are often defined as those that focus on creating and exploiting intellectual property products such as music, books, film, and games, or providing business to business creative services such as advertising, public relations and direct marketing. Aesthetic live performance experiences are also generally included, contributing to an overlap with definitions of art and culture, and sometimes extending to include aspects of tourism and sport. Economic activities focused on designing, making and selling objects or works of art such as jewelry, haute couture, books of poetry or other creative writing, or fine art also often feature in definitions of the sector because the value of such objects derives from a high degree of aesthetic originality.

How has a Kenyan creative economy progressed, both before and during the post-colony period? When art ceased being made 'for the tribe', for whom then was it being made? An examination of two directions that have evolved might shed some light. One direction took the form of collective action led by the creative members of community, and the second direction witnessed the emergence of activity by individual artists – some of whom received formal schooling in the arts, while others were self-taught.

Collective creative activity (sometimes termed by arts researchers as a movement) can be seen in the evolution of arts& crafts among the Akamba and the Kisii. (Other similar movements in the East & Southern Africa region include Makonde and Tingatinga from Tanzania and Shona sculpture from Zimbabwe). In these two communities it can be seen that when art & crafts ceased to be made predominantly for community purposes, when it lost its direct integral relationship with community life, it did not die away but instead entered the wider economy. Kamba wooden figurines entered the public market as early as 1914, (Von D. Miller, 1975). The impulse, it is reported, came from exposure received by the Kamba carver Mutisya Munge to Zaramo carvings from Tanzania, while he was there on duty with the Carrier Corps during World War I. The Akamba crafts movement organized itself to participate effectively within the wider economy: they selected which designs to produce, they set pricings, they established working and packaging spaces.

The shift from an ethno-centric craft to one that became more broadly defined as Kenyan craft happened, from an aesthetic perspective, through change in the design motifs selected, and a consciousness of the market's tastes – Kenyan wildlife, human figures, (old men, male and female busts) and contemporary everyday household items such as spoons and bowls. According to Von D. Miller, the external market for Akamba carvings opened as early as the period of the First World War with missionaries and foreign visitors as the consumers. Trade continued to grow, so much so, that "by the late 1950s soapstone carvings could be purchased all over East Africa and in various places overseas."

Kisii carvings followed a similar path. Carvings in soapstone, for public consumption, also began to be produced around World War I (Von D. Miller, 1975). Again, aesthetically, universal themes and motifs were settled upon and these were innovated with time, according to market needs. Commonly used household items such as soap dishes, vases and decorative figurines, were and continue to be popular with markets.

Like with the Akamba, the idea of working under a cooperative was adopted. But over the years, arts & crafts cooperatives have seen on and off successes, constantly requiring revitalization. Still, they have made a contribution towards the production of handicrafts that can be identified as *Kenyan* rather than ethnic-based crafts. Market opportunities undoubtedly contributed to the development and innovation of new product ranges in arts and crafts, but the same markets do also dictate what will sell and what will not. Thus the arts & crafts artist or artisan's creativity can be limited.

The second direction that the arts have taken is individual creation, which are quite unlike arts movements or cooperatives which in reality operate like mini- factories, employing many artisans who churn out designs in quantity, in a repetitive process. The individual artist typically creates one-off originals or only a limited edition of the creative product. This evolution of the artistic skills, that begins to move away from handicraft and into 'fine art', can be seen, for example, in the works of individual artists Kioko Mwatiki and Elkana On'gesa, respectively. Both are inheritors of the particular creative skills of their ethnic communities, (Mwatiki having dual heritage—Akamba and Maasai) and Ong'esa hailing from Tabaka in Kisii. Both are Kenyan artists of international repute.

What is of interest about the individual artist in the post-colony, is that their expression, deriving from their unique personal vision and coupled with their technical mastery, defies being placed within any particular ethnic locus. Again, it is in part, the contemporary and universal themes and imagery portrayed by these artists that lift their creative expressions from being ethno-centric to becoming part of a dynamic *Kenyan* creative economy. Mwatiki's life-size elephants at the Jomo Kenyatta International Airport roundabout in Nairobi, or Ong'esa's 'Dove of Peace' at the Joseph and Sheila Murumbi memorial in Parklands, Nairobi are examples of work that can definitely be termed *contemporary Kenyan*; none of these works can be described as Akamba or Kisii art. For both artists, the influence of formal arts training and exposure to international work has influenced not only their personal styles, but also their strategies to enter the arts markets locally and overseas. It is Kenya's loss, but obviously a gain for these two established artists, that the economies that consume their creative products are for the most part not Kenyan. For each, the export market, international commissions, and invitations by overseas galleries, are key end-destinations of their work.

Indeed, when one considers the overall contemporary visual arts sub-sector in Kenya, it is evident that any tendencies toward ethnic visual arts have been over-ridden by the complexity of modern Kenya. As far as the building of a Kenyan creative economy goes, the visual arts output, whether at craft level or fine art level is aimed for the present at external markets, although one can also begin to see the (very) slow emergence of local consumers of products from this sub-sector.

We now move to consider music. One finds here as well, progression towards pan-Kenyan sounds, a particularly good example being *benga*. The *benga* style of music was and still is a pervasive expressive form across practically all communities of Kenya, originating in the late 50s and early 60s (Osusa, Kelemba, Muhoro, 2008).

In the same way that Akamba carvings drew inspiration for innovation and wider markets from contact and exposure to sculptures outside their own community, *benga* spread through contact and encounter between Kenyan musicians of diverse ethnicities. In Nairobi of the mid 60s to mid 70s, recording studios were the meeting point between Luo musicians (from whom *benga* is said to have originated) and Kikuyu and Kamba musicians, and through 'session-ing' together, musical cross-fertilization began to take place. The spread of *benga* into Kisii was due to the geographical proximity of Luo and Kisii, with Luo musicians playing frequently in Kisii town, thus eventually influencing the development of a *benga* among the Kisii.

With the wide adoption of *benga* as a common-denominator musical form across communities, markets began to grow across ethnic boundaries. Daniel Kamau Mwai, popularly known as DK, and hailing from Gatanga in Kenya's Central Province, crossed over to Luo Nyanza with his hit song *Murata* because it incorporated the *benga* structure and sound. (Osusa, Kelemba, Muhoro, 2008).

Through the *benga* formula, artistes whatever their ethnicity, now had the potential to reach Kenyans beyond their own ethnic community, because, as with the popular *lingala* music from Zaire, it was not the only the lyrics that were the hook; the rhythm, dance pace and the recognizable role of the lead guitar were equally important in attracting audiences.

Today, as *benga* continues to be a common musical form across communities, other forms with the potential to become pan-Kenyan as well, are also emerging. The various musical forms from within and outside Kenya are collectively providing a repertoire of musical idioms that the contemporary popular Kenyan musician uses at will, in a genre increasingly referred to as afro-fusion. Contemporary musicians like Eric Wainaina and Suzanna Owiyo work in this genre and their appeal and primary markets are with multi-cultural urban audiences.

The economy of music, perhaps more than any other creative sub-economy, can be greatly enriched by creative exploitation of the diversity of ethnic music in Kenya. As long as the creator, for the purposes of economic gain, or to refresh inspiration, makes conscious effort to find a sound that can be shared and enjoyed alike by the majority of Kenyans. Such creation, as already exemplified by *benga* and *lingala* music, need not reduce the writing of lyrics to a national language, vernacular can still be used.

Part Two: Riding the rainbow

The economies of ethno-cultural arts

In this section, we return to the multicolored quality of the rainbow. In the first part, we tried to make the case for the value of overriding the rainbow, where a higher common platform of identity — we termed it Kenyan-ness - can be seen to readily yield socio-economic returns. And we tracked forces and directions taken by creators of Kenya's crafts, visual arts and popular music, looking at how they are delivering references more representative of Kenyan-ness, and with potential to reach wider markets. Yet, it is also true within the concept of creative economies, that there is individual value in each of the colors of the rainbow – in other words, the distinctive cultures of different ethnic groupscan also bring economic returns. After all, unity in diversity is not about same-ness, but rather a recognition and celebration of perspectives provided by different cultures.

The economies of ethno-cultural arts today are mainly managed under government departments of culture. Developing museums, cultural centres and historic sites, for cultural tourism is an important aspect of the creative economy. And to be sure, Kenya does not lack for places, things and events of ethno-cultural interest. What seems presently to be missing is proper investment in, and development and branding of such opportunities. A fine example of an ethno-cultural and historic site is Lamu Island. Lamu town is an old Swahili settlement on Lamu Island. It features original Swahili architectural structures, ancient building methods and a unique urban layout. It was recently declared a World Heritage site by UNESCO. For over five years now, the island has also held an annual festival that showcases the cultural activities and historic sites of Lamu – henna art, Swahili food, dhow races, donkey races, visits to the old Fort and the Lamu museum. But the opportunity presented here is yet to be maximized. Instead, interest on the island has come from Western foreigners; many own villas on the island. Lamu is steadily evolving into an exclusive resort for the rich, as local residents sell and move out.

If government has plans to develop cultural centres in different communities around the country, it must be prepared to 'go all out' and begin by selecting and developing the best sites, ensuring that curating and the program development of these centres is carefully thought through, and that the branding and publicity around such centres are given sufficient attention. In Johannesburg South Africa, there is a site very well branded as the Cradle of *Humankind*, and marketed as a key attraction for visitors to the city. Kenya too has important archeological sites that are known as the Cradle of *Mankind*. But one could come away entirely unaware of this because of the poor publicity and packaging of these sites for cultural tourism.

Another opportunity that presents itself is the gradual positioning of some cities as 'cities of culture'. This no doubt requires careful thinking and planning about existing assets that could be maximized and those that might be newly introduced to achieve such a positioning. The city of Nairobi, for example, is uniquely located next to a National Park. But is this fact really leveraged enough for cultural tourism? In addition, the cultural life that sustains a cultural city - music concerts, exhibitions, local cuisine, theatre, etc - would also need to be boosted, and to achieve this, one would need to draw from both ethno-cultural and contemporary creative economies.

Conclusion

While it seems entirely feasible to develop a robust creative economy both by riding and overriding our ethnic diversity, the dynamics of a creative economy must be properly studied and understood in order to better support it. So even as one reflects on the role of ethnic diversity in the Kenyan creative economy, the following issues and their implications for policy are also of concern:

Firstly, a comprehensive mapping, analysis and interpretation of the sector, qualitative and quantitative, ought to be carried out: knowledge of who are engaged in the creative economy, how and why they are engaged; an account of which training and capacity-building opportunities exist, and an understanding of the range of activities in the capital (Nairobi), out-of-capital and in rural.The specific locations of these activities ought to be known as well.

Secondly, there is need to consolidate Kenyan creative economy and its sub- sectors. The sector's value chain – from creation to production to distribution - is not only fragmented but has many missing links. Active encouragement of the private sector, with incentives to invest and engage with the creative sector value chain should be done. And the public sector should step up in delivering the necessary civic infrastructure such as concert halls, galleries, museums, cultural centres and training institutions.

Thirdly, is an examination of the financing of the sector- where might grants and subsidies be required? Where may micro-financing be more suitable? In what ways might government raise money for the arts? In some countries, for example, national lottery schemes are used to help fund the arts.

Fourthly, the arts must be re-instated in the education system as a core subject in schools. At the same time, a broader offer of vocational training, one that would include creative sector-related courses in areas such as arts management and technical courses such as sound engineering and lighting design ought to be developed.

And last but not least, if Kenya is to fully embrace the creative economy paradigm, it must also ensure that the policy-making processes and legal frameworks pertaining to the same are dynamic and timely.

References

Anheier H.K & Isar Y. R. (2008). "The Cultural Economy." *The Cultures and Globalization Series 2*. Los Angeles: Sage Publications.

Meyer, L. (1994). *Art and Craft in Africa*. Paris: Pierre Terrail Editions.

Osusa T, Kelemba & P, Muhoro N. (2008). *Retracing the Benga Rhythm*. Nairobi: Ketebul Music.

Razlogov, K. (2008). "Countries in Transition: Which way to Go?" *The Cultural Economy, The Cultures and Globalization Series 2*, pp. 172 -177. Los Angeles: Sage Publications.

Reed, A. W. (1965). *Aboriginal Fables and Legendary Tales.* Adelaide: Griffin Paperbacks.

Von D. Miller, Judith. (1975). *Art in East Africa.* Great Britain: Whitsable Litho Ltd.

Leveraging Africa's Diversity for an improved Image and Branding

Mary W. Kimonye

Introduction

The twenty-first century has presented nations of the world with unique challenges which, if not adequately and appropriately addressed, may negatively affect the livelihoods of the world's six billion people and throw the entire world into a crisis. Already we are experiencing the effects of global warming, international terrorism, substance abuse, environmental degradation, and of course globalization and run away technological development.

Whereas some of the developments of the century are positive and have eased the way nations of the world relate to the exchange goods and services, for example—others are causing tensions and each nation is wondering: "How do we survive?" Technological developments have shortened distances but also complicated commerce and industry. The poor nations of the world, most of which are in Africa, cannot keep up until they get their share of resources.

Globalization has opened up interactions, smashed psychological and physical boundaries and intensified competition for investments, tourism, inward migration of factors of production and individual nation's influence in world affairs.

The question that most nations of Africa are grappling with is where to find the competitive advantage that is so much needed to remain relevant in world affairs. Much of this relevance is dependent on how others see and perceive Africa. Africa stands out in the minds of certain sections of the world as the Dark Continent—a backward place where disease, poverty, ethnic strife, crime and poor governance are the defining characteristics. Whereas all these exist and African governments are struggling with these challenges, there is a lot of good coming out of Africa.

The richness of African cultures, great endowments in minerals, good agricultural climates and warm friendly people present unique and positive assets which can be propelled to position Africa as truly the next frontier for development in the world.

First-world nations and emerging economies in Asia and the Middle East are currently the most developed of the world, and have the tallest buildings and the biggest factories. The fastest growing economies are now to be found in Asia.

Africa can be positioned to be the next frontier. The huge deposits of unexploited wealth, youthful dynamic populations and the resiliency of the continent will in coming years present Africa as the preferred option for investments, trade and industry as well as sources of labor. But for this to happen and for the African people to benefit fully, well-thought strategies of improving Africa's image must be put in place. Africa must take the lead and tell her story. Africa must consciously direct the content that reaches the ears of the world whether through the net, print or electronic media. Africa's leaders must begin to think "image" and take the lead as the public relations agents for their respective countries and for the continent as a whole. In sum, Africa must look to leverage her diversity to create and maintain the desirable image. Africa must brand and rebrand herself.

The stories and challenges of the East African countries cannot be divorced from those of the rest of Africa. In terms of branding, what the Eastern African countries need to worry about is how to wriggle themselves out of the generally-held perceptions of Africa as the backward continent. Successful attempts have been made elsewhere. Egypt is able to attract tourists and investments, and South Africa has been working on its brand. "Alive with Possibilities" is a common phrase to many of us. Because of their similarities, the East African countries would benefit more from joint branding efforts.

This chapter will present proposals on how the East African countries could leverage their ethnic diversity to create a competitive advantage that will turn the region into an attractive place for business, work and leisure and improve the inflow of the much needed foreign exchange.

Africa's diversity: A blessing or curse?

Africa is truly a continent of contrasts; a mosaic of colour, that in a manner of speaking could be said to "capture the world in one". Popularly known as the "Motherland", Africa is the cradle of mankind and the home of ancient civilizations occupied by some 900 million people of diverse cultures over a large expanse. Africa is the third largest continent and Africa's personality and character are very well captured in its rich diversity.

The climates of Africa range from deserts to rich tropical rainforests. In these are huge deposits of all types of resources: the oil rich North, expansive gold and copper belts of the South-western and Central Africa, and a diversity of agricultural products grown throughout the continent.

The people of Africa speak over 2,000 languages with diverse cultures and heritage. These cultures and heritage remain some of Africa's greatest attractions to the world. Those who know Africa most possibly know the sounds of the African drum, which virtually every African community beats to signify good things like harvest, winning of conflicts, the birth of children and of course marriage and many other good fortunes. Africa has an awesome experience, informed by the many struggles of her people, through history: colonialism, slave trade, ethnic conflicts, neocolonialism, and more recently, globalization which has left African leaders struggling with ways of generating enough capital to develop their countries within world monetary and trade systems which they have little or no say, but where so much is expected of them.

One would also need to consider Africa's natural beauty: the alluring beaches, the snow-capped mountains right on the equator, the variety of wildlife, the ruggedness of the savannah and the Great Rift Valley. The question is why Africa, despite all these, suffers negative images. Why does a continent that is so richly endowed still house the world's poorest people? Why has the richness of Africa's diversity not been fully exploited to position Africa where it should ideally be?

In his book *Africa Rising*, Vijay Mahajan presents a very encouraging view of Africa. Despite all the attention it has received for its social, medical, humanitarian and political challenges, it is still undervalued as a consumer market. Africa has 900 million consumers who need all manner of goods and services. The world cannot afford to ignore Africa or even to brush it a side as the "backward" continent. According to the Population Reference Bureau 2007 World Population Data Sheet, 41 percent of Africa's population is below the age of 15 years. This makes it one of the youngest markets in the world. These young Africans are dynamic and are connected with consumer demands that mirror those of the West. In these young people's energy, enthusiasm and resilience lies the true brand assets of Kenya.

Through music and sports this young generation of Africans is slowly but surely leaving their footprint on the world. Africa's strength and its greatest competitive advantage does not lie in its many minerals like oil, diamonds and gold but in the youthful talent and vibrant creativity of its people.

Africa has produced countless entrepreneurs, business people, academicians, sportsmen and political leaders. The nations of Africa and indeed East Africa must tap into this hidden "soft" wealth to transform themselves into domitable global brands.

Africa's branding and image building

The branding of nations and regions can be looked at within the context of place branding. This covers all initiatives of giving places—be they cities, towns, nations or regions—distinctive and attractive characters based on the unique characteristics of these places.

What is place branding?

The concept of place branding is fairly new and often confused with traditional advertising and promotion. Place branding is, however, a more encompassing concept that deals with developing a place's image and identity consciously in order to improve the place's attractiveness. It is a holistic concept that demands the involvement and contribution of everybody. In a continent like Africa, political, religious and community leaders, together with business people, policy makers, citizens and investors would all be critical in the continent's branding.

By definition, place branding involves applying the concepts and practices of marketing to the social, political, economic, and cultural development of a place. The result is an improved image of the place, whether it is a country, city or even a continent. It also results into an improved identity, i.e. how the citizens and others in the place see and conceive of the place. *Place branding, then, assumes that a place can be treated just like a product by a critical mass of people.* Such people hold a generalized perception about the place which then informs or determines the nature of their interactions with the place. Through the use of strategic communication and marketing, and backed by reality on the ground, the place can then generate awareness about itself, as well as affection and preference towards itself.

When people express their preference for Indian cuisine, Italian shoes, French perfumes, German engineering, Egyptian heritage, African culture, they do so as a result of the brand images of these places. Is it then possible for a critical mass of people, say investors, to express their preference for a continent? Yes, depending not so much about what is said of that continent but rather the context within which the continent exists and in which its messages are received. Branding a continent is then driven by the reality of the continent's context.

The fundamental question to ask is, *"What is the prevailing perception of African context or culture?"* If it is predominantly negative then people respond negatively: no desire to visit, wariness/suspicion, less resources etc. It is within that context and these reactions that Africa, and indeed East Africa, must find and secure a vantage place for herself in the world. This in essence is where branding comes in.

Why brand Africa?

Fundamentally African countries are not only in competition with each other but with those in other regions. African nations need compelling reasons to present to the world. A deeper look at the majority of African countries gives both positive and negative reasons to embark on branding.

Positive reasons (Drivers of the continent branding)

First, Africa possesses an array of strong brand assets whose potential has not been fully exploited:

- People (African icons)
- Cultures/heritage
- Climate
- Minerals
- Geographical features
- Wildlife
- Sports

Secondly, some countries of Africa such as Botswana and Mauritius have built strong social and governance systems which can be sold to the rest of the world as useful models. Thirdly, due to the geographical and climatic conditions of Africa, some of the world's highest quality agricultural products are to be found here. There are strong exports, but rarely do they carry the names of their countries of origin (tea, coffee, cut flowers, cocoa etc). Lastly, the African population remains an important source market not only for skills but also for talent in such areas as music, dance and technology. Companies looking to house their corporate headquarters away from the very expensive cities of the world would find Africa a very viable option. Already, industry and the private sector are thriving in many African states.

Negative reasons why we must rebrand Africa

- Limited or nonexistent African voice in world affairs
- Wanton exploitations of Africa's natural resources by others, led especially by multinational corporations
- Low levels of pride, confidence and patriotism among a majority of Africa's people towards their motherland
- Challenges of poverty, unemployment and diseases
- Predominantly negative perceptions held worldwide towards Africa
- Lack of control and limited control of content on Africa leading to over-projected notions of insecurity, corruption and inequality, poverty and general deprivation as well as understated achievements and positive values
- Socio-economic challenges among them overstrained infrastructure, basic services and unemployment.

To what extent does Africa need branding?

Put very simply, to the extent that the continent is low in "place value", i.e. uniqueness and distinctiveness, fundamental questions need to be asked. For example to what extent can the nations of Africa make claims of being unique, distinctive and attractive? What is their competitive advantage over others? If they are lacking in these, then they can be viewed as depressed or distressed places which need a new image. Put against the key measures of attractiveness, i.e. livability, investability and visibility, Africa can generally be described as depressed though some nations may not fully fit this classification.

What model should African nations use towards branding and improving their images?

Nation branding is not a short term, quick fix process, but a strategic and consciously thought-out process that is systematic in its very nature. The situations and challenges African countries are experiencing and which are denting their image, cannot be advertised away. Solutions must be sought and deliberate actions taken to improve the context in which they exist.

To succeed at nation branding, a country must design a home-grown approach that takes cognizance of its uniqueness as well as the needs and aspirations of its people and potential target audiences. In general, however, a generic approach could be employed. This approach may be guided by the following steps.

a) It is advisable for the branding initiative to be within a high level agency led by a collaborative planning group of visionaries from diverse disciplines and groups (investors, business people, academicians, policy makers and professionals).

b) The planning group should begin by dissecting the country to extract its DNA, i.e. to clearly isolate the country's strengths, weaknesses, principal assets, key brand-builders and also brand-destroyers. The process should lead to the development of a catalogue of the country's problems and their causes as well as the countries attractions and their status, resources, values and opportunities.

c) Based on this diagnostic, the planning group should then develop a clear vision of long term solutions to the country's problems, taking into account all key aspects, i.e. politics, economy, social policy etc.

d) Out of this vision the planning group should develop a strategy for the country's transformation in terms of:

- Investments
- Basic services
- Infrastructure
- New attractions
- Behavior and attitude
- Charge

e) The country should then roll out a communication program both internally and externally to communicate its improved status and image.

f) Finally, real-time collaborative mechanisms of support and image monitoring and evaluation should be put in place, and brand champions (identified to convey and embody the vision) should be identified.

Ethnic diversity tools for branding

Our ethnic diversity is a unique tool that can be used to propel African nations to more prominent standings in world affairs.

Among these are:

National attitudes and values

A country's national psyche can be a strong differentiator and a formidable source. Kenya's transformation in the period 2003-2007, when it attained a 7 percent rate of economic growth had, among others things, a lot to do with the then prevailing attitude of optimism among the population. Countries with strong nationalistic attitudes have been known to evolve cohesive and stable societies; Tanzania is such a state. The "English way of life" has often been cited as one of the reasons for Britain's economic decline in the last century. This way of life is characterized by "stable, cozy behavior". The now-saving culture of America, informed by over-confidence and a high sense of security in the might of their nation, has seen many suffer greatly under the current world financial crisis. Needless to say a welcoming friendly attitude is a big image booster. Kenya has been a beneficiary of this for many years.

Music and dance

The love for music across all cultures is indisputable. Music has become a universally unifying force and indeed a strong income earner for many communities in Africa. This is the one product that Africa must use to communicate herself and tell the world her story.

Sports

Africa is awash with all manner of captivating sports, many from ancient African traditions. From football to long distance running, the might of the African people has left the world awe-stricken. Ethiopian runners on the tracks of America and Europe are truly spectacular and if modernized and institutionalized sports can change the face of Africa.

Art

African art constitutes one of the most diverse legacies on earth. Though many casual observes tend to generalize "traditional" African art, the continent is full of peoples, societies, and civilizations, each with a unique culture. The definition also includes the art of the African diaspora, such as the art of African-Americans. Despite this diversity, there are some unifying artistic themes when considering the totality of the visual culture from the continent of Africa. African art with its emphasis on the human figure, visual abstraction, sculpture, performed art and non-linear scaling can be a real image booster.

African Cuisine

Africa is home to hundreds of ethnic and social groups. This diversity is also reflected in African cuisine from the ingredients used to the preparation and techniques of cooking. From the culinary dishes of North Africa to southern

Africa's braais and Eastern Africans Swahili and traditional dishes, Africa is truly a banquet ready for the world to feast on.

Religion

Religion in Africa is multifaceted. Most Africans adhere to either Christianity or Islam. This does not mean that other religions are not represented; they are, but in smaller percentages. Religion plays a big role in African culture and through it identities and ways of life are shaped, thus resulting in a diverse and enriched population. This makes Africa a vibrant place as anyone in the world can easily fit in.

Dress and fashion

Every continent has its distinct sense of style and Africa has not been left behind. Africa has become a leader in some fashion trends and has influenced fashion in America, Europe and the rest of the world. Examples include West Africa's *agbada* and *buba*, Eastern Africa's *kikoy, kitenge, umshanna, omwenda* and *gomesi* and the North African's *bui bui* and *kanzu* (which has been modernized to today's fashion trend). Africa's fashion industry is growing and diversifying each day, thus boosting the economy and image of the continent. Some examples of country brands

1. Singapore

Context

- Has no natural resources
- Possesses only a harbor
- It has transformed itself into what can be referred to as a city state.

Approach

The government intervenes directly and heavily in the direction of political, social and economic policies and programmes. The focus is moved away from foreign loans to foreign investments.

2. South Africa

South Africa has managed to transform itself from the image of the apartheid nation to an attractive destination offering investment tourism and corporate headquarters. To do so, South Africa has told her story in the way best beneficial to her. Despite having such challenges as high HIV and AIDS prevalence, crime, discrimination, South Africa stands strong as a brand. South Africa has used effectively their iconic leader Nelson Mandela to build their major brand.

Conclusion

Clearly, Africa can rebrand itself through an exploration of its diversity. The continent should not be viewed as a depressed continent but as a vibrant and diverse one. To reverse this depressed state, certain fundamental steps must be taken by African states. These steps are mapped directly on those aspects of the countries that give them a bad image:

- Governance must be addressed;
- Infrastructure must be improved;
- The costs of doing business must be addressed;
- Challenges of security must be addressed;
- Urban congestion and provision of basic services must also be addressed;
- All the symptoms and causes of society's decay must be addressed, among them crime, idleness, debt, poor services, inequality etc;
- The country's products and services must be delivered in an efficient and accessible way.

When all these are dealt with, the nations should be in a position to take up the two critical actions towards repackaging themselves by:

- Designing the right mix of each country's attractions;
- Setting attractive incentives for potential visitors, investors and buyers of goods and services. Until these are in place, African countries can use communication to challenge the notion that Africa is risky and unsafe and also reinforce the fact that Africa is an attractive place to visit, live and invest.

These activities require that citizens become active participants in changing attitudes and images about Africa. By drawing on our diversity and ensuring greater image of African can be greatly enhanced.

References

Mahajan, V. (2009). *Africa Rising*. Upper Saddle River, NJ: Pearson Education/ The Wharton School Publishing.

Ethnicity in Politics

Ethnic Diversity, Democratization and Nation-Building in Ghana

Kenneth Agyemang Attafuah

Introduction

The processes of creating the single geo-political entity known as Ghana out of hitherto multiple, diverse and independent ethnic states have been well told elsewhere and do not bear a detailed exposition here: colonial conquest, subjugation, purchase, trickery and domination.[1] Virtually all African countries, with the exception of Ethiopia and Liberia, are artificial products of the same instruments of incomplete and inadhesive cementation for colonial political and economic convenience.

Nowhere in Africa did the tools of colonial coercion, subterfuge and penetration result in nation-building, or in the crystallization of a sense of nationhood. It is now clear that the introduction of schools, the construction of development infrastructure such as roads and railways, and the extension of missionary works into the heart of the continent principally aimed at serving the material interests of colonial powers.

Admittedly, in some measure, these innocuous processes, such as participation in colonial education and civil service, had the unanticipated consequence of bringing persons from diverse ethno-cultural backgrounds together, especially in urban areas, and forging new networks of friendship, amorous relationships and interdependence that occasionally transcended the strength of ethnic ties and other primordial loyalties and, as a corollary, created a sense of *nationhood*, even under colonialism.[2] Many such relationships provided the initial platforms for the anti-colonial political movements that subsequently enveloped the continent. Nevertheless, the emergence and continued relevance of voluntary ethnic associations as instruments for meeting the material, emotional and social security needs of new entrants to the urban milieu underscores the power, resilience and relevance of the ethnic group in the urban setting. In the urban context, strong in-group solidarity is often correlated with strong out-group hostility. Ethnocentrism or ethnic prejudice grounded in the belief that one's ethnic group is superior to another group or all others combines with ethnic discrimination or tribalism to impede nation building and national development efforts in Ghana. Tribalism continues to bedevil the *emergent nation*. Formation of political parties, patterns of voting in presidential and parliamentary elections, political appointments and termination of public sector appointments, formulation of development policies and programs, and distribution of development projects are all heavily influenced by ethnic considerations.

Focus of paper

Against this background, the fundamental questions discussed in this chapter are two-fold:

1. How is Ghana developing nationhood and tapping on the richness of its diverse cultures and communities?
2. How can Ghana nurture diversity and make the best out of it through, for example, strengthening democratic institutions?

Prior to engaging with these issues, it is important to explore briefly the challenge of nation building within the context of ethnic pluralism within a country, as well as the meaning and elements of the very concept of nation-building. This brief excursion is important in order to clearly situate the subsequent discussions in a proper conceptual framework.

The challenge of nation-building amidst ethnic diversity

Despite its significant strides in nation-building, Ghana, like many other African countries, remains severely fragmented, fractured and mired along ethnic lines, with other primeval ties and loyalties binding most people far more tightly than the state can currently dream of or claim. The classic example is the traditional Asante-Ewe hostility which has been capitalized upon by nefarious politicians since Ghana's independence in 1957. This is in spite of great personal friendships and business partnerships across the two ethnic divides, as well as numerous flourishing marriages between women from matrilineal Asante and men from patrilineal Ewe ethnic groups that are considered hugely advantageous to the children of such marriages. A great number of Asante-Ewe concubinages also abound in Ghana. Yet, it appears that the two ethnic groups are considered the most fearsome ethno-political enemies, with mutually strong suspicions and attributions of ill-will. And in their traditional settings, fantastic myths abound that justify out-group hostility, in-group solidarity, and, by extension, the maintenance of social distance and social exclusion.

Mutually negative stereotypes and prejudicial attitudes also assail relationship between the large clusters of ethnic groups from the Northern parts of Ghana and those from the Southern parts. Partly rooted in the nature of the colonial and post-colonial political economy, the systems of resource mobilization for economic production, and the unfair distribution of educational and development facilities, all of which have benefitted the resource-rich South to the disadvantage of the relatively resource-starved North, have largely been maintained to date. "Northerners" as individuals and groups often tend to be the object of vile discrimination in employment, housing and the provision of social services by "southerners", while the former also tend to find a scapegoat in the latter for virtually every personal or group failing. At the root of the problem also lies the fact that the development of the resource-endowed South has been made possible by and with the critical supply of labour from the resource-deprived North.

The challenges that have attended the business of forging a sense of nationhood in Ghana have been daunting, longstanding and occasionally debilitating. Ethnic competition, rivalry, conflict, domination and marginalization often characterize inter-group relations in Ghana. In parts of the country, particularly in the Bawku municipal area of the Upper East Region and parts of the Volta Region, contiguous ethnic groups are still caught up in pre-medieval rivalries and inter-ethnic warfare even in the face of long traditions of intermarriages and joking relationships. These internecine conflicts are often fuelled by incendiary politicians and acted out by idle armies of unemployed youths who are misled into the belief that their long-term economic prosperity is tied to the political fortunes of the politicians.

Occasionally, the inter-ethnic violence is spurred by arguments and conflicts arising from the mundane activities of living. Indeed, in 1994, disputation deriving from haggling over the price of a guinea-fowl sparked off latent strife in one part of the Northern Region of Ghana, which quickly transformed into an explosive, full-blown war between two anciently contiguous ethnic groups – the Konkombas and the Nanumbas. More than four thousand people died in that war and numerous others became internally displaced persons. Thousands moved to the heart of Accra and established a "temporary" slum settlement, known as Sodom and Gomorrah, for its scale of unspeakable immorality, crime and violence.[3]

The point is that Ghana has its fair share of inter-ethnic difficulties that frustrate and complicate the process of building a formidable nation out of the many distinct ethno-cultural groupings. Yet tensions in ethnic relations in Ghana have been sufficiently well-contained and well-managed; the country continues to pursue with zeal, even if at present lopsidedly, the agenda of nation-building. A veneer of inter-group hostilities is discernible in social and political life, especially as evidenced in voting patterns and free speech on the more than 320 private FM radio stations in the country.

Despite these major deficits in national integration, democratization and nation-building, the centrifugal forces of ethnic diversity have not been allowed to degenerate into full-scale armed conflicts as witnessed in many African countries such as Liberia, Ivory Cost, Nigeria, Kenya and Rwanda.

The meanings of nation-building

Nation-building as state reforms and reconstruction

In one sense, nation-building refers to broad efforts to promote political and economic reforms with the objective of transforming a society emerging from conflict into one at peace with itself and its neighbors. In Europe, the end of the Cold War provided the occasion for the United Nations, NATO, the United States and a range of other states and nongovernmental organizations to engage directly and increasingly in nation-building operations.

In post-conflict societies, nation building equals *state-building*. It often entails the massive investment or deployment of financial resources and humanitarian aid. Indeed, in the contemporary world, nation-building is often a strategy of *modernization* modeled after the Marshall Plan – the magnificent reconstruction effort initiated by the United States in 1947 to rebuild some European nations devastated by the World War II. The implementation of that plan cost $12 billion between 1948 and 1951 under President Truman. Nation building also frequently requires the use of armed force to ensure law and order. As in Liberia, Sierra Leone, Democratic Republic of Congo, Iraq, Afghanistan, Bosnia and Belarus, armed force was considered vital to securing the appropriate environment for the pursuit of other restorative and national reconstruction measures.

Nation-building as national identity formation

The concept of nation-building has a second, *broader* and probably more compelling meaning. In its broad sense, nation building refers to the process of constructing or structuring a *national identity* through the use of state power. The exercise of state power in aid of nation-building commonly finds expression along two key dimensions, namely social psychological engagement and infrastructural development. The aim of nation building is to foster a *shared* and coherent national identity, orientation and unification among the people or peoples of a state in order to ensure the long-term political stability and viability of the state.

Typically, nation-building in this broad sense entails the simultaneous use of strategies of mass reorientation, including propaganda, *and* major infrastructural developments to foster social harmony and economic growth. The second variant of nation-building also emphasizes the development of the social sector comprising education, health and family welfare, water supply, sanitation, housing, social welfare, nutrition, rural employment and minimum basic services.

Symbolic efforts and manifestations of such orientation in aid of nation building may include (a) the introduction of superficial national paraphernalia such as flags, anthems, pledges and currencies, national identity cards; (b) the institution of national holidays; (c) the establishment of national colleges and universities, airlines and stadiums; (d) the institution of a *lingua franca* or national language for the state; and (e) the production, articulation or propagation of national myths. Nation-building is thus a complex and dynamic process with ideological, philosophical, political, socio-economic and cultural dimensions.

This broad view of nation-building, then, is a deliberate political and cultural process of constructing or moulding a common nation out of hitherto independent political and ethno-cultural groups or tribes. In other words, the task of nation-building in broad sense is the creation of a universal national identity and sense of common destiny for people who previously belonged to different social formations and who defined and perceived their destinies as diametrically opposed. Thus, for instance, at the time of independence in 1957, the Gold Coast was a motley collection of different nation-states previously formed from the magma of wars, political alliances dictated by fear of military conquests, colonial annexation and impositions. Indeed, the Asante Kingdom, for example, was an amalgam of several smaller nation-states that came together to form a single political, military and religious entity "because of war" – *osa nti*. [The Asante nation gained its name from the corruption of the *"Osa nti"* to "Asante"].

Nation-building in much of Africa commenced in the post-independence period as a reaction against the divide-and-rule tactics of the colonialists. It is an enterprise of persuading, manipulating, moulding, cementing and bonding diverse peoples into a nation with a common emotional relationship to the state and modernizing and improving their material socio-economic circumstances. That process continues to this day. This form of nation-building thus requires the subordination of all competing ethno-cultural, primordial loyalties in a state to an emergent nationhood and "supra-ethnic" identity.

Evidently, this meaning of nation-building as national integration is a more daunting phenomenon. Thus understood, nation-building appears to be a difficult and lifelong process. Canada has been treading the path of nation-building since its founding fathers signed the Independence Proclamation and Constitution in 1877. A key challenge facing Canada today consists in finding ways to harmoniously integrate the two dominant "founding groups", the French and the English, as well as the First Nations of Canada and the large numbers of immigrant and visible minority populations whose labour and other contributions helped build the country's magnificent economic development infrastructure and sustain its enviable level of human well-being.

Today, the United States is grappling with a different kind of nation-building founded on revitalizing the relatively shattered American economy, saving industries, jobs and banks, paying for education, rebuilding families, and generally restoring hope to millions. Building on the dreams of Dr. Martin Luther King, Jr., America under President Obama is also building a nation that is more inclusive and fairer, kinder and gentler. And the United Kingdom is now re-inventing itself in an effort to accommodate its increasing minority populations.

On the African continent, Liberia, Sierra Leone, Guinea, Cote d'Ivoire, Burkina Faso, Ghana, Togo, Benin and Nigeria are all entrapped in what appears to be in a state of perpetual infancy in nation-building and the facilitation of economic development. Malawi, Burundi, Democratic Republic of Congo, Kenya, Rwanda, South Africa, Uganda and Zimbabwe are examples of other countries on the continent that failed to build nations when they should have, and are still grappling with the painful costs of development without nation-building.

Elements of nation-building as identity formation and governance

Fundamentally, nation-building is about building one identity out of many; it is about harnessing and utilizing state resources to deliberately create a shared and broad-based sense of belonging to a socio-legal entity that is greater than the sum of its parts, i.e. to the nation, with all its emotional, spiritual and symbolic ramifications and connotations. It is about using good governance and democratization to foster a new common identity for the citizenry. In other words, it is to engender inclusivity and national integration.

What, then, may be described as the essential elements of this variant of nation-building in Ghana as a counterfoil to the divisive centrifugal forces of ethnic diversity? Thus conceived, the foremost elements of nation-building in Ghana, in my view, include the following:

a. Fostering a sense of national identity and belonging

b. Pursuing socio-economic development vigorously, equitably and responsibly in order to enhance the overall quality of life of people in all parts of the country in a sustainable manner

c. Promoting inter-group harmony to reduce ethnic prejudice and discrimination

d. Advancing and protecting human rights, administrative justice and integrity in private and public life

e. Nurturing an open society to engender transparency and reduce all forms of tyranny and caprice

f. Fostering respect for the rule of law, transparency and accountability

g. Ensuring individual and public safety and security, and

h. Creating the social and political space for a vibrant civil society to flourish and participate in the process of governance at the local and national levels.

Nation-building, as with all processes, aims at the production of a preferred outcome; namely, a society in which most citizens emotionally and intellectually identify themselves with the salient manifestations of its nationhood, and the citizens evince a sense of unity, a common outlook, and a sense of shared destiny.

Strategies employed in Ghana to manage ethnic relations and promote nation-building

Since independence, Ghana has worked toward the development of nationhood by developing and implementing several legal, social and economic policies and programmes aimed at integrating the country's wealth of diverse ethnic groups into a mosaic of cultures. It has also instituted measures to tap on the richness of its diverse cultures and communities. The following are illustrative:

Adoption of affirmative action policies and programs

At the start of the Nkrumah's pre-independence Government in 1950, there were significant differences in levels of development between the South and the North. Even to this day, there are portions of the North that are derogatorily referred to as "overseas" because of their acute levels of underdevelopment. The Nkrumah Government introduced and implemented an Accelerated Development Plan with in-built elements of corrective affirmative action. The policy continued throughout the reign of Nkrumah in the post-independence era till his overthrow in 1966. The result was a preponderance of physical development structures, including factories and schools, all of which aimed at facilitating the expeditious development of the North. This included a policy of free education for students from the North, and scholarships for bright students from the North to pursue secondary education at first class and prestigious schools in the South. Regrettably, not enough attention was paid to the qualitative output from those structures, and the affirmative action policies, like all such truly affirmative action measures, should have been time-bound, implemented within a specified time frame, monitored and periodically evaluated to ensure that they were indeed addressing the educational imbalance it was introduced to address. This was not done, and the whole programme became a sorry subject of criticisms as, by 1966 (i.e., 15 years later) there was no evidence that the gap was closing.

Use of a mandatory constitutional framework for nation-building

Ghana's constitution compels the deliberate implementation of efforts and initiatives to achieve national integration. Socio-economic development and nation-building are constitutional imperatives in Ghana. Indeed, Ghana's Fourth Republican Constitution (1992) provides the legal framework for the pursuit of socio-economic development and nation building.

In the Preamble to the Constitution, the people of Ghana assert their conviction that the purpose of establishing a democratic framework of government is to "secure for [themselves] and posterity the blessings of liberty, equality of opportunity and prosperity". Article 1(1) also provides that the welfare of the people of Ghana constitutes the basis for the exercise of governmental power. The essence of that welfare is elaborated upon in the Directive Principles of State Policy (DPSP) found in Chapter Six of the Constitution which, in Article 34(1), calls for the use of law and state power to establish "a just and free society."

Accordingly, Article 34(2) specifies the realization of the following fundamental conditions of liberty and human welfare for Ghanaians as the foremost job description of the State:

a. Basic human rights

b. A healthy economy

c. The right to work

d. The right to good health care, and

e. The right to education

Given the great importance the framers of Ghana's Constitution attached to these cardinal conditions for ensuring the welfare of the people, Article 34(2) obliges the President to report to Parliament at least once a year all the steps taken by Government to ensure their realization. Indeed, for Ghana, these foundational elements of human liberty and prosperity constitute the key benchmarks of socio-economic development, which the Government of every President must earnestly strive to achieve. This article therefore provides the compulsory template for the essential contents of the President's Sessional Address to Parliament. The Constitution also obliges the President to pursue, and report to Parliament on, other key policy objectives contained in the DPSP. And I must add that the President does not have to report to Parliament *only* once a year, but *at least* once year! Minimalism is not a best practice when it comes to public sector accountability.

Significantly, Article 17 of the Ghanaian Constitution prohibits discrimination on several grounds, including gender, race, colour, ethnic origin, place of origin, religion, creed, political opinions, occupation, social status or economic status. The nation will be well built when every Ghanaian is allowed to feel that they *really belong* in Ghana—when no one is unjustifiably discriminated against on the basis of race, colour, ethnicity, ancestry, place of origin, sex, age, political affiliation or belief, physical or mental disability, economic status, social status, and family status. When no competent public officer is dismissed from employment because of their real or perceived political colour, the nation will be deemed to be well built because it will be truly inclusive.

Article 35(3) of the Constitution provides as follows:

> "The state shall promote just and reasonable access by all citizens to public facilities and services in accordance with law."

In a most progressive pursuit of nation-building, Article 35(5) of the Constitution charges the State with the obligation to "actively promote the integration of the peoples of Ghana; it charges the State to prohibit discrimination and prejudice on the grounds of place of origin, circumstances of birth, ethnic origin, gender or religion, creed or other beliefs".

Towards this end, the State is further required in Article 35(6) to pursue and implement appropriate measures, among other things, to:

(a) foster a spirit of loyalty to Ghana that overrides sectional, ethnic and other loyalties;

(b) achieve reasonable regional and gender balance in recruitment and appointment to public offices; and

(c) provide adequate facilities for, and encourage, free mobility of people, goods and services throughout Ghana.

The State is also obliged to take steps to eradicate corrupt practices and the abuse of power, and to promote political tolerance among Ghanaians.

In Article 36, the State is enjoined to competently manage the national economy with a view to maximizing the rate of economic development and securing the maximum welfare, freedom and happiness of every person in Ghana. It must also provide adequate means of livelihood and suitable employment for the people, as well as public assistance to the needy.

In particular, Article 36(6) requires the State to afford equality of economic opportunity to all citizens, and to take all necessary steps to ensure the full integration of women into the mainstream of the economic development of Ghana. These, then, are the core goals of nation-building as enshrined in the Ghanaian Constitution. Nation-building in contemporary Ghanaian society, as in the contemporary world generally, thus includes the active promotion of good governance, including the eradication of corruption and the prevention and control of administrative injustice and abuse of power. Indeed, it may be said that nation-building today is fundamentally about good governance, and good governance is best assured when it is anchored in sound leadership, equity and accountability.

Nation-building in Ghana will be advanced when Ghanaians sincerely and prudently "protect and safeguard the independence, unity and territorial integrity of Ghana," in accordance with Article 35(2) of the Constitution, and "seek the well-being of all." The nation will be built when, as required by Article 35(2), Ghanaians sincerely "promote just and reasonable access by all citizens to public facilities and services in accordance with law." We further build the nation when we enable people to achieve their goals without placing frustrating impediments in their way.

We build the nation when our chiefs set personal examples of tolerance and acceptance of diversity by engaging in high-level cultural diplomacy — when the Agbogbomefia of Anlo pays a courtesy visit to the Asantehene, the Nayiri of Mamprugu exchanges visits the Nzimahene, the Wa Na visits the Ga Manste, or the Drobohene visits the Krobohene, and when chiefs forge friendships in real and substantive ways. What positive impact on inter-group relations there is, when ethnic groups join forces to stage food festivals in celebration of each other's cultures and organize language clinics for members of the other ethno-cultural group.

We build the nation when we protect and defend the civil rights of all persons from discrimination and unfair treatment regardless of their political orientation or affiliation, or their religious persuasion or creed. We build the nation when we do not abuse our power or authority at the workplace. We build the nation when we do not subject our subordinates at the office, factory or church to bullying, sexual harassment or other form of demeaning treatment or humiliation.

We build the nation when we cultivate among all Ghanaians "respect for fundamental human rights and freedoms and the dignity of the human being." The dignity of the human being, we are told in Article 15(1), is "inviolable". That means that human dignity is sacred. A nation is built and sustained when it respects the dignity of all persons within its boundaries.

Use of socio-economic development as a strategy for nation-building

Socio-economic development provides an impetus for nation-building. Much racial bigotry and ethnic prejudice melt away when the processes of socio-economic development plunge strangers from different social groups into unavoidable cooperation or collaboration on such platforms as school-based formal education, the workplace, sports teams and military battalions and police contingents.

The introduction of the boarding school system in Ghana, for instance, served as a training ground in inter-group tolerance, peaceful co-existence and social harmony. More than the university, the factory or the church, it was in the boarding schools of this country that the most enduring inter-ethnic friendships were forged, and where long-term political alliances were incubated and nurtured. Respect for religious diversity and tolerance was better fostered among our peoples from interactions in the boarding school than from the state propaganda apparatus.

In some measure, the attainment of higher education and economic success reduces ethnic bigotry. The ethnic bigot with a superiority complex accords genuine respect to the rich or successful business executive from a despised ethnic minority background. Such an executive is treated with a greater sense of fairness than his/her compatriots or other in-group members. It is evident from the foregoing that socio-economic development is the handmaiden of nation-building.

Commitment to fairness in the distribution of national development

Ghana's pursuit of sound economic development, likely to be boosted by the exploitation of crude oil from the South from the year 2010, can be best anchored and sustained in a well-considered strategy of nation-building, which will ensure a just and equitable distribution of development projects. A country with a lopsided social and economic development structure based on geography and ethnicity is not building a nation but commotion. To this end, Government in 1993 established the University for Development Studies as the first tertiary institution in the North, which has a catchment area of approximately 41% of Ghana's land mass. This was part of broad efforts by the State to bridge the yawning educational and developmental gap between the South and the North. This was partly founded on the recognition that literacy is empowering, and illiteracy and ignorance are often perceived, rather sadly, as a ticket to ill-treatment. The University was also to open up the North to vibrant intellectual activity and increased engagement with civil society. Similarly, in 2009, Government established the Northern Sector Development Authority (NSDA)—a special statutory agency devoted exclusively to overseeing the development of the Northern parts of Ghana. Although Government has pledged to provide significant seed money, the NSDA has the power to mobilize resources to finance approved development projects.

Development and promotion of a national peace architecture

Between 2005 and 2007, Ghana developed and tested a comprehensive Peace Architecture, with the support of the United Nations Development Fund, which contributed immensely to the management of ethnic and political conflicts in the country.[4] The key elements of the peace architecture included specific roles for the following statutory bodies, including the National Peace Council which was deliberately created, to (a) serve as an early warning system, (b) ensure continuous monitoring of conflict situations and "conflict spots", (c) intervene in conflict situations and pursue such measures as are reasonably necessary to arrest and redress the situation, (d) make appropriate recommendations for action by Parliament, the Executive and other statutory agencies such as the Ghana Police Service, and social dialogue bodies such as the Council of State, CHRAJ, NCCE and the National Media Commission; and (e) make recommendations to enhance democratization in a particular institution, community, district or region as may be appropriate.

The social dialogue and deliberative bodies that have played important roles in preventing and managing ethnic conflicts and building peace in Ghana include:

a. Affirmative action policies of the Nkrumah Government, establishment of boarding schools, fair and equitable distribution of scholarship across the country, and multi-ethnic appointments

b. Broad civic education on citizenship, rights, obligations and national cohesion by constitutional and social dialogue bodies such as the:

- Erstwhile Centre for Civic Education of the late 1960s;
- National Charter Secretariat of the 1970s; and
- National Commission for Civic Education – the constitutional body charged with the promotion of civic awareness about duties and responsibilities of the citizenry;
- National Commission on Culture;
- The Council of State;
- National House of Chiefs
- National Council of Religious Bodies
- National Peace Council
- Committee of Eminent Chiefs
- National Media Commission;

d. The role of Parliament and Municipal and District Assemblies in enacting legislation and by-laws that promote nation building

e. The role of the Commission on Human Rights and Administrative Justice (CHRAJ), pursuant to Article 218(b) of the Constitution, in investigating complaints *concerning the functioning of the Public Services Commission, the administrative organs of the State, the Armed Forces, the*

Police Service and the Prisons Service in so far as complaints relate to the failure to achieve a balanced structuring of those services or equal access by all to the recruitment of those services or fair administration in relation to those services." The typical focus of concern in such complaints and investigations are ethnicity, gender and regionalism

f. The role of the National Reconciliation Commission in excavating Ghana's history of human rights violations, administrative measures and other acts and omissions that fractured the nation or otherwise undermined national cohesion

g. The role of the Judiciary in the progressive interpretation of laws during adjudication in order to advance socio-economic development, national cohesion and unity

h. The role of political parties in serving as national platforms for the articulation of common ideologies, visions and aspirations for the governance of the nation, and

i. The role of the National Identification Authority in establishing a credible national identification system to accelerate socio-economic development and promote a symbolic sense of belonging through the use of the national identity card.

Use of traditional social mediators

The chieftaincy institution is an integral part of traditional and contemporary systems of governance in much of Africa. In *The Position of the Chief in the Modern Political System of Ashanti*, Prof. K.A. Busia demonstrated the centrality of the role of the chief in resolving a large variety of conflicts, both intra- and inter-ethnic. In Ghana as elsewhere, chiefs continue to be veritable instruments for conflict resolution and peace-building, even if some of them, through their insincerity, incompetence and unbridled wealth acquisition, are the engineers of the perennial chieftaincy and land disputes. But the role of the Committee of Eminent Chiefs led by the Asantehene Otumfou Osei Tutu II in exploring solutions to the long-standing Yendi Chieftaincy Affairs has been most lauded, although the inability of the State to effectively resolve the criminal justice dimensions of the dispute has thrown a heavy damper on the Committee's otherwise glorious efforts[5].

There is also cross-cultural diplomacy by traditional rulers/authorities. Sincere cultural exchanges and courtesies between rival traditional leaders, such as the Asantehene in the Ashanti Region and the Agobgbomefia of the

Asogli State in the Volta Region of Ghana, were instrumental in neutralizing and abetting ethnic tensions between their peoples in 2004. Our chiefs must institute internal diplomatic cultural exchanges. We will register significant breakthroughs for peace and inter-ethnic respect if, for instance, paramount chiefs pay courtesy State visits to the "rival" chiefs, and learn over a week or several days, the ways of the other. Such domestic diplomatic missions by our traditional rulers would serve to bridge the gap between our different cultures and tone down the inter-tribal prejudices if they are seen by the populace to be sincere and gratifying. Let our traditional leaders take up the staff of new cultural leadership and forge genuine multiculturalism in Ghana, Kenya, Nigeria and Uganda, and the impact will transcend intercultural symbolism and contribute to the establishment of a society of genuine belonging. In entrenching a welcoming society of genuine belonging, we must emphasize the values of tolerance, toil and teamwork, as the famous African scholar, Professor Ali Mazrui, would put it.

Teaching conflict prevention and conflict resolution skills to youths

Teaching young people to eschew conflict (whether ethnic or political), to prevent conflict, to avoid being drawn into armed conflict, and to resolve conflicts when they arise, is one of the most important duties of Government and society. As former United Nations Secretary General Kofi Annan puts it, "There is no higher goal, no deeper commitment and no greater ambition than preventing armed conflict." This must simply be one of the core concerns of the State, through such agencies as the Ministries of Justice, Education, Youth and Sports; independent national human rights institutions; National Youth Council; civil society groups and competent individuals across Africa. Indeed, in the context of the Konkumba-Nanumba conflict, the personal intervention of Dr. Mohammed Ibn Chambas, now President of the Economic Community of West African States (ECOWAS) was crucial to ensuring sustained peace. [6] Dr. Chambas recognized that, beyond the usual ceasefire, peace-keeping and other official interventions by security agencies, enhanced youth awareness of the triggers of conflicts, the possession of critical skills in conflict prevention and alternative dispute resolution such as negotiation, mediation and conciliation, were critical to sustaining inter-ethnic peace and avoiding retrogression to armed conflict. Thus, in 2001, at his invitation, Dr. Chambas and I worked quietly with Konkomba and Nanumba youths, part in hotel conference rooms, part on a soccer field in the township of Bimbilla in Northern Region, and part in the traditional areas of two opposing communities. The goal was to enhance their youth leadership skills, equip them with appropriate tools for preventing and resolving conflicts, and to foster in them a sincere appreciation of the humanity of each other and the acceptance of their diversity as intrinsically and mutually beneficial.

Civil society has not been left out of the process of equipping youths to effectively engage in conflict prevention and conflict resolution. In March 2009, the Accra-based West Africa Civil Society Institute (WACSI), an agency of the Open Society Initiative for West Africa (OSIWA) founded by multi-millionaire George Sorros, organized a three-day training in conflict resolution, human rights, and post-conflict reconstruction for youths from all over the West African sub-region at the Kofi Annan International Peace-Keeping Training Centre.

Institutionalization of public educational programmes

Strategies for managing ethnic relations and promoting nation-building in Ghana have also included educational campaigns by constitutional and statutory national bodies such as the National Commission for Civic Education (NCCE) and the Commission on Human Rights and Administrative Justice (CHRAJ). For instance, the NCCE in 1998 staged several town hall meetings on identity, civic responsibilities and nation-building. Similarly, in August 2001, to help deal with the challenges of nation-building in the face of evidence of growing tribalism,[7] CHRAJ organized a national consultation on combating tribalism and promoting nation-building.[8] The program line-up included the following topics and issues:

a. Preventing racism/tribalism, xenophobia and related intolerance through the promotion and enforcement of human rights principles and norms;

b. Overview of ethnic and racial conflicts in Ghana: causes, origins and factors contributing to inter-group violence;

c. Voices of victims;

d. Dealing with racism/tribalism
   i.   Multiculturalism: the strength of the nation;
   ii. Embracing diversity in the school and workplace;
   iii. Cultural competency and skills for cross-cultural communication;
   iv. Characteristics and skills of effective interculturalists.

e. Prevention of ethnic and racial conflicts through the creation of mediation, conciliation and social dialogue bodies;

f. Social inequality: trends, pattern and impact on national unity and development;

g. Strategies for promoting national integration and ethnic harmony – the role of civil society:
   i.   Traditional authorities;
   ii. Youth associations;
   iii. The media.

h. Realization of economic, social and cultural rights and the right to development as a strategy for preventing ethnic and racial conflicts;

i. Correcting persistent patterns of inequality affecting ethnic groups;

j. Enhancing ethno-cultural and religious harmony through good governance, lawfulness and social equity;

k. Strategies for combating racism/tribalism and related intolerance at the workplace and the school—the role of:
   i.   Employers;
   ii. National association of teachers;
   iii. National union of Ghana students;
   iv. Trades union congress.

l. Basic skills in mediating inter-group conflicts;

m. Voices of hope.

The CHRAJ fostered a sense of community ownership of the program through an expansive engagement of civil society actors in the planning process; it also drew resource persons from all sectors of Ghanaian society, and replicated the program across the ten administrative regions of the country. These events were given wide publicity through the print and broadcast media, particularly through radio and television, in English and many local languages across the country.

Establishment of Truth, Justice and Reconciliation Commissions

In Ghana, one recent method of national re-tooling for nation-building was the institution of a national reconciliation process that sought to excavate the truth about gross human rights violations and abuses of the past, offer opportunities for healing, apology, reparation, forgiveness and reconciliation. The object was fairness and inclusivity.

Several countries that have undergone cataclysmic political change have found resort to transitional justice mechanisms as important ways of freeing up the bottled energies of the people occasioned by the pains of conflict in order to create a space for them to contribute meaningfully to the development of their countries, and to focus on nation-building. Such other post-conflict societies as South Africa, Nigeria, Morocco, Sierra Leone and Liberia have experimented, with different degrees of success, with truth and reconciliation commissions (TRCs) as mechanisms for healing and nation-building. Cote d'Ivoire, Togo, Kenya and Zimbabwe are at different stages of establishing transitional justice mechanisms.

Creating an educational system that produces nationalists

In promoting nation building and national integration, it is imperative that Ghana consciously implements an educational system that produces supra-ethnic nationalists who are well-informed, cosmopolitan, tolerant, understanding and accepting of diversity.

Adopting a policy of multiculturalism

Multiculturalism emphasizes the value of, and contributions to the development of the state by, each cultural group being a constituent part of the state. It is a policy that encourages the recognition and celebration of the principle of unity in diversity. It is a policy that partly underpins the relative peace of such countries as Canada and Switzerland. Encouraging individuals and groups to learn the language and culture of persons who are culturally or linguistically different from themselves could help advance the purposes of national integration and cohesion. It is desirable and fulfilling to celebrate ethnic diversity not as calamity but as opportunity.

Moreover, deliberately planned and well supervised excursions of students and youth groups to schools and communities different from their own could also contribute to fostering inter-group harmony, trust, respect and cooperation. In many places, student and youth group excursions already exist, and these must be purposely expanded to cover more young persons in order to broaden the scope of coverage and the scale of beneficiaries.

Abolishing the first-past-the-post system of governance

The popular practice of winner-takes-all on which the electoral systems of much Africa is based in inimical to national integration and nation-building. It provides an excuse and justification for bloc ethnic voting that invariably allows ethnic groups that are in the numerical majority to not only win elections but also to sweep and grab all public and political offices in a manner akin to sharing the spoils of war after raping and plundering the countryside. It is politics of exclusion and marginalization, and it is a politics that is inherently against the grain of constitutionalism and good governance, even if it is legal by virtue of being the law of the land. In place of this legalized rape and plunder and marginalization, which in Africa means the exclusion and marginalization of a large number of ethnic minority groups, must be replaced with the system of voting known as proportional representation (cf. Chege, volume).

Expediting decentralization

It is imperative that the process of decentralization of government be accelerated, with appropriate devolution of power, and the provisions of adequate financial resources and responsibility.

Future directions in nation-building

Our country will make significant advances in nation-building if we tailor our development strategies closely to the DPSP contained in Chapter Six of the Ghanaian Constitution. As outlined in the DPSP, the key principles that must be earnestly promoted in order to achieve effective nation-building are:

(1) Pursuit of a viable socio-economic development agenda;

(2) The cultivation of a vibrant and competent crop of leaders imbued with focus, high ethics and liberal, republican democratic values;

(3) Fair and equitable distribution of the benefits of development;

(4) Promotion of inclusivity, acceptance and shared sense of belonging;

(5) Prevention of discrimination based on the prohibited grounds enumerated in Article 17(2) of the constitution and elsewhere;

(6) Ensuring responsible media reportage of potentially divisive ethnic remarks; and

(7) Promotion of fundamental human rights, social justice and the rule of law.

To succeed with nation-building efforts generally, there must be a firm commitment on the part of Government and civil society to social justice—a view that everyone is entitled to fair treatment, equitable access to the opportunities and resources of the State, and to prosperity. It is also a view that those who are disadvantaged by circumstances and the accidents of birth must be helped along the ladder of personal growth and development. It is a view that the nation is better built and made even stronger when no one is left behind; when, in the language of the times, "we *all* move forward in the right direction."

Conclusion

Nation-building is not an event but a process; it is not a revolution, but it is no fancy needle-work either. Nearly twenty years after the fall of the Berlin Wall, German unification is still a struggle, although from the outside, it seems like a seamless process of integration and socio-political harmony. Failed families and suicides, increased vulnerabilities and crime, and a sense of anomie and purposelessness were among the initial burdens that many former nationals of East Germany shouldered in the early phase of the unification. South Africa continues to experience the pangs of racial unification and the promotion of multiculturalism. In Ghana, the task of promoting ethnic tolerance and political harmony continues to be as difficult today as it was in the 1960s.

The answers, as I have emphasized, lie in continued democratization, the promotion of good governance, human rights, multiculturalism, cultural diplomacy, sound economic management and social justice.

Notes

[1] See Adu Boahen, Albert, *The Ghanaian Sphinx: Reflections on the Contemporary History of Ghana*. Sankofa Educational Publishers, 2002.

[2] See Kenneth Little, *Urbanization as a Social Process*. London: Routledge, 2004.

[3] Fifteen years later, the Government is now hell-bent on tearing down the slum which has always served not only as a haven for criminals but also as a brewery for odious forms including ethnic rivalry, gun and machete battles between the two dominant ethnic and political groups in the slum.

[4] Dr. Ozonnia Ojiello, Senior Governance and Rule of Law Advisor to the UNDP Representative in Kenya, was the brain behind the development of the Ghana Peace Architecture which has now become a model for the UN in assisting other similarly-situated countries.

⁵ The Committee of Eminent Chiefs was appointed by President Kufour in March 2001 following the killing of Ya Na Yakubu Andani, King of Dagbon, and 28 others in feuding between members of two opposing royal gates in Yendi, capital of the Dagbon Traditional Area in the Northern Region of Ghana. Although a Commission of Inquiry, chaired by a Justice Wuaku, a retired Supreme Court judge, investigated the matter over several months, the day-light killers of the overlord, who was beheaded, have not been found and apprehended.

⁶ Indeed, the announcement of Dr. Chambas appointment and elevation to the post of Executive Secretary of ECOWAS came on the eve of our arrival in Bimbilla to train Konkomba and Nanumba youth in leadership and conflict resolution skills. One of the most unifying moments I have ever seen was the presence of a large retinue of elders from the two opposing communities who trooped to the home of Dr. Chambas in the small hours of December 31, 2002 to prostrate themselves before him in worship of "their son" for that great elevation. It was truly humbling!

⁷ As measured by the growing number of ethnic discrimination complaints filed with the CHRAJ.

⁸ The two-day meeting also formed part of Ghana's preparation toward the World Conference on Racism, Xenophobia and Related Intolerance which took place in Durban, South Africa, in September 2001.

Ethnic Diversity in East Africa: The Tanzanian Case and the Role of Kiswahili Language as a Unifying Factor

Huruma Luhuvilo Sigalla

Introduction

Ethnic distinction can be based on language, geography or kinship. It is a form of identity. This chapter attempts to discuss some social factors useful in the process of building national identity, peace and political stability. It explores the development of Kiswahili from a historical and anthropological point of view including how the language has been developed in Tanzania. The chapter will focus on some factors such as trade, political decisions and policies as well as cultural factors especially joking relationships, religious beliefs and practices, the educational system and the national services which among others have contributed to the development of Kiswahili as a national language and one of the unifying factors in Tanzania. Although there are other factors which facilitated the process of nation building, peace and stability in Tanzania, the focus of this chapter will be on the contribution of Kiswahili to this process. In addition, it will discuss the development of Kiswahili in East Africa, and its possibilities as a lingua franca in Eastern Africa. Towards the end, the chapter addresses some challenges Tanzania is facing with Kiswahili as a national language.

Internal and historical factors

Tanzania is a diversified country with over one hundred ethnic groups and different religions. Whereas some ethnic groups are big in size others are small. There is also differentiation in political, military and social organization; for instance between the Nyamwezi, Sukuma, Hehe and Chaga. Although, the Nyamwezi under Mirambo were strong politically and militarily, they did not seek to conquer others and control them. Some scholars for instance, Svendsen and Teisen[1], have pointed out that Tanzania's ethnic groups "were loosely organized with many leaders; thus, tribalism failed to become a significant political factor". Therefore, from sociological and anthropological points of view this organizational structure can be described as a decentralized type of political and governance system. The pre-colonial tribal relationships and interactions were built in peace rather than conflict. The pre-colonial communities, despite their ethnic diversity, lived in harmonious relationships due to various socio-cultural factors. But, the word "harmonious" does not mean there were no conflicts or/and eruptions of wars. Although, there is a limited body of literature on the factors which held different ethnic groups together before colonialism in Tanzania, some socio-economic and cultural factors such as social organization, the size and number of ethnic groups, their spiritual life and practices *(matambiko)* and trade may have contributed in building cohesive relationships.

Another factor is the joking relationships *(Utani/Mtani)*, a type of ideology which existed in Tanzania between various ethnic groups and built friendships between them. *Utani* created a strong sense of solidarity, neighborhood and later on shared identity between groups. There were several factors which created this type of relationship. The most common factor was neighborhood, especially, among tribes which shared boundaries[2]. The second factor was conflict. For instance, the Ngoni created joking friendships with other tribes in southern parts after being in conflict (wars) with them. Some tribes formed alliances as *watani* such as Matumbi and Ndengereko in order to protect themselves against enemies. Others developed *utani* between them based on the belief that they are related by blood in the sense that they share ancestors. Ethnic groups around Lake Victoria such as Haya, Kuria, Zanaki, Luo among others became *watani* through trade and fishing. It was necessary for them to have good relationships in order to successfully and peacefully carry out their activities. Conflict between them would have excluded some of them from using and extracting resources from the lake, and consequently undermine their social development. Therefore, hostile and conflictual relationships could have caused more harm, destruction and causalities in their undertakings than peace and harmonious relationships. Fishing was smooth mainly because of the *utani* between them. This social relationship and ideology of *utani* laid a foundation for peace, and gradually facilitated a process which undermined the tribal feelings and identity and created the thrust for good neighborhood, and national identity and solidarity. Nyamwezi for instance, established joking relationships with a number of tribes from Tabora to the Coast, in the process of trade. They created and maintained *utani* relationship with some tribes along the trade routes. Gradually, such relations together with other factors laid a foundation for future national unity.

It is also important to consider *Undugu* as a form of social organization particularly communal life based on equality in contrast to feudalism *(umwinyi)*. The former promoted neighborhood, interdependence and harmonious life while the latter encouraged competition, formation of classes and inequalities. In addition, traditional spiritual life and practices (*matambiko*) were similar and common among different tribes in Tanzania. In some cases, for instance, within the southern part of Tanzania, some tribes had commonalities in their spiritual and religious practices to the extent that a person could go and practice his spiritual life together with other tribes. Similar religious ceremonies have been common among the southern tribes such as Zaramo, Matumbi, Makonde, Makua, Bena and others. In southern Tanzania, almost all tribes paid tribute to *Kolelo*[3]. This shared beliefs and ceremonies reduced the gap between ethnic groups.

Kiswahili as an identity and unifying factor in Tanzania

Samuel Huntington (1996: 59-67) suggests that "the central elements of any culture and civilization are language and religion…people define their identity by what they are not".

One of the factors which facilitated the cohesion of ethnic groups in Tanzania, and later a national identity, is Kiswahili. Many scholars such as Whiteley (1969) and Ohly (1978) have traced the origin of Kiswahili language from the coast. They have associated it with Arabic and Bantu languages. However, it is worthwhile to emphasize that Kiswahili evolved out of Bantu languages, and that it is an African indigenous language. It developed like any other language in the world, and was used by different people from different racial and national backgrounds; borrowing some words from other languages especially Arabic and Portuguese. Before colonialism, Kiswahili evolved and developed as a medium of communication between traders of different races and ethnic groups especially Arabs, Africans and Europeans.

Let us consider for a moment the early caravan routes from the coast to the mainland. The major trade routes started from coastal areas such as Bagamoyo, Saadani, Mboamaji, and Kilwa through Ugogo to Tabora or south-westwards to Uhehe and the areas between Lake Nyasa and Tanganyika. From Tabora, caravans went to north-west to Karagwe and Uganda or north to Lake Victoria close to Mwanza. In his discussion about Kiswahili and its function in East Africa in general, and Tanzania in particular, Steere (1870)[4] suggests that:

> There is probably no African language so widely known as Swahili. It is understood along the coasts of Madagascar and Arabia, it is spoken by the Seedees in India, and is the trade language of a very large part of

central or inter-tropical Africa. Zanzibar traders penetrate sometimes even to the western side of the continent, and they are in the constant habit of traversing more than half of it with their suppliers of Indian and European goods.

In the some context, Omari (1995) points out that Kiswahili has played an important role in making Tanzania a nation. It has also been claimed that Germans were the best promoters of Kiswahili. [5]

Colonial administration and promotion of Kiswahili

From the turn of the century, and increasingly with time, the educational and administrative implications of colonial policies determined the choice to speak Swahili. Though educational policies in Uganda, Kenya, and Tanganyika converged for a time in the 1920s, in general quite different policies were pursued in relation to Swahili, both in the British-administered areas and in the Belgian Congo, and quite separate treatment were accorded to them. (Whiteley, 1969:56)

It is worthwhile at this point to suggest that despite social and cultural factors which have contributed to the process of national unity and identity in Tanzania there also have been political factors worth serious consideration. The vision and policies of national leaders have been influential in strengthening unity and building stability and peace. Specifically, policies were developed to promote Kiswahili and this had the effect of weakening ethnic identity, at least politically on the one hand, and strengthening national unity and identity, on the other. From the economic point of view, Tanganyika under German administration was not aimed at establishing a strong and sustainable economy, it was rather meant to produce raw materials for metropolitan industries. "Such colonial economic policies did not create a stable and vibrant economic structure which would have caused prosperity of some ethnic groups than others which later on could have caused competition to access or/and control such economic fortunes as it has been the case in other African countries"[6]. Unlike Kenya, Tanzania did not have a large settler community and urbanization was slow.

Politically, colonial policies promoted Kiswahili in different ways. For instance, it is argued that Tanganyika had more Swahili newspapers which were produced in the countryside (regions) than those in Dar es Salaam.

Kenya has always had few Kiswahili newspapers and magazines. Whiteley (1969:67) for instance, suggests that:

> ... in short, if Swahili was the language of the country in Tanganyika, in Kenya, it was the language of towns, especially Nairobi, where people from all parts of the country found it as convenient bulwark against the loneliness of a city life as well as a reality tool to exploit attractions which the city offered

German administration promoted Kiswahili in various ways. At the educational level, schools were established to train Africans to work as junior officials in the administration. Kiswahili was to be the language of the administration and great efforts were made to promote and document it. For example, governor Rechenberg (1906-12) spoke the language and his successor, H. Schnee, had attended courses on it in Berlin. Not only administrators but also settlers and missionaries became competent in the language (Whiteley, 1969). By 1911, missions were responsible for primary education. Because a school population required textbooks, these were produced in increasing numbers. In this context, the British missionaries of the U.M.C.A. played an important role. The Mission at Magila produced the classic *Habari za Wakilindi*, the first newspaper, *Msimulizi* by 1888 and *Habari za Mwezi* around 1894. In the year 1910, German missionaries produced the German Protestant Mission's monthly *Pwani na Bara* whose circulation rose to 2,000 by 1914. This was followed by the Catholics with *Rafiki Yangu* in the same year with more religious content. By 1914, Kiswahili was developed and expanded to the extent that the German administration was able to conduct much of its correspondence with local people and authorities in Kiswahili. The language was supported by the administration to a level that letters which were not written in Kiswahili or German were likely to be ignored. This also meant that the Junior officials especially Africans were not restricted to a regional setting due to language difficulties. They could be transferred without difficulty from one part of the country to another and be assured of finding people who were fluent in Kiswahili, particularly around the households. In the same context, this undermined ethnic loyalty and promoted the feeling of belonging to a unit which is more than the ethnic group. Thus, it also facilitated the cohesion of different communities.

Explaining this development, for instance, Whiteley (1969:61) suggests that:

Over the whole colonial period Swahili was used throughout the District Administration as a means of communication between people and officialdom, not only where this was the only possible means of communication but also, in some cases, where English could have been used. It was thus a mark, if only secondarily, of social distance; a means of reaching down to people, rather than of enabling them to reach up to the administration. Whereas in German times the acquisition of Swahili represented a first stage towards participating in Government through membership of the junior Civil Service, no further stage in this participation could be achieved through the language.

Sharing a similar point of view, Ohly (1978:12) suggests that Germans introduced Kiswahili as the only official administrative language. He asserts:

> In fact, the Germans were unable to control the whole Tanganyika territory to-be, therefore Swahili fulfilled rather the function of a regional official language. The British standardized Swahili and enlarged its vocabulary with modern terms. Like other domains of social life, Swahili was underdeveloped in respect to its vocabulary, because of the intention that within the educational system English would increasingly displace Swahili. At this time, however, Swahili satisfied the needs of social control, being used, beside English, as the official language of the legislative council.

By the mid-fifties it was widely and more vigorously applied than before. For example, there were as many as forty newspapers in regular circulation. Most of the newspapers were run by the government and some were produced by missions, and one or two, like *Zuhra* in Dar es Salaam were independently run.

With regard to Government newspapers, we should distinguish between the 'regional' and the 'national' press. The regional papers, which were more than twenty, usually appeared monthly, and were concerned almost exclusively with local, i.e. district, news. Whitelely (1969:62-64) provides some examples of the regional newspapers as follows: *Kulichi* based in Sumbawanga was distributed monthly and had four pages, *Mara Gazeti* based in Tarime, was also distributed monthly and had four pages, *Irgobawe* which was from Mbulu, was also a monthly paper and had six pages. The national papers included the famous *Mambo Leo* which appeared monthly since 1923 and *Mwangaza* which by 1957 was already a daily. These newspapers performed a number of valuable services; they did not only support the establishment of Swahili as a means of national communication but also introduced

Tanganyikans to the problems involved in running such papers and provided adults with much needed reading material. In addition to the newspapers, some government departments such as agriculture too were at this time producing a considerable volume of Swahili materials. Furthermore, some endeavors were taken to start translating some legal terms and the compilation of technical word-lists. These were essential preliminaries if Kiswahili was to assume the status of a modern African language. In the same vein, the Tanganyika Broadcasting Service (TBS) reached a wider audience with its Kiswahili programmes. Finally, the important step under colonial administration was taken in 1955 when Kiswahili was officially introduced in the Legislative Council and members were permitted to speak in it.

The process of building the nation after independence in Tanzania

Prior to and during the colonial era, Kiswahili had an important role to play as a means of communication particularly for trade and administration. Building an identity was not a priority at the time, although it did contribute to the process. The need to develop Kiswahili as a national language was more apparent after independence probably for political and cultural reasons. After independence, Kiswahili was made the language of political power and nationhood. Tanzania, in contrast to its neighbors, adopted the language as the national language. The first revolutionary change was the transformation of different Kiswahili dialects and local (ethnic) languages into languages of statehood. The second revolutionary change was the transformation of Kiswahili into a supra-ethnic language during and after colonialism. The third revolutionary change occurred at a time when Kiswahili took over the function of a national language, integrating most Tanzanians linguistically. The country managed to overcome its ethnic heterogeneity with the help among other factors of an Africa language (Ohly, 1978). Ohly (ibid) further points out that this development was facilitated by a peculiar Tanzanian language policy which entails a socio-linguistic phenomenon on world-wide scale; creating a promising model for other heterogeneous countries. Other scholars such as Whiteley (1969) have suggested that when Tanzania African National Union (TANU) was founded in 1954 it deliberately used and maintained the long-established language policy. In connection with this, for instance, Whiteley (1969:65) further points out that:

> "the value of Swahili to TANU was quickly demonstrated, and President Nyerere once boasted that during his many tours of the country he had had recourse to interpreters only on two occasions. Not merely were they Swahili-speaking but they also served as an excellent example when

the party wished to organize its own country-wide branches. It might be true that President Nyerere's status as a leader was enhanced by his ability to negotiate for independence in English, on terms of linguistic equality, but in this role the fact that he represented so large a proportion of the people of Tanganyika was due in large measure to the efficacy of Swahili as a means of communication on a national scale.

The ability to operate in Kiswahili became a source of national pride, even though it did not mean that one operated in it more efficiently than previously. It must be emphasized that the great strength of the language in the pre-independence period was the fact that it was associated with no single ethnic group; it was neutral and integrative. The national culture of Tanzania is, in a sense, the sum of its regional cultures expressed in more than one hundred and twenty local languages and tied to the local customs and situations. After this historical background, it is worthwhile at this point to discuss how Kiswahili was institutionalized to give it status as a national language. The following part will focus on the way in which Kiswahili was institutionalized politically.

Institutional development

After independence two ministries namely, Education and Community Development and National Culture, were closely involved in the development of the language. On the one hand, the Ministry of Education was responsible for teaching Kiswahili at all levels of the educational system. Some sub-committees were established as well in order to study and revise the secondary school syllabus as well as to find ways of extending the teaching of the language up to University level. Politically, it was also promoted by politicians and policy makers. For instance, Whiteley (1969:105) suggests that "late in 1964, the second Vice-President sent a circular to civil servants and others urging them to desist from the habit of mixing Swahili and English...Civil Servants were urged to remedy the weakness" of being unable to express themselves elegantly in the national language. Several institutions and departments were established during 1960s and 1970s to promote and support Kiswahili at the national level. Among others, the following institutions had played a vital role in the development of Kiswahili as a national language which also supported nation building. Whiteley (1969:110-113) mentions and summarizes some of these institutions.

The Association for the Advancement of Swahili (*Jumuiya ya Kustawisha Kiswahili*) was founded in 1963. Its main objectives were:

(a) To discover the origin of Swahili words, in the belief that understanding the origin of something is to understand its quality, and indeed is the basis for loving and respecting it;

(b) To cherish Swahili, by correcting the misleading use of words;

(c) To co-operate with similar-minded bodies;

(d) To promulgate preferred usage;

(e) To correct existing grammatical descriptions;

(f) To translate and write books.

In addition, Society for the Enhancement of the Swahili Language and Verse (*Chama cha Usanifu wa Kiswahili and Ushairi*) founded under the leadership of the leading poet, M.E. Mnyampala had the following objectives:

(a) To preserve the language, encourage its poetry and also purity of form and style: to develop the language in Bantu terms and encourage poetry as a special study which contributes to acknowledging Swahili for national benefits;

(b) To awaken and stimulate people who wish to be experts in the language and poetry;

(c) To awaken the efforts of those who wish to write books on various subjects in Swahili, and in verse, and to find ways of publishing their work;

(d) To set about compiling a dictionary and grammar more adequate than the present ones;

(e) To encourage dramatic performances, and other cultural features.

In August 1967, a National Swahili Council (*Baraza la Kiswahili la Taifa*) was set up. Its functions included:

(a) To promote the development and usage of the Swahili language throughout the United Republic of Tanzania;

(b) To co-operate with other bodies in the United Republic which are concerned to promote the Swahili language and to endeavors to co-ordinate their activities;

(c) To encourage the use of the Swahili language in the conduct of official business and public life generally;

(d) To encourage the achievement of high standards in the use of the Swahili language and to discourage its misuse;

(e) To co-operate with the authorities concerned in establishing standard Swahili translations of technical terms;

(f) To publish a Swahili newspaper concerned with the Swahili language and literature;

(g) To provide services to the Government, public authorities, and individual authors writing with respect to the Swahili language.

Moreover, other scholars, for instance, Mulokozi (2003:68) have pointed out some governmental structures which were deliberately established to facilitate the development of Kiswahili and implementation of new policies on language. These included:

(a) Creation of the Ministry of Culture, 1962
(b) Creation of the Institute of Kiswahili Research (TUKI) , 1964
(c) Creation of Tanzania Publishing House, 1966
(d) Creation of the national Kiswahili Council (BAKITA), 1967
(e) Creation of Department of Kiswahili at University of
    Dar es Salaam, 1976
(f) Establishment of EACROTANAL, 1976
(g) Establishing of Institute of Kiswahili and Foreign Languages Zanzibar (TAKILUKI), 1978
(h) Establishment of the Zanzibar Kiswahili Council (BAKIZA), 1986
(i) Creation of Mfuko Wa Utamaduni Tanzania (Tanzania Culture Fund), 1998

These institutions, as their objectives indicate, were aimed at providing technical support to the governments and individuals who promoted and supported an endeavor to spread Kiswahili as a national language throughout the country.

Another political initiative which contributed to the process of "nation building" was the education system, especially the secondary and post secondary education system. Secondary schools were institutions which brought young Tanzanians from different parts with different cultural and religious backgrounds together. As it was the case, partly due to the scarcity of schools, students were selected to join secondary schools, and were located in different parts within the country, in most cases, far from home. For example, students from southern parts attended secondary education in Mirambo (Tabora), Ilboru (Arusha) Pugu (Dar es Salaam), Zanaki (Dar es Salaam), Old Moshi (Moshi), Tanga Schools (Tanga) etc. Likewise people from Northern, Western, Eastern and central parts of Tanzania went to southern parts of the country such as Rungwe (Mbeya), Malangali (Iringa), Tosomaganga (Iringa), Songea Boys and Songea Girls (Songea), Mazengo (Dodoma) and so forth. This further weakened tribal, ethnic and regional feelings on the one hand, and strengthened the feelings that they were all Tanzanians. In the long run this process paved the way toward intermarriages between couples from different ethnic groups and religious backgrounds.

There was also, within the education system, the establishment of National Service. It provided a venue for a young educated generation in Tanzania to learn more about their country and serve it. All students regardless of sex, religion, and race were supposed to serve in the national service. Initially, they served for two years; then later, the period was reduced for one year soon after completion of their high school. Again, they were distributed all over the country in most cases, away from where somebody did his/her secondary education. This also exposed young educated Tanzanians to different environments and cultures. It in turn, merged individuals from different ethnic and religious backgrounds together, and with the help of a well established and widely used language (Kiswahili), nation building with strong beliefs of being Tanzanian was further cemented. The education system and national service in my view had "latent and manifest functions" as far as ethnic identity and nation building are concerned in Tanzania. On the one hand, one of the objectives of these institutions was to provide education and knowledge to young Tanzanians. National service, among other things, aimed at preparing the young generation to be good civil servants who will serve their nation with commitment and integrity. On the other hand, it brought many educated young Tanzanians together. They could easily communicate using one language and it further facilitated intermarriages between people from different ethnic and religious backgrounds. This is a very important factor in consolidating national unity. Intermarriage paved a way to a generation to whom Kiswahili was a first language or /and a mother tongue.

Ujamaa philosophy and villagization policy

Apart from all the factors discussed above, an endeavour to build a nation based on justice and equality played a vital role to building social cohesion and stability in Tanzania. Nyerere had a vision to build a nation based on the African tradition of living together as an extended family. According to him, as Komba (1995:36) suggests, the *ujamaa* setting was supposed to be governed by three fundamental principles; namely "living together, working together, and sharing equitably the fruits of their work as well as the means of production. Their culture encouraged them to think of themselves primarily as members of a large group, a community, and thus the needs of each as an individual tended to be superseded by his needs as a member of society".

Last but not least, it is worthwhile to argue that, despite all the factors that Tanzania seems to have had, which might have created a conducive social-economic and political environment to transform Kiswahili to a national language, one point must be emphasized, that the political vision, commitment and pragmatic measures and policies adopted by the government, especially after independence played a vital and unique role in building a stable and unified nation. In the same vein, I wish to argue that the role played by Mwalimu Julius K. Nyerere was remarkable and he is the real founder of this unity and stability in Tanzania. His reputation as the Father of the Nation (*Baba wa Taifa*) signifies a peculiar psychosocial and political feeling and meaning that Tanzanians associate with him. As Mazrui (2008:41-47) suggests "The late Julius Nyerere, for example, has bequeathed young Tanzanians a greater self-confidence and national pride…" than most other leaders have done.

Kiswahili as a language of Eastern Africa

Today, Africa finds itself subdivided into three major linguistic blocks; namely; Francophone (the French Speaking countries); Anglophone (the English speaking countries); Lusophone (the Portuguese speaking countries) and Arabophone (the Arabic speaking countries).

This subdivision shows how Africa is still dependent on foreign cultures. Mulokozi (2003) argues that the opponents of Swahili language as medium of instruction in Tanzania is based on the argument that "English is a doorway to science and technology, it is an international language and thus we need to learn it in order to be able to communicate with other people." These arguments according to Mulokozi are "technical and international". On the other hand, proponents of Kiswahili as a medium of instruction emphasize that language has "a pedagogical aspect; that children learn better in a language that they know best". Ryanga (2002:2) suggests that "Africa would do well to take, and go for linguistic emancipation instead of continued linguistic dependency, by adopting an existing indigenous language." One of the problems with the use of "borrowed languages" is the fact that we are not competent with them and the languages exclude the majority of citizens in the process of discussing and participating in decision making on vital issues which affect their lives because these languages (English, French,

Portuguese) are languages of the elite, who are the minority. Ryanga (ibid) further argues that "we need to accept the realization that the formation of economic regional bodies and political affiliation alone have failed to unite the African thought." Language may be the missing link in continental unity. Kiswahili is the only African language which has proved that it has a potential and unifying power. The commitment and vision to transform it to a national language has been successful in Tanzania. Africa in general and East Africa in particular needs such an indigenous language. Several scholars have acknowledged that Kiswahili is a potential language to develop internationally particularly in East Africa.

In contrast to other indigenous African languages such as Hausa, Arabic, Luganda, Chiluba and Lingala, Kiswahili is seen as neutral and harmless. It has neither ethnic nor political connotations; and is an easy language to learn. Ryanga (ibid) suggests that Kiswahili is a language which is easier to further develop from where it is currently in order to give it a "wide stature than most of other indigenous languages in east and central Africa". Similarly, Mulokozi (2003) points out that the growth and spread of Kiswahili as a national language in Tanzania was supported by economic and social factors, and these factors still exist at the East African level. Thus, it is worthwhile to expect and suggest that it will also develop and expand as an international language, starting with the East African sub-region. Decision makers of these countries have a vital role to play in the development of Kiswahili.

The viability of Kiswahili in East Africa

Kiswahili is one of the three African indigenous sub-continental languages. Other two languages are Hausa and Arabic. However, Kiswahili has been gaining more acceptance and sympathy than Hausa and Arabic throughout Africa and abroad. It is the African lingua franca" (Bull, 2003:234) and it is estimated that over 110 million people speak it (Mulokozi, ibid: 73; Ryanga, ibid: 6). There are more than eleven countries in eastern and central Africa where Kiswahili is widely spoken and understood. This group of Kiswahili speaking countries include Burundi, Comoros, Congo, Kenya, Malawi, Mozambique, Rwanda, Tanzania, Uganda, Zambia and Zimbabwe (Mulokozi, 2003:73; Ryanga, 2002:6; Bull, 2005:234). This region may be appropriately called Swahiliphone Africa.

As far as East Africa is concerned, it is worthwhile to point out those political and economic endeavours in Africa such as Africa Union (AU) in general, and East Africa Community (EAC) in particular cannot be successful and effective in their purposes if they do not deal with cultural and language issues which could glue their unity. People's participation, in the sense that ordinary people take part on debate and decision making on important issues affecting their lives, can best be facilitated by a common language.

The current challenges

There are various challenges which Kiswahili has been facing as a national language in Tanzania. The first one is educational. There has been an attempt to suggest that Kiswahili should be further promoted and used as a medium of instruction at secondary and post-secondary levels. The challenge is that resources and expertise to translate the basic literature especially science subjects at this level, remains problematic. Another challenge is the fact that we are living in a world where technology and economy are globalizing. English remains the widely used language especially in commerce. Thus, opponents of the use of Kiswahili at these levels of education use this argument to discourage its development. There are more social factors as well, especially the current wave of commercial activities after the liberalization of social services since 1990s, where the education system was not bypassed.

The introduction of private schools from kindergarten, primary, secondary and tertiary level of education has caused the mushrooming of many private schools which use English as medium of instruction. In the same vein, there is a tendency among parents nowadays (led by the elite) to regard competence in English language as a necessary condition for the academic excellence of children. Unfortunately in my view, there is an increasing number of parents who speak English with their children and consequently, discouraging competence in Kiswahili. Mastery of Kiswahili is being devalued. A change in the importance attached to an ethnic identity may reflect a political change. For example with the introduction of neo-liberal policies and multiparty politics in Tanzania, ethnic feelings have been on the rise although they do not manifest themselves in discriminatory practices. Another issue relates to the social aspects of globalization. Socially, globalization has been associated with the spread of western culture and way of life, television and the internet. Since English is the dominant means of communication in popular culture from the West, it creates a challenge for the development of Kiswahili. Supporting popular culture in Kiswahili would be of immense benefit in the consolidation of nationhood and regional consciousness.

Conclusion

This chapter has attempted to discuss the socio-economic and political factors that have contributed to nation building and stability in Tanzania. It has focused on some cultural factors which can be traced to pre-colonial period, which facilitated the establishment of social cohesion, peace and stability between different ethnic groups and religions. It is argued that Kiswahili was able to evolve and develop to become a national language. Trade and colonial policies promoted the language across different ethnic groups. After independence, the government deliberately promoted and transformed it into a national language and several policies, measures and institutions were put in place to support its development. The chapter also argues that the late Mwalimu Julius Nyerere played a vital role in building a stable nation despite its ethnic and religious diversity. As far as East Africa is concerned, the current wave of globalization through trade liberalization, promotion of Foreign Direct Investment, economic integration of countries and sub-continents offers unprecedented opportunity for Kiswahili to develop, expand and penetrate all spheres of life.

While recognizing that a national language is not enough in creating cohesion and integration in multi-ethnic settings because issues related to governance, equity, quality of leadership and national values must be addressed, it does provide an important avenue for the entrenchment of local and national development. Investing in Kiswahili could have important political economic and social consequences for East Africa.

Notes

[1] Quoted from Omari, C.K. (1995) "The Management of Tribal and Religious Diversity".

[2] These information were derived from my personal conversation with Prof. Mugyabuso Mulokozi of the Institute of Kiswahili, University of Dar Es Salaam, 15th September 2009.

[3] A spiritual figure which united them.

[4] Steere (1870) A Handbook of Swahili Language as Spoken at Zanzibar. Quoted from Whiteley, W. (1969) *SWAHILI: The Rise of a National Language*, London: Methuen & Co. Ltd.

[5] Derived from author's personal conversation with Prof. Luanda of the Department of History, University of Dar es Salaam.

[6] Derived from my discussion with Prof. Mugyabuso Mulokozi, Institute of Kiswahili, University of Dar Es Salaam.

References

Bull, A.F. (2005). "Looking back thirty Years and Forward: The Story of the East African Swahili Committee". *Journal of the Institute of Kiswahili Research*, pp. 232-234.

Chacha, D.M. (2006). "Kiswahili and The African States: The Legacy of Mwalimu Julius Kambarage Nyerere". *Journal of the Institute of Kiswahili Research*, Vol. 69.

Huntington, P.S. (1996). *The Clash of Civilizations and the Remarking of the World Order*. Sydney: Simon and Schuster.

Komba, D. (1995). "Contribution to Rural Development: Ujamaa & Villagization". In Legum C. and Mmari, G., (Eds.) *Mwalimu: The Influence of Nyerere*. Dar es Salaam: Mkuki na Nyota.

Mazrui, A.A. (2008). "Conflict in Africa: An Overview". In Nhema, A & Tiyambe Zeleza, P., (Eds.) *The Roots of African Conflicts: The Causes and Costs*. Pretoria: UNISA Press.

Mpangala, P.G. (2000). *Ethnic Conflicts in the Region of the Great Lakes: Origins and Prospects for Change*. Dar Es Salaam: DUP.

Mulokozi, M.M (2003). "Kiswahili as a National and International Language". *Journal of the Institute of Kiswahili Research*, Vol. 66, pp. 68-80.

Ohly, R. (1978). *Language + Revolution= Kiswahili*. Dar es Salaam: DUP.

Omari. C.K. (1995). "The Management of Tribal and Religious Diversity". In Legum C. and Mmari, G., (Eds.) *Mwalimu: The Influence of Nyerere*. Dar es Salaam: Mkuki na Nyota.

Ryanga, S. (2002). "The African Union in the Wake of Globalization: The Forgotten Language Dimension". *Journal of the Institute of Kiswahili Research*, Vol. 65, pp. 1-15.

Whitelely, W. (1969). *Swahili: The Rise of a National Language*. London: Methuen & Co Ltd.

Critical Reflections on the Challenges and Prospects of Ethnic Diversity Management in Democratization

Eric Aseka

Introduction

An increasing number of countries are beginning to appreciate and value the richness and strength imparted by cultural and ethnic diversity. Nevertheless, idiosyncratic histories of African countries have shaped contemporary politics and inter-ethnic relations in these countries in a negative sense. For effective development policies to be formulated that meet accepted principles of diversity management, an understanding of the social and political contexts of inter-ethnic relations is crucial. The agenda of societal transformation should encapsulate an analysis of the role played by public policies in mitigating ethnic tensions and the promotion of the spirit of accommodation and pluralism in nation-states.

The need to perceive the nature of the intersection of consciousness and historical experience as the basis of identity construction cannot be gainsaid. We need to appreciate the fact that identity is a product of complex processes of historical interaction between people, institutions and their social practices in expressing selfhood (Aseka, 2007). These processes require defined midwifery roles of transformational leaders and not political charlatans whose social actions have no basis in good principles of socio-political management. To build a well-ordered society, principles must come before politics. As Strappado Wrack says, political charlatanism has no incentive to tell the truth and its discourses are all deceptions to get such leaders elected and to sustain their political survival. This, therefore, makes cheating the mark and fundamental function of political charlatans (Wrack, 2003).

It is this kind of leadership that has a knack of promoting the demagoguery of manipulation and instrumentalization of ethnicity. It may be noted that there has been a recent upsurge in ethnic conflict in a number of African countries where such unmediated charlatanism thrives. The paradox of ethnic identification is that ethnicity typically becomes most destructive when its subjects feel threatened in conditions of manipulation and politicization of ethnic identities. Therefore, in order to reduce ethnic tensions it is necessary to protect people's rights to form ethnic loyalties, and not to repress ethnic identification (see Chege, this volume). In a number of respects, this does not mean, however, that policies entrenching ethnicity in formal social and political structures should necessarily be put in place. Ethnicity naturally evolves, and in the process of good diversity management previously important ethnic markers become insignificant, and new bases for identification are created (UNRISD/UNDP, 1994).

Re-thinking, conceptualization and theory-building on alternative statehood ought to be done in order to understand the specific situations of particular polities and/or historical periods in relation to configurations of coterminality or discoterminality of cultural and political communities. As such, an understanding of the nature of ethnicity when negatively manipulated as well as of the origins and evolution of ethnic conflict is essential for an understanding of ways to address and prevent such conflicts in a proper framework of ethnic diversity management. Ethnicity, of course, is only one of the many ways in which people identify themselves among other specificities of family, community, nation, class, occupation, gender, age and other group characteristics. These social specificities form different layers of identity thereby generating their own peculiar mindsets, attitudes, social cleavages and antagonisms.

In a quest to construct a better foundational basis of alternative statehood which can effectively address idiosyncrasies of such mindsets, attitudes, social cleavages and antagonisms, it makes sense to state that there is need to equip governments, development agencies, grassroots organizations and scholars with better tools for diversity management. These entities need to develop a better understanding of how development policies and processes of economic, social and environmental change affect different social groups within their respective jurisdictions.

I do not agree with scholars who argue that ethnic diversity is an important impediment to economic and political development. Ethnic diversity becomes an impediment to socio-economic development only if it is mishandled. Ethnic diversity cannot be harnessed if it is not viewed positively as a useful element of a country's social capital (see Kamonye, this volume). We must begin to trace the cultural origins of social capital within ethnic cultural permutations of beliefs, values and social practices and begin to evaluate the political consequences of various forms of social capital emanating from these sources. Social capital is, at its core, a set of institutionalized expectations, purviews, tendencies and practices whose origins are largely religious, ideological and cultural, and for this matter, social capital stocks vary across countries and communities. Nevertheless, we need to begin to account for the mechanisms that link social capital with good governmental performance since good repertoires of social capital make it possible to sustain social cooperation (Boix and Posner, 1998).

It has been claimed that economic growth rates are slower in ethnically diverse countries. As such, what is needed in much of Africa goes beyond mere economic restructuring as to embrace transformational social policy, ethnic diversity management strategies, as well as the provision of a good moral foundation for public policies. Much of the continent requires serious interventions to bring about the desired national character transformation of citizens through character education (see, Attafuah, this volume). Designing and implementing of transformational civic education programmes and leadership retaining initiatives is necessary in creating alternative citizenship. In this sense, there is need to examine the relationship between ethnic diversity management and local collective action, public goods, public services, as well as social capital outcomes in societal re-engineering social policy applications. There is a fundamental relationship between citizenship, nationality and ethnicity. As Worsley (1984) would say, broadly speaking, there are distinct modes of conceptualizing the relationship between citizen and state necessitating the linking of nationality and citizenship (cf. Greenfeld and Chirot 1994: 79-130).

Challenging coterminality as a central legitimizing principle

The African experience gives us a basis of faulting the Western idea of nation that is highly individualistic. Within this individualistic framework, individuals and hence citizens have been recognized as the basic units of polity. Here, multiple nationalities and single citizenship have co-existed within the polity called nation. The nation was conceived as a collectivity of individuals, comprising distinct people, a collective individual and a sovereign collectivity as in the German, Russian and Italian cases. Unfortunately, this coterminality gave birth to the chauvinism of the collectivistic-ethnic idea of nation and nationality. If the collective individual is the nation, fusion of citizenship and nationality is the logical corollary in this mode of statehood. This mode of conceptualizing the relationship between citizenship and nationality assumes cultural homogeneity of the nation and denies political autonomy and voluntarism to the citizen. Citizenship is bestowed on the individual by virtue of her membership in the nation and hence the two cannot be bifurcated. It is this mode of conceptualization, which can, and it did, lead to ethnic bigotry culminating in criminalization of statehood as witnessed in Hitlerism and Mussolini's fascism.

Observably, the Westphalian definition of the era of nation-state with its thrust on homogenization seems to have heralded the advent of patterns of uniformity in state-citizen relationship thereby occasioning a coterminality between nation and state that socially excludes the other. Established on the basis of a different imperial calculus, such coterminality was virtually absent in many countries of Africa except Botswana, Somalia, Lesotho and Swaziland. In most of Africa, the state is a convergence of many 'nations'. We are particularly concerned with the Westphalian notion of sovereignty by which the concept of nation-state sovereignty was based on two principles, namely; territoriality and the exclusion of external actors from domestic authority structures. These Westphalian notions have not been totally eliminated by globalization and have impacted on the world today in terms of:

1. *The principle of the sovereignty* of states and their fundamental right to political self-determination. Under this Westphalian cloak, countries have continued to violate principles of human rights in the name of the sovereignty of nations. It has provided a cover for impunity for every kind of abuse of power and office within the nation-state. Pursuit of this principle has contributed to the possibility of dominant cultural groups marginalizing minority cultural identities.

2. *The principle of (legal) equality* between states. This principle contributes to the continued failure to forcefully intervene in member states to implement the common principles in line with expected best practices of managing national public affairs. We clearly need mechanisms of enforcing transnational civil procedure and behaviour by leaders of countries.

3. *The principle of non-intervention* of one state in the internal affairs of another state. Despite modern sovereignty being characterized by an increasing interdependence between states, the prohibition of non-intervention in internal affairs of a state renders fellow states helpless in event of violations of human rights and failure by regimes to devise and implement civilized approaches to ethnic diversity management.

When re-thinking globalization in a quest to lay foundations of alternative statehood, there is need for establishment of minimum standards in the management of ethnic diversity. The world needs the necessary treaties and the effective mechanisms of enforcing their respective protocols given that the situation cannot simply be seen as a matter of treaty violation. Therefore, the question becomes: what can be done to correct situations when states cannot fulfill their obligations? Indeed, the ability to fulfill international obligations is one of the constitutive requirements of a state in a globalizing world. However, the question of what happens in the event of the inability of a state to discharge international obligations has not been explored by the international legal system. This situation is particularly apparent in the cases of failed states, but it is not limited to them.

Inescapably, there is need to demonstrate the role that ethnic diversity plays in exacerbating national conflict. The need for the designing appropriate steps to devise diversity governance strategies to hedge against unnecessary ethnic conflicts given the discoterminality of nation and state in Africa, unlike other parts of the world where such coterminality is a central legitimizing principle of the modern state, is apparent. Some scholars have pointed to ethnic and other social divisions as a leading cause of economic underdevelopment, due in part to their adverse effects on public good provision and collective action. Nevertheless, there is a need to be creative in devising ethnic diversity management models that would adequately address contentious questions in encounters between ethnic identification and the state. Attempts ought to be made to provide a comprehensive conceptual framework for the study of ethnic nationalism and devise adequate safeguards against the danger of ethno-nationalism and criminal politicization of ethnicity.

There is need for leaders and citizens to rise above an apparently pervasive criminal psychology through the embrace of viable premises of ontological transcendence and identity transformation. The idea of transcendence is critical to identity transformation since it can enable us to rise above the fallenness of human nature by raising a new man whom Martin Heidegger calls *Übermensch* (overman or superman) in a Nietzschean sense. The Heideggerian *Übermensch* was depicted as a responsible being who was meant to be life-affirming and creative. In today's Africa, we need an epistemological transcendence that takes us beyond Heidegger and Nietzsche and formulate a basis of raising a new type of citizen who will rise above mediocrities of such tendencies as ethnic chauvinism, bigotry and corruption. As Heidegger would say in the moment of fellness, ontological transcendence as a quest for meaning does provide us with the basis of original unity of the future, the past, and the present which constitutes a basis for manifesting of authenticity as it expresses itself in being (cf. Heidegger, 1964).

Consequently, Heidegger argues that the truth of being, its openness, is not something which we can merely consider or think of. It is not our own production. We need to consider the character of thinking which does not attempt to dominate, but engages in disclosing and opening up what shows itself, emerges, and is manifest (Heidegger, 1964). Politics in Africa is known for its banalities. As Heidegger's student Hannah Arendt (1964) reminds us, negative ethnicity is a banal form of evil, which hangs on the practitioners of politics.

The very reality of political banalities which Arendt would label as banality of evil should accentuate the quest of transforming the whole sphere of power relationships in African states. Unless we are taught, trained and mentored, the banality of evil has a commonplace in each of us (cf Arendt, 1964). As one who is strongly convinced about the value of transcending ethnic chauvinism, I reiterate the precariousness of contemporary politics of identity in Kenya which seems to affirm the philosophical insights of Frantz Fanon when he states in *Black Skin White Masks* that the colonized subject cannot make a meaning for himself. Leadership and intellectual projects of social transformation are supposed to be critical projects in national development in creating such meaning, which, if carried out on the basis of a near sightedness of exclusionary identity politics, inevitably leads to forms of resentment and resistance that generate and sharpen terrains of social conflict (Aseka, 2007).

Africa needs leaders who are political engineers, astute statesmen and stateswomen than charlatans who are sheer political demagogues. As Saad Z. Nagi (1992) asks; what conditions strengthen or diminish ethnic identification? What conditions foster or inhibit the transformation of ethnic identification into nationalist movements? What patterns of development do these movements follow and what repertoires of expression do they exhibit? What aims do ethnic nationalist movements espouse? What are the reactions of governments to nationalist movements? And, what are the outcomes of these movements?

Although the coterminality of nation and state was the central legitimizing principle of the modern state, in Westphalian statecraft, it has recently come to be challenged by a variety of ethnic groups across the world. There are two such challenges as alluded to heretofore, namely a) the claim of alternative statehood and b) the claim of alternative citizenship. We see evidence of the claim of alternative statehood in Somalia, an apparent failed state, which is faced with the apparent breakaway of Puntland. This challenges the hitherto endorsed coterminality of cultural and political community of this nation-state in the Horn of Africa. It also challenges the political boundaries of existing nation-states laying down grounds for secessionist demands in a nationalist quest that undermines the congruence between nationality and state. We see evidence of the claim of alternative citizenship in the nation-building proclivities of Julius Nyerere. This was a nation-building effort which did not threaten the nation-state because it was encased in a unifying national ideology of national construction which Nyerere tirelessly enunciated to create a united and cohesive Tanzanian society. He cobbled out a citizenship which sought not only the security of the nation but also the protection for the special requirements of cultural community, for which it demanded autonomy, agency and rights of self-determination (see Chege, Huruma, this volume).

These two challenges need to be properly worked at as they may tend to submerge the individual and uphold the rival claims of states and cultural communities. It may be argued that the failed promise of pluralism in modern multi-ethnic societies demands a rethinking of the notions of statehood and citizenship in new terms. Extending citizenship from its location in polity/state to society as such in a transcendentalist sense, and providing space for affiliative and affinitive identities which have been worked out ideologically have an identity transformational imperative that may help to strengthen civil society, within a non-majoritarian and non-homogenizing political framework (cf. Niraja Gopal Jayal, 1993).

Effective management of ethnic diversity

Nation building which ought to address the above two challenges of alternative statehood and alternative citizenship has been very high on the agenda of postcolonial governments of multi ethnic societies. Nevertheless, as Asante (2004) aptly states, the management of ethno-regional and other conflicts as well as nation building has been very high on the agenda of post independence governments. For him, politicians and policy makers are faced with different types of constraints. Thus, different types of ethnic structures and inequalities as well as the nature of ethno-regional rivalry may require different combinations of reform instruments in order to manage diversity and to build stable and inclusive society. Indeed, there is a link between ethnicity and governance reforms. While governance reforms have been lackadaisical, they should fully address the challenges and constraints of ethnicity.

Douglas North (1991) defines institutions as the humanly devised constraints that structure political, economic and social interaction. The leadership function should be energized by consultative proclivities and synergistic decision-making that is embellished with diversity management competencies if the intellectual and material outputs of various components of our statehood and national citizenry are to be meaningfully brought into play in national reconstruction and development. It is in this sense that the need to identify the role the intelligentsia, the political class and bureaucrats should play in a new cultural politics of national construction becomes apparent (cf. Aseka, 2007).

We need a new phenomenological approach to the study of ethnicity, corruption and all those social conditions which exacerbate our fellness in social, economic and political behaviour and hinder us from raising a new type of citizen. Phenomenology as a study of the structuring of consciousness is a current in philosophy that takes intuitive experience of phenomena (what presents itself to us in conscious experience) as its starting point. It tries to extract the essential features of experiences and the essence of what we experience, creating a basis of what Heidegger called ontological transcendence and epistemological transcendence. Apparently, transcendence is a dimension of experience that holds enormous promise for escape from the mundane levels at which some leaders and citizens operate. The search for transcendence should be prompted by the desire for a deeper and more profound meaning of life and for a sensitizing and intensification of human experience.

We superfluously talk about democratization of multi-ethnic societies without giving sufficient consideration to demands of effective diversity management in democratization. Although it is germane to explain and problematize the concept of identity as an idea that can encapsulate a lot of definitions, we need to explore how some of these definitions only trigger off ambiguities of social adventure where there is no sense of national vision to offer a basis of construction of statehood and citizenship. The concept of identity needs to be reworked to create a national sense of purpose, political community and also form a new basis of fostering social cohesiveness (Aseka, 2007).

It is clear that the international community has increasingly become prepared to openly intervene in specific internal affairs of states on grounds of human rights protection and humanitarian assistance. However, it appears that it is still reluctant to openly engage in discharging other international and external obligations without a precise mandate. It makes no sense to try to eliminate diversity or pretend that it does not exist. This merely provokes resistance and has long-lasting destructive effects. Efforts to recognize and accommodate diversity ought to be part of the quest to construct alternative statehood and citizenship and can offer a basis of resolving seemingly irreconcilable situations and create opportunities for innovation and progress (Kimonye, this volume; Gashi, 2000).

Many democratizing states of Asia and the Pacific have effectively responded to ethnic diversity and ethnic conflict by political engineering and institutional reform. In recent years, some of the contemporary world's most ambitious and innovative attempts at political engineering have come from the Asia-Pacific region. During the 1990s, democratizing states such as Indonesia, Thailand, the Philippines, Fiji and Papua New Guinea have embarked upon far-reaching overhauls of their political systems via refashioning of their executives, electoral laws, party systems and other key democratic institutions. Many of these reforms were driven, in large part, by the need to manage the consequences of social diversity on political stability in the design of political institutions (Reilly, 2005).

If reprehensible attitudes and practices associated with the domestic political class can be avoided by all professional caucuses (who in turn can sensitize the various categories of people under their influence), authentic processes of development, social change, and public policymaking can shape new identities in people's public life. Such groups can serve as cardinal epistemic communities as well as actively engaged policy networks. We need to focus on the concepts of development in terms of our Africanity rather than our differences, and there is need to identify the thrusts of our national interests.

In my view, there is need to distinguish false transcendence from true transcendence because the latter is driven by clear epistemological and ethical motivations. A lasting transcendence is ideologically worked as a means of proper socialization of citizens. Transcendence means that human beings can move psychologically from one state of consciousness to another. Such self-transcendence is needed as a basis of overcoming the idiocies of corruption and tribalism. Without it human beings tend to be less than human in their behaviour towards one another. Citizen transformation ought to bring citizens into a new social awakening, into a new ontological transcendent realm that self- transcendence provides.

The primacy of the national interest in citizen transformation

In Kenya no serious discussion of national interests has taken place despite the fact the salient message of National Anthem bespeaks the national interest in the form of the following pillars of *Pax Kenyana*:

1. *God-centredness*: We are committed to uphold national integrity as a sacred trust. There is need to spawn an aura and respect for God-centred governance. We need a God-centered governance and spiritually-motivated leadership since we invoke the God of all creation to bless our land and nation. Our behavioural tendencies in our interactions with others at work and in social settings need to be transformed and there is need to spell out national ideals and purposes upon which management tools can be developed which provide action plans on how we can get along better with everyone within the nation-state and in our work places.

   If we embrace God-centred leadership as a national interest it means giving prominence to the platinum and golden rules which have a transcendental imperative as a basis of effective diversity management in our country. These rules demand a great deal of rationality and conscientiousness. As Douglas Hofstadter states, irrationality is the root of all evil. Implicit in this is the fact that rationality is the root of all good–that to be rational about being rational is to be good.

2. *Justice and fairness*: The transition to democracy is more feasible and sustainable when a country has an established track record of rule of law. The rule of law and not rule by provides a stable basis for democracy to develop. We need to operationalize the principles of justice and fairness in a regime of governance that guarantees human and ecological security. National transformation necessitates the proper understanding of the social form of which law is a critical contributor to its emergence.

   We need to institutionalize the enforcement of distributive and retributive justice in a country which is yearning for an elusive fairness. The process of mainstreaming the concept of inclusiveness into national project designs must be keenly worked out to reflect our sense of justice and fairness. This will minimize the political charades and behavioural absurdities of "it is our turn to eat" which undermine the very foundational basis of sound diversity management.

3. *Progress and prosperity*: Democratization which does not tackle challenges of poverty can only be described as delusional democracy. Widespread unemployment is an enormous human tragedy and a

destabilizing social force, but it is also the largest obstacle to democratization. The transition to democracy is more feasible and sustainable when a country has a vibrant middle class, a healthy employment market, a dynamic and independent entrepreneurial community and vigorous economic development. We need to re-engineer institutions of national integrity and provide them with an architecture which defines, protects and nurtures national integrity fired by the quest for diligence and honesty as basis for our individual and collective progress. We need a national work ethic and should punish malpractices including corruption and tribalism.

4. *Security: Peace, law and order*: Responsible leaders and their parties ought to necessarily presume peace as a necessary condition for democracy. There is a correlation between democracy and peace. Genuine democracy has social justice as its social foundation for peace. We need to establish a culture of peace-making, peace-building and peace-keeping while recognizing the intrinsic links of peace to sustainable democracy. The formulation and evolution of our legal architecture must address all the challenges there are to the creation of an enabling environment for security of the nation in law, and this should be the basis of realizing a new social order that values peace and tranquility.

5. *Liberty and respect for human rights and dignity*: It is the responsibility of the government to make people freer, increase their liberty, and make them happy. As Friedrich Hayek would argue liberty is freedom from coercion. Liberty and self-government are critical components of democracy. But as Robert Dahl (1985) says, liberty is a good of supreme importance, perhaps indeed a good greater than equality; but the love of equality is stronger than the love of liberty. The rule of law and the due process of law should aim at maintaining and advancing individual freedoms and liberties as well as human rights and dignity. That is why we need to consider the importance of ethics in law enforcement.

Our identity is not restricted to our blackness, brownness or whiteness. Neither is it only a matter of ethnic or religious belonging, despite the fact that ethnicity and religion have been labeled as critical markers of identity in improperly mediated perceptions of the essence of being (Aseka, 2007). The essence of being is more productively conceived in terms of the preservation of human dignity and the upholding of a social order in which fairness and social justice to all citizens is respected. Our blackness or ethnic grouping is not an end in itself; it is a mere representation of majoritarian or minoritarian fractions of our geographical location in which certain senses of identity are developed.

Improper use of majoritarian and other social categories has led to misdeeds that have contributed to Africa's fractured geographies as marked by not only its ethnically and racially diverse citizenship but also by the presence of a wounded cadre of transmigrated citizens we call refugees. Mismanagement of the African polity has led to a swelling of the ranks of refugees, and these émigrés have contributed to the making of global Africa embodied in the Black Diaspora. It has also contributed to the evolution of ethnic and national identities in the struggle for social justice. But that evolution need not detain us here. There is more relevance in accounting for how the end of the struggle for decolonization were sabotaged or reconfigured by political agents who undermined the whole purpose of resisting the economic and political changes wrought by colonialism (Aseka, 2007).

It is evident that for decades, scholars have recognized that ethnicity is an important factor in the political life of a nation. Nevertheless, there is the need to ask the question: how does the relative homogeneity or ethnic diversity of a state's population relate to democratization and state-building? Those who point to ethnicity and culture as important factors in the democratization process, such as Robert Dahl and Joseph Rothschild, consider the political actions of ethnic groups to be important factors in the development of a state (Basch, 1998). Having invoked the concept of ethnic diversity considerably, it is important to indicate my perception of diversity as simply the uniqueness of every individual, which encompasses different personal attributes, values and organizational roles. The notion of diversity is also loaded with connotations of the mix of differences and similarities at all levels of an organization or social entity. This may encapsulate differences in abilities, culture, ethnicity, race, age, physical characteristics, values, sexual orientation, religious inclinations, educational achievements, marital status, etc. Inclusion therefore is a means of creating harmony. In the quest to build a good framework for ethnic diversity management, there is need for creation and nurturing of a new social ecology of inclusion.

In a sense, there are links between processes of social exclusion and violence. Even mild forms of social exclusion provoke aggression in most people. As such, social exclusion is a process which brings about serious social ruptures, therefore detaching groups and individuals from social relations and institutions and preventing them from full participation in the normal activities of the society in which they live. This shows a lack of diversity management insights. That is why in this social ecology, diversity in the civil service has to emerge as a key issue in the initiative to reassess the role of government in constructing viable statehood. Demands for equity, equality and fairness in a time of growing demographic diversification indicate a parallel need to diversify public bureaucracies and make them sensitive to principles and demands of diversity management. The unprecedented challenges to public policy making and management set in motion by the forces of globalization and democratization require governmental capabilities which can effectively embrace diverse cultures and perspectives (Caiden and Caiden, 2001).

Diversity management is, therefore, a strategy of good public management practices. It builds on good governance principles that have been formulated to embrace human rights as positive managerial tools meant to facilitate the broader inclusion of all groups at all levels of governance. In a well governed state, the state ought to be a guarantor of social, political, and economic stability. It sets norms and creates precedents for inter-ethnic interactions. As such, both institutional competence and personal competence are key for governments to manage diversity and the implementation of these policies (Gashi, 2000).

Challenges of managing diversity

A new politics of ideological becoming must be deployed to bind the wounds of a highly fractious Kenyan society with a goal to spur a new prospective process of identity formation given the failed promise of pluralism. This process is necessary in confronting the senselessness of ethnic separateness and bigotry which bedevils the psychology of leaders and citizens in different social locations of an otherwise beautiful country. This calls for a re-thinking of the notion of citizenship and nationhood. Diversity may challenge the long-cherished domination of bureaucracies by one group and entrenched ways of doing business. The achievement of diversity would require changes in hiring and promotion practices, as well as structural changes to ensure mobility and opportunity for previously excluded or under-represented groups (Caiden and Caiden, 2001).

With proper mechanisms of social intervention and empowerment, citizens can be effectively led out of the trappings of a criminalized ethnic psychology. Criminal tribal mind-sets may have developed because of lack of good leadership mediation and the development of a congenial culture of tolerance of the so-called "other". The absurdity of this criminal psychology is exhibited by persons from different social backgrounds who appear in essence to stand in different relationship to structures and systems of power, privilege and authority in a country whose contours of the problem space we need to understand adequately (Aseka, 2007).

It has been stated that good diversity management challenges stereotypes about people and their capacities. It shatters myths about the superiority of certain groups and the inability of certain identities such as women, people with disabilities, the elderly and minorities to compete and succeed if only they have a real opportunity to do so. Managed well, diversity can be an instrument for democratizing the state. It may safely be stated that cooperation between ethnic groups can significantly affect, and in some cases become the key determinant in the formation of a pluralist democracy. Ethnic groups can work together to demand accountability and transparency among leaders at the community and national levels.

Effective diversity challenges the power of entrenched groups by opening up to others the careers, responsibilities, decision-making, and advantages previously reserved for them. Such diversity management disturbs and breaks ethnic structures of privilege and should aim at achieving social cohesion and unity through diversity approaches which see diversity as a common value. It strengthens community social capital and enhances governmental capacity for decision-making and government legitimacy and also ensures more responsive service delivery.

Many states are struggling with their internal diversity and face growing challenges from restive ethnic minorities in their midst. The future of deeply-divided societies dominated by ethnic politics presents the most important political and ethical issue of the contemporary world. In view of the need for political accommodation in deeply divided societies—if democracy, equality, human rights and self-government are to advance in a new global governing code—there is a need to create a framework that will allow humanity to move toward efficacious solutions. In a very fundamental way, well-formulated diversity management challenges exclusiveness. It combats prejudices against people who do not fit fixed images or stereotypes of bigoted leadership. It presents opportunities to individuals, who previously had seen public service as closed to them. A more diverse civil service workforce expands concepts of trustworthiness and confidence to include the broader citizenry, beyond a self-selecting elite (Caiden and Caiden, 2001).

Diversity management efforts should be driven by a rationalized work ethic in the nation and all its workplaces to facilitate the exchange of new perspectives, improve problem solving by inviting different ideas, and create a respectful accepting work environment. Diversity challenges conformity, and the insistence that those in public bureaucracies assimilate to a single norm of behaviour, attitude, and thought. It brings a fresh approach to the organization of work, the structure of careers, the potential contribution of differences, and the formulation of public policies. There are critical challenges to political stability as well as democracy, and this suggests that there is a need for solutions that move from the management of ethnic conflict to policies that are not only democratic but also fair. Justice can become our defender if we institutionalize proper mechanisms of diversity management. Leaders need to devise means of accommodating their ethnic minorities. Diversity management challenges formalism, in which sheer process substitutes for result. Means are valorized rather than the ends. Diversity management opposes procedures and forms which on their face are neutral, but really act to exclude people. Instances of such hypocrisies are not few among leaders.

Worthwhile diversity management ought to be formulated not in narrow terms of sheer organizational workplace and recruitment criteria. Recruiting and retaining diverse leaders is important but effective diversity management means much more than that. Leaders have such a strong influence on any organizational endeavour and perhaps that is why a first step in diversity management is recruiting and retaining a culturally diverse leadership team. It is assumed that having a diverse management team that showcases the positive side of people being different is a reminder to all staff that the organization's diversity goals are in the forefront. They will see that it makes economic sense to increase diversity in top level management positions. Moreover, it is assumed that more diversity in management was necessary if the needs of ethnically diverse employees were to be met. But beyond doing ethnic arithmetic to balance numbers of people, there is need for a profound identity transformation.

Diversity not only involves how people perceive themselves, but how they perceive others. An organization's success and competitiveness depends upon its ability to embrace diversity and realize the benefits. In this sense, diversity is different from affirmative action since affirmative action is a mere framework for a diversity management that may not demand any ontological transcendence in operationalizing the platinum principle which states that we should treat others as they want to be treated. The platinum rule is germane because in effective diversity management, rationality must guide us in developing durable ideals. These ideals will guide us in our interaction with others because there is no limit to the number of people we can encounter, and we must establish a standard which embraces diversity as much as it embraces harmony. The platinum rule lies at the centre of a diverse and inclusive work environment. Our understanding of diversity requires involving the use of the platinum rule. A transformational leader ought to realize that a key role in transforming the national or organizational culture, so that it more closely reflects the values of our diverse citizens and workforce, requires skills in effective diversity management including:

1. An understanding and acceptance of diversity management concepts and principles of justice, fairness and inclusion

2. Recognition that diversity ought to be threaded through every aspect of management in our institutions

3. Development of a profound sense of national self-awareness, in terms of understanding our different cultures, identities and seeking to transcend our biases, prejudices, and stereotypes

4. Readiness to demonstrate willingness to challenge and change national and institutional practices that present barriers to different groups.

Diversity management has been described as looking at: 1) the mind set of an organization or social institution 2) the climate of an organization or social institution 3) the different perspectives people bring to an organization or social institution due to race, workplace styles, disabilities, and other differences (Reichenberg, 2001).

Leadership as social capital and leadership as intellectual capital point to the importance of competency—building as a way of tapping into these forms of capital. Performance competencies draw from the spiritual, mental and emotional reservoirs of our personality types (Aseka, 2009). Leadership is a means of mobilizing and deploying social capital. Despite the acknowledgment that leaders spend most of their time interacting with others, the social capital of leaders is perhaps the most ignored, under-researched aspect of leadership. In contrast to human capital constituted as traits and behaviours, social capital refers to relationships with other actors and the accompanying access to information, resources, opportunities, and control. Because organizational leadership involves accomplishing work through others, it is critical that we assess the social capital of leaders given the importance of networks and of the civic norms which leaders institute.

The key indicators of social capital include social relations, formal and informal social networks, group membership, trust, reciprocity and civic engagement. There is the prospect of developing good social capital through leadership and the fostering of community partnerships. Good quality partnerships can be developed through a new style of leadership called "enabling leadership". Leadership dynamics should produce social capital and social capital should build a strong national political community. Responsible leadership springs out of responsible citizenship. According to Bass, authentic transformational leadership on whose proper diversity management proclivities can be discharged is grounded in moral foundations that are based on four components:

1. *Idealized influence:* Idealized influence describes leaders and managers who are exemplary role models for associates. Leaders and managers with idealized influence can be trusted and respected by associates to make good decisions for their communities or organizations.

2. *Inspirational motivation*: Inspirational motivation describes leaders and managers who motivate associates to commit to the vision of the organization. Leaders and managers with inspirational motivation encourage team spirit to reach goals of increased revenue and market growth for their communities or organizations.

3. *Intellectual stimulation*: Intellectual stimulation describes leaders and managers who encourage innovation and creativity through challenging the normal beliefs or views of a group. Leaders and managers with intellectual stimulation promote critical thinking and problem solving to make their communities or organizations better.

4. *Individualized consideration*: Individual consideration describes leaders or managers who act as coaches and advisors to the associates. Leaders and managers with individual consideration encourage associates to reach goals that help both the associates and their communities or organizations.

In the above sense, diversity should improve cultural sensitivity toward client groups, as well as incorporating a greater variety of viewpoints into policy making, broadening the range of possibilities for consideration, and providing more realistic insights into complex, dynamic problems. As such, there is need for African leaders and citizens to demonstrate a sense of national responsibility by showing an extensive interest in articulating the relevance of place and position as well as the resources required for the construction of a new sense of identity in the country. This is particularly critical as we begin examining the power dynamics that can be made possible in cultural geographies that have long been fractured by socio-economic exigencies and discriminatory policies, policies which have criminalized difference while undermining politics of alternative thought. This community must take stock of the social, human and financial capital at its disposal and begin to focus on their use and deployment for development purposes. As pointed out by Caiden and Caiden, effective civil services cannot stand aloof, sheltering behind a neutral facade of technical competence, from the vicissitudes of the societies of which they form apart. They are an essential component of governance, and should conduct themselves so as to help prevent conflicts and integrate populations that are increasingly divided among different races, nationalities and ethnic groups. Diversification in civil service should contribute toward policies of inclusiveness toward all members of our societies.

Conclusion

One need not overemphasize that an understanding of cultural dynamics is essential to the proper perception of what is needed to be done in confronting and meeting our society's quests and desires to promote health, prevent disease, improve literacy levels and spur people into productive actions and amicable social relations. There is a need for dialogue, debate and cultural conversation in order to produce social knowledge which equips us with understandings of our cultures. It should also enable us to devise strategies that provide us with not only the social, cultural, and economic environments that influence human health, economic productivity and behavior but also with the means of incepting the necessary processes through which these environments can positively exert their influence. Consequently, in figuring how ethnic diversity as part of a country's social capital can be turned into a resource for political, economic, social and cultural development and how to manage it through structures and community engagements, we need to consider how diversity management ought to be guided by sound principles.

References

Arendt, H. (1964). Eichmann in Jerusalem: A Report on the Banality of Evil, http://www.bu.edu/wcp/Papers/Cont/ContAssy.htm.)

Asante, R. (2004). The Politics of Managing Ethnic Cleavages, Inequalities, Nation Building and Democratization in Ghana, http://www.newschool.edu/tcds/Richard%20Asante.pdf.

Aseka, E. (2005). *Pitfalls of Ideology, Social Policy and Leadership in Africa.* Nairobi: New EME Research Initiatives and Publishers.

Aseka, E. (2007). "The Role of the Kenyan Diaspora in Constructing a New Politics of Culture and Identity", in *African Affairs*, The Zeleza Post, http://www.zeleza.com/blogging/african-affairs/role-kenyan-diaspora-constructing-new-politics-culture-and-identity.

Aseka, E. (2009). (Re) "Defining Leadership Models", a paper presented at the Goethe-Institüt, Maendeleo House, Loita/Monrovia St. Nairobi on the theme (Re)membering Kenya: Governance, Citizenship and Economics supported by The Ford Foundation and Goethe-Institüt Kenya and in partnership with Twaweza Communications, held on 15th April.

Basch, R. (1998). *The effects of ethnic separation on democratization: A Comparative Study*, East European Quarterly, June.

Benjamin, R. (2005). "Democratization and Ethnic Politics in the Asia-Pacific" Paper presented at the Annual Meeting of the International Studies Association. Hilton Hawaiian Village, Honolulu, Hawaii.

Caiden, N.J. & G. E. Caiden. (2001). *Strategies for Meeting the Challenges of Diversity Management in the Civil Service.* United Nations Headquarters, New York: School of Policy, Planning and Development, University of Southern California.

Carles, B. & D. Posner (1998). *The Origins and Political Consequences of Social Capital*, http://www.princeton.edu/~cboix/bjps98.pdf.

Chidozie, O. (2009). Diversity Management: Its Challenges in the Workplace, http://ezinearticles.com/?Diversity-Management—Its-Challenges-in-the-Workplace&id=1498059.

Giorgetti, Fulfilling International Obligations by International Organizations in the Absence of State Control, http://www.esil-sedi.eu/fichiers/en/Giorgetti_343.pdf.

Heidegger, M. & Krell, David Farrell; *Basic Writings: From Being and Time (1927) to the Task of Thinking (1964).* (San Francisco: Harper, 1993).

Heidegger, M. (1977). 'The End of Philosophy and the Task of Thinking' translated by Joan Stambaugh. In *Basic Writings*, edited by David Farrell Krell (New York: Harper & Row, 1977), 375.

Ian, F. (2000). Leadership in Vocational Education and Training: Developing Social Capital Through Partnerships, Centre for Research and Learning in Regional Australia (CRLRA) University of Tasmania, Australia.

Ibrahim, G. (2000). Democratization of Multi-ethnic societies-avoiding conflicting logistics: the Case of Kosovo, http://www.kosovotimes.net/kosovo-pdf-library-download-section/doc download/43-democratization-of-multiethnic-societies-avoiding-conflicting-logics.html.

Ilan, P. (2007). *Democratizing the Hegemonic State: Political Transformation in the Age of Identity*. Cambridge: Cambridge University Press.

Neil, E.R. (2001). *Best Practices in Diversity Management. United Nations Expert Group Meeting on Managing Diversity in the Civil Service*. New York: United Nations Headquarters.

Niraja, G.J. (1993). *Ethnic Diversity and the Nation State*. Centre for Political Studies, New Delhi: Jawaharlal Nehru University.

North, D.C. (1991). "Institutions", Journal of Economic Perspective, Vol. 5.

UNRISD/UNDP (1994). Ethnic Violence, Conflict Resolution and Cultural Pluralism, Report of the UNRISD/UNDP International Seminar on Ethnic Diversity and Public Policies, New York.

Saad Z. Nagi (1992). Ethnic Identification and Nationalist Movements, in *Human Organization Issue*: Volume 51, Number 4 / Winter 1992, pp. 307-317.

Smith, A.D. (1986). *The Ethnic Origins of Nations*. Oxford: Blackwell.

Strappado, W. (2003). The high cost of claiming: CHOSEN, http://batr.org/wrack/061303.html.

Media and National Identity: Should National Media be Relegated to the Backseat?

Nassanga Goretti Linda

Introduction

This chapter explores media's influence in creating national identity, particularly focusing on "national media". With the changes in media structures resulting from globalization and the rise of computer mediated communication (CMC), the question of interest is whether national media are still of relevance today or should they be relegated to the backseat. A case will be put forward for rethinking the role of national media, particularly the public service broadcasting (PSB) and community/citizens' media. These media outlets offer citizens chances of participation, a sense of belonging and togetherness, thus enhancing the national identification process.

By way of putting the discussion into context, the chapter looks at the concept of 'I' or how the individual acquires his/her identity. It is after having an appreciation of how the individual identity is derived that we can then talk about national identity. The identification process occurs when the individual interacts with others, starting with the family, peers, tribal and ethnic groups, expanding to the national level and beyond.

Traditionally in Africa, we largely depended on oral interpersonal communication, but this has not been spared by the influence of *Information and Communication Technologies* (ICTs) in order to have mediated communication. Even in the rural areas that do not have much ICT penetration, radio coverage there is fairly high. Radio continues to be the fundamental communication technology for much of the planet (Downing 2007) and has been the most appealing tool for participatory communication and development throughout the world, making it the ideal medium for change (Gumucio-Dagron 2001). Community radio has been a practical and cost-effective means of reaching and connecting the world's poorest communities (AMARC 2003).

In Uganda, like in many other African countries, ethnic groupings have played an important role in shaping media's agenda especially with the privately owned commercial media. Much as the public media is expected to cater for the interests of the various ethnic groups, it has not to a large extent achieved this. Several communities have started their own community or citizens' media to fill this gap.

Since media structures are similar in most developing countries, Uganda will be used as a case study, but the discussion should be applicable to other developing countries. The major question of interest will be whether national media is still of relevance in the national identification processes given the global and regional media networks. Globalization will be used as the conceptual framework, for the discussion and the chapter will explore how this has affected national identity. Issues of how media influence the identification processes through inclusion and exclusion or 'we' and 'them' as well as the resultant sub-national communities will be highlighted. The paper will look at how CMC has facilitated the narrowing of gendered spaces through creation of online identities.

As a way forward towards enhancing national media playing its rightful role in the national identification process, the chapter calls for reforms in the national media, specifically focusing on PSB and community/citizens' media. Due to their participatory nature, these national media can turn ethnic diversity into a resource that can enhance the democratization process by creating an all-embracing national "we".

Personal identity and national identity

One gets his/her identity from communication (verbal or non-verbal) with others, implying that without communication, it would not be possible for identification to take place. Family and social ties remain the cornerstone and scaffolding for individual existence in Africa. As channels for the transmission of values and norms in the rural communities, in the spirit of 'it takes a village to raise a child', they guide and encourage individual action. In this setup, individuals are seen as a product of the environment within which they live (Megwa 2007:54) or their culture. Traditionally culture referred to the organic way of life of a certain people fixed in a certain place (Sinclair 2004:73), so identity is seen in terms of a cultural set-up. We cannot talk about identity in isolation or in a vacuum as people have identity because they are part of a community (Ake, 1993).

Hoijer (2007:33) differentiates between self-identity and collective identity or individual/personal identity and social identity. While the former refers to personal experience, the latter is associated with belonging to certain social groups, constituted by different factors - age, gender, religion, ethnicity, nationality etc. She points out that the two are not mutually exclusive but are inter-woven.

A person derives his/her identity primarily from a name, which signifies certain attributes. For example in many societies first names carry a male/female gender connotation. The surnames, however, tend to be distinct and meaning is attached by the particular tribe or ethnic group. Thus ethnic naming is a key aspect in any identity discourse. Ethnic identity may be based on ethnic groups which can be referred to as 'a historically formed aggregate of people having a real or imaginary association, a specified territory, shared cluster of beliefs and values connoting its distinctiveness in relation to similar groups and recognised as such by others' (Okuku 2002:8).

Uganda's ethnic groups are most broadly distinguished by language. In southern Uganda, most of the population speak Bantu languages. Sudanic speakers inhabit the northwest and the Nilotic speakers, the northeast (*Encyclopedia of the Nations*). There are 13 major ethnic groups (Kurian & Thomas 1992) with the Baganda in the central region being the largest at 16.2% of the population, followed by Iteso and Banyankore at 8.1% and 8.0% respectively. The rest of the ethnic groups are shown in the table below.

Table 1: Major ethnic groups in Uganda

Group	%	Group	%
Baganda	16.2	Bagisu	5.1
Iteso	8.1	Acholi	4.4
Banyankore	8.0	Lugbara	3.6
Basoga	7.7	Batoro	3.2
Bakiga	7.1	Banyoro	2.9
Banyaruanda	5.8	Karamojong	2.0
Lango	5.6	Others (est.)	20.3

From these ethnic groups, the identification process occurs. Identity has to do with feelings and conceptualizations of oneself and one's belonging to certain groups of social categories (Hoijer 2007:33). A person's identity is comprised of their individual or personal identity, and their group or social identity (Thurlow et al. 2004:67). Identity has been likened to a centreless web of beliefs, values and attitudes plus cognitive components that are characterized by relative stability (Oulasson 2007:53). Research on identity initially was premised on the assumption that a person had an essential or natural identity, which usually was supposed to be formed by adulthood. This identity was believed to be unitary, implying that each one has a 'true' identity that is fixed, staying basically the same throughout (Thurlow et al. 2004:97).

New focus by scholars like Stuart Hall (cited in Thurlow et. al. 2004:97) regard identity as being more flexible, dimensional and socially constructed, such that people now talk of identification, rather than identity as this identity, is a life-long process. In post-modern theory, it is accepted that people can have more than one cultural identity at the same time or cultural affiliation existing at different levels. The theory conceives of the individual subject, not as composed of single relatively constant identity, but rather multiple identities that become mobilized within different cultural discourses. In these situations, people are on the move with cultural affiliations at various levels and the cultural ties of nationhood become ever less credible and binding (Sinclair 2004:74).

Apart from its physical location or geographical boundaries, a nation must have a group of people or a community. In order for a community to develop, there have to exist a number of common interests and a sense of common identity (Oulasson 2007:67). Four processes through which a community emerges are identified (Thurlow et.al. 2004:111):

1. the forms of expression like talking

2. the sense of shared group identity

3. norms or the rules and conventions for living that are agreed upon, and

4. relationship or connections and interactions with others in the community.

A nation like Uganda has all these characteristics of a community so one can talk about a Ugandan community with a national identity. Olousson (2007:54/ 57) notes that such a nationalized community constructs meaning essentially along the horizon of the national "we". The national identity position is nourished by the notion of "sameness" or the experience of being similar to others in the community and different from those outside. Waisbord (2004:376/8) submits that nations provide a sense of unity and identity, yet they also establish differences among cultural groups. He adds that nations simultaneously aggregate and separate people on the basis of cultural forms such as language, religion, history and symbols. However, as he points out, intense migration and movements have undermined national visions of "one race, one language, one culture" that shaped modern national identities. These movements have not only been physical but also movements of global media networks.

Media and shaping identities

In order to appreciate media's role in shaping national identities, we need to look at how we get information. While we get some information through personal and interpersonal communication, we are dependent upon a wide range of information that we receive through the media. As Dennis Everette (1991:88) points out, the power of the media does not come from single messages, but from the cumulation of messages and from the domination of the information environment by the media.

Media exercise cultural power which among others gives the media power to define which issues will enter the circuit of public communications, how the issues will be debated, and who will speak on the issues in the media. In this process, media "install themselves" as dominant in the production and distribution of culture, even if the events will not be systematically encoded in a single way, they will tend to draw on a limited ideological or explanatory repertoire which will tend to make things have meanings within the sphere of the dominant ideology (Golding & Murdock, 1997:491). What is seen as the national culture is the "preferred culture" of the dominant group, not the nation as a whole (Sinclair 2004:72). The national identity position constitutes a fundamental mechanism in the interpretation of media, whether or not the making of meaning will draw upon dominant ideological or oppositional counter-ideological repertoires (Oulasson 2007:66). There tend to be forces in the national identification process that encourage the feeling of either being part of the national community or excluded from it.

Oulasson (2007:56/63) notes that national identification processes tend to discriminate against minorities within the national borders. The minorities, be they ethnic, religious or other social group, experience some kind of threat and exclusion from the national environment. Thus, they form sub-national communities, based on their common denominator identity position. He further notes that the conflicting relationship with the national environment among sub-nationalized communities seems to be closely connected to experiences of exclusion from national media. These communities experience oppression or domination in various situations within the national context.

This leads sub-national communities to create meaning in an oppositional manner, compared to the nationalized community and in relation to public structures of power. In Uganda where we have several interest group-based media, this has been applicable to a large extent.

Overview of media development in Uganda

After independence in 1962, government maintained control over the media, with the country having one radio station (Radio Uganda, now UBC Radio), one television station (Uganda Television, now UBC TV) and a few newspapers. The government monopoly was broken with the liberalization era in 1990s, and we now have media pluralism with private media co-existing alongside government/public media. The media industry has experienced rapid expansion since liberalization, especially the electronic media. According to the Uganda Communications Commission, there were 204 radio stations and 48 television stations licensed as per February 2009. There are 4 national daily newspapers and about 8 weeklies, most of them in English. Internet access is still very low with only 2.4% users of the population (World Internet Usage Statistics 2009).

While television has become a very important information source for developed countries, radio is the most accessible media for most developing countries. In Uganda, there is almost universal access to radio (99%), with television having average access (55%), (*National Electronic Media Performance Study,* 2004:36/44). Newspaper readership is still fairly low with an estimated combined daily circulation of about 80,000 copies.

Uganda's media landscape conforms to the political economy theory, where media are largely market-driven and serve interests of the minority urban elite (13% urban population). Media are concentrated in urban areas and content is about urban affairs mainly. There is vertical integration, horizontal concentration, and transnational expansion, with 2 major players dominating the media sector—The Nation Group and the government. The public/government has the following: UBC Radio, Vision Radio, Bukedde Radio, Star FM, Mega FM, Radio West, UBC TV, Vision TV, *New Vision, Bukedde, Etop, Rupiny* and *Orumuri.* The Nation Group, which is a regional media has the following: In Uganda, Monitor/KFM Radio, Nation Radio, Nation TV, *The Monitor* and *The East African.* In Kenya Nation Group has: Nation Radio, Capital FM, Nation TV, KTN TV, *The Nation, Taifa Leo, Coast Express* and *Standard.* The Nation Group in Tanzania has: *Citizen, Mwananchi* and *MwanaSpoti.*

There is also concentration on a smaller scale amongst several other private owners including: Top Radio, Kampala FM, Radio Rhino and Top TV, owned by Pastor Ssenyonga; Capital FM and Beat FM owned by William Pike; Hot FM and Simba FM owned by Aga Sekalala; Radio One and Radio 2 owned by Maria Kiwanuka; NBS TV and NBS Radio owned by Nabeta Nathan.

Such concentration creates a big barrier to new entrants in the industry as they find it difficult to compete. In addition, advertisers prefer to deal with the media conglomerates, and media content is targeted at meeting the interests of the advertisers, instead of the public interest.

Is national media still relevant in the globalization context?

Media's primary role is to keep society informed by reporting about what is taking place, thereby acting as a reflection of society. As Waisbord (2004:387) contends, the relevance of the media lies more in their having a great capacity to offer representations, and interpretations of the nation on a daily basis. These representations contribute to the sustainability of nations by institutionalizing national cultures. Nations need institutions like media that permanently remind members of their commonality and cultural allegiance or which have institutional retention. Waisbord further notes that media reinforce national belonging by constantly making reference to places, symbols and memories that anchor national cultures and identities. In addition, in shaping a sense of time and space commonality, such as when the country is listening or watching the same event, media coordinate the life of a nation.

Media were able to perform these functions effectively when we still had national media that targeted local/national audiences principally and when countries had fewer media outlets. For example in Uganda, the nation relied on Radio Uganda and UTV. With more outlets under a liberalized policy, audiences are fragmented across several media, nationally, regionally and globally. The audience fragmentation and media diversity notwithstanding, there is a tendency for "pack-journalist" to cover the same events and produce similar news stories, even if there are differences in approaches or styles used. For instance, whenever there is a policy before Parliament or an issue of public concern, a press conference is organized, to which various media houses are invited. As Waisbord (2004:387) deduces, while we have media fragmentation and audience segmentation, unlike in the past when technological options were limited, national media still manage to reel in dispersed audiences and shape common collective experiences.

It is noted that the nation-state that exists now is no longer such an intact entity as before, given the large scale movement and settlement of people across national borders. This change has been influenced by among others, the liberalization trade policies and de-regulation of national markets and inroads of foreign capital, changes in technology, urbanization, transportation, increased literacy, rising standards of living and growth of the advertising industry (Sinclair 2004; McQuail 1997). Given that media are increasingly extending beyond national frontiers to create global audiences, which get lost from their original communication sources (McQuail 1997:62), does national media still contribute to building national identity as before? It is noted that the local or national has become detached from physical space as a result of the movement of populations who carry with them a symbolic space but leave behind the geographic space, in addition to the ubiquitous diffusion of the information infrastructure (Braman 2003:115).

Critiques of the concept of nationalism point out that the conditions that propelled nations and nationalism to exist have changed so much that nation-states are becoming irrelevant. The argument is that if modernity was the cradle of nations, the end of the modernity era brings about the "passing of the nation" as the intensification of the movements of capital disrupts nations and the sense of home community (Waisbord 2004:384). However, present-day nationalists have countered and argued that despite the rise to power of the global corporations; the fluid movement of media, people, and goods across borders; the growth of supranational institutions like the IMF and the UN; it has not been possible to overtake the nation-state. The nation remains the effective unit of economic, political and socio-cultural authority, even if now there are many forces struggling above it as well as a plurality of social and cultural differences that have opened up below it (Sinclair 2004:79). Initial fears that the increased movement of social groups taking place within a political context would lead to 'second world' nation-states to disappear, while international governmental organizations would flourish (Wilkins 2003:246), have proved unwarranted. Since the nation-state still has a role, the national media too is still of relevance, though in a different context.

Cosmopolitanism and national identity

Cosmopolitanism signifies a commitment to cosmopolis or world society, a celebration of global citizenship where identification and political engagement transgress national borders (Waisbord 2004:385; Oulasson 2007:67). The earlier theories on globalization closely linked the process to cultural imperialism, based on modernization theory's promise of rapid development and they tended to emphasize the trend towards cultural homogenization or "Americanization". Post modernist theorists like Arjun Appadurai rather emphasize the cultural fusion or "hybridity" that occurs as global influences become absorbed and adopted in a host of local settings, producing cultural heterogeneity (Sinclair 2004:66). It is therefore important to examine how globalization and cosmopolitan culture have affected national identities.

There is an on-going debate on whether cosmopolitan identity is replacing national identities. Proponents have pointed out that due to labour migrations, most of the world's developed countries are now diverse, multiethnic, and able to create global citizens. The analysis of the resultant hybrid identities, border communities and mobile or virtual populations are important examples of the impact of global communication not interpretable within a solely state-centric frame (Bramann 2003:115) or within national geographies. The massive increase in the movement of people across borders caused by globalization has increased the cultural and linguistic pluralism in each nation-state's populations, which are now less culturally homogenous than before (Sinclair 2004:72).

The anti-cosmopolitan groups have downplayed the impact of cosmopolitanism's threat to national identities. Anthony Smith (cited in Waisbord 2004:385) notes that cosmopolitanism or global culture lacks a "vital ingrained sense of historical experience, a sense of temporal continuity and shared memories." Tomlinson (1999:101) ably sums up global culture as being a "constructed" culture; it is historical, timeless, and memoryless, and is constructed out of various features which have nothing to bind people together in common integrated cultural experience.

Similarly, Waisbord (2004:384/5) argues that cosmopolitanism is devoid of common symbols and a shared history through which cultural cohesion could be possible. He also notes that cosmopolitanism lacks the institutionalization evidenced in national media, since global media are not designed to preserve common symbols and memories in order to sustain post-national sentiments. It is noted further that in contrast to national citizenship, cosmopolitanism does not offer social and political entitlements. Citizenship rights continue to be rooted in specific states. He acknowledges that although global communities exist like for sports, music fans, academics, religious groups etc. these do not appeal to historical or cultural bonds to have political recognition so they remain "imagined communities". Rather than eliminating individual and social identities, he contends, transnational cultures and identities add new layers to them, or the concentric circles of belonging and identity. Thus, he concludes that globalization has not offered group identities or cultural groupings that supersede national identities. Relating this to the East Africa region, while a protocol for cooperation in various areas has been signed, each country still retains its system of national identification like national identity cards and passports.

Together with developments in transportation, the media have emerged as a potential aid to cosmopolitanism by eliminating distance and offering a new global public sphere in which a cosmopolitan culture could be nurtured. (Waisbord 2004:385). This spatial displacement of mediated social relations and behavior has been described as "deterritorization" whereby migrants can receive news from their countries of origin, say from satellite TV, even when away from 'country home' (Sinclair 2004:67). So, much as media has been an influential factor in building cosmopolitanism, it is still a force in reinforcing national identities.

Computer mediated communication and online identities

In their study on the dynamics of computer mediated communication (CMC), Thurlow et.al. (2004:99) advance the notion that CMC offers liberation due to the relative anonymity, whereby an identity was no longer dependent on physical appearance. They saw the internet as giving opportunity for those whose voices had not been heard, including the marginalized and disenfranchised. Sherry Turkle (cited in Thurlow 2004:99) foresaw the great potential for people to reinvent themselves via CMC, and describes the computer as a "second self". She said that this gives an "online identity" as opposed to the real or "offline identity", explaining that;

> you can be whoever you want to be. You can completely redefine yourself if you want. You do not have to worry about the slots other people put you in, as much. They do not look at your body and make assumptions. They don't hear your accent and make assumptions. All they see are your words.

Thurlow et. al. (2004:97) posit that depending on the situation we are in, the people we are talking to, the stage of life we are at and the mood we are in, we choose to present or represent different aspects of ourselves. This implies that a person has multiple identities. As has been noted, to have feelings of belonging to a national community does not exclude simultaneous feelings of belonging to local or supranational formations (Waisbord 2004:384).

The concept of replacing roots with aerials tallies with the global communication environment, where we have technologized our lives to the point of their becoming unrecognizable (Downing 2007:8). These views are similar to Manuell Castells' concept of 'space of flows' where spatial location only matters in terms of the relation of a place to other locations in the patterns of global flow or the Network. In this 'power geometry', while physical location in space may matter less, location in social hierarchies, notably class and gender continue to be determinants (Sinclair 2004:68).

The evolution of media has decreased the significance of physical presence in the experience of people and events and the physically bounded spaces are now less significant as information is able to flow through walls to great distances. As a result of this permeability, where one is has less to do with what one knows and their experiences since electronic media have altered the significance of time and space for social interaction (Tomlinson 1999:154). These transformations in social relations have been facilitated by computer networks combined with mobile telephones, satellite broadcasting, with easier systems of storage and distribution of sound and pictures.

Communities can be physical or geographical and they can also be virtual communities that are not tied to a specific location, but all members of communities share a sense of belonging and togetherness. Correspondingly, we can have physical identity and virtual identities, which can be on-line. To Benedict Anderson (cited in Thurlow et. al. 2004:111), communities are not about numbers or places but about activities and feelings, all communities larger than the primordial villages of face-to-face contact are "imagined communities". Tracing developments in computer systems, Plant (2004:839) says that as the computers have moved from the military ware they were initially designed for, to desk tops, laptops, and pocket-size mobiles; they have lost their individual isolation to become a global web. This is through the e-mail connections, bulletin boards as well as multiple-user domains which compose the net.

From a gender perspective, Plant (2004:835) notes that although network culture is still dominated by men as well as masculine designs, women are accessing the circuits on which they were once exchanged and are discovering their own post-humanity. In her research on feminism, Luce Irigaray (cited in Plant 2004:836/8) submits that initially, the internet was an extension of the patriarchal system, or an economy in which women are treated as a commodity. In such a system, exchanges take place exclusively between fathers, husbands, brothers and sons and a woman was left without the sense of identity, which accrued to the masculine. Irigaray explains that it was out of the question then for the women to go to the market alone to profit from their own value or talk to each other without the control of the seller-buyer-cum-owner. With the advent of networks that need no centralized organization, the lines of commerce and communications have changed allowing women a relative degree of freedom. With computerized markets, she notes, women can now escape the isolation that they were subject to before as women can now access the "virtual markets" independently, just like the men.

Thurlow et al (2004:135) observe that CMC creates a space for women to air their concerns to the world. Women's organizations are trying to narrow the gender gap by building online communities to increase supportive dialogue, exchange of information and promote activism. In Uganda there are several women's online communities like the Women of Uganda Network (WOUGNET). Considering the very low internet penetration in most African countries and Uganda in particular of 5.6% and 2.4% respectively (World Internet Statistics 2009), the few online communities are still located largely in the urban centers. Elsewhere in the semi-urban and rural areas, people are mainly part of communities that access tele-centre facilities, internet cafes and community or citizens' media. There is also use of SMS_on mobile phones for circulating simple messages. The next section looks at ethnicity and community media.

Community media, ethnicity and conflict

Scholars like Jerry Muller (cited in Weinstein et. al. 2008) have argued that ethnic diversity tend to generate violent conflicts. Because some community media is set up by ethnic groups, there is a fear that such media will also be a source of conflict. However, this explanation has been discounted as a simplistic and hasty way to make sense of African conflicts (Ake 1993) as ethnic diversity is not always negative and will not always lead to conflicts.

There is an assumption that the task of nation-building calls for uniting all the forces in society, thus the ethnic diversity is seen as inherently negative and obstructive to successful nation-building and devel-opment (Okuku 2002:10/15). This is contrary to what Ake (1993) finds in his study on ethnicity in Africa. He notes that ethnic groups are often the major engine of development in rural Africa. He further submits that although Africa should not return to the past or stagnate in the present that promises no future, Africa must mobilize ethnic networks in the name of development, for "those who do not know who they are cannot really know where they are going."

Waisbord (2004:375) explains that, based on the complex and contradictory history of nations, nationalism can be equally associated with sentiments of human solidarity as well as with feelings of intolerance and exclusion. Thus nationalism remains ambiguous as it means different things to different people. The implication is that even the issue of ethnicity is complex and different groups have devised various means to cope or to express their ethnicity, including setting up community media. While the majority of community media are locally based, they nevertheless have internet connection, so they become both local and global (Lewis 2008:12). The penetration of localities which connectivity brings is thus double-edged. It dissolves the securities of locality and offers new understanding of experiences in wider global terms (Tomlison 1999:30).

Community media may sometimes be set up as a result of a group (which may be based on ethnicity) perception that national media are not catering for them adequately. The local or national in this context can include local commercial media or public service media. As Gumucio-Dagron (2004:44) notes, most of the social movements, their bids to advance their causes in the public sphere started their own community or alternative media.

In Uganda, similar to other developing countries, the community media or alternative media that is most widespread is community radio. Most districts in the country have at least an FM radio station, which often acts as community media. The radio gives listeners a sense of community and identity and creates action space for people to link with community power structures and access to resources (Megwa 2007:53). Community radio stations are not only started to serve minority rural communities. Urban communities often create their own means to express a culture that is suffering from "adaptation stress and deprivation" (Gumucio-Dagron, 2004:46). While there are a few cases when the community radio stations have been a source of ethnic conflicts, most of the time they have been used to mobilize people positively for development.

Looking at Central Broadcasting Service (CBS) FM radio, which is owned by the Buganda Kingdom, (Uganda's largest ethnic group) it used to broadcast in Luganda and had been used to reach both the elite and rural areas in the central region. The radio had several talk shows daily and two of the most popular public debates (*Ekimeeza*) that were broadcast live. *Parliament Yammwe* (Your Parliament) featured on Saturday mornings and *Mambo Bado* on Saturday afternoons. Both programs drew participants from both government and opposition parties, Baganda and non-Baganda ethnic groups.

Because of its immense influence and capacity to mobilise the subjects of the largest ethnic group (Baganda), CBS radio was sometimes seen as working against government and paying more loyalty to the Buganda kingdom. The radio being situated in Kampala, which is the country's administrative and commercial capital, brings together different ethnic groups, and this further enhanced its advantaged position. The radio has been used to sensitise people on various government programs like immunization campaigns and education of HIV infections. However, in some cases the radio has been used negatively.

On 12th July 2009, *The New Vision* (government paper) published an article on the *Kabaka* (King of Buganda). The article claimed that the Kabaka (King of Buganda) had mortgaged the kingdom's land title for a loan. CBS radio launched a media campaign calling on people not to buy *The New Vision* and a sister newspaper, *Bukedde*, which is published in Luganda. The CBS claimed that the Kabaka was being belittled and Baganda as an ethnic group were being marginalized. This created some tension and violence. Some people were beaten up when they were found reading the two papers. For the three weeks that the boycott lasted, sales figures for the two papers went down considerably (exact figures in the drop could not be disclosed due to tight competition in the media). The impasse was only settled when *The New Vision* made an apology.

Soon after this incident, on 11th September 2009, government prevented Kabaka from going to officiate at a youth function citing security reasons. CBS called on the Baganda to go out and provide security for their king. Several road blocks were mounted, where non-Baganda were harassed and prevented from passing resulting in ethnic clashes. In the ensuing riots, ten people were killed. The radio used tones likely to create ethnic conflict and violence and was subsequently closed along with three other radios broadcasting in Luganda - *Akabozi ku bbiri, Ssubi* and *Serpentia*. These latter 3 have since been re-opened, but CBS remains closed.

Commenting on the closure of the radio stations, President Museveni said that "some of the radios had made it a habit to promote genocide like Rwanda's Radio Mille Collines did in 1994. Like the day we closed CBS, they were promoting insurrection; telling people to take up *pangas* and fight ... you who are working in the media collectively have got a duty to enjoy your rights. But you have to respect the rights of others. You have no right to promote positions which are injurious to the rights of other people" (*Sunday Vision*, 18 October 2009:9).

This scenario shows 2 differing interpretations of allegiance or nationalism. It was a test of who the Baganda ethnic group owed more loyalty—their king/Buganda or the nation/Uganda. The government and Broadcasting Council's priority was on national unity so the calls to Baganda to support the Kabaka's position were seen as divisive and anti-nationalistic. On the other hand, CBS radio considered loyalty to Buganda kingdom as paramount so used the kingdom's radio to rally support for the king. Among conditions government has given for re-opening, is that the radio makes an apology and acknowledges responsibility for deaths and property lost during the riots. However, CBS radio remains adamant claiming it was not the one responsible but government that in the first place prevented Kabaka from making the visit.

The influence such community radios have on their communities, including ethnic groups, should not be underestimated. These radios can be used positively to facilitate participatory communication that enhances group identification and one's sense of belonging. Such community media allow for cultural expression, community discussion, and facilitate political engagement (AMARC 2003). However, they can also be used to fan ethnic violence as happened during the riots when people were killed and property was destroyed. Media thus have to be very mindful of the consequences of their reports especially in times of tension and conflict when emotions are high and irresponsible media reports can spark off ethnic violence. The media reports should be geared towards peace journalism and should be balanced, rather than stressing exclusion of some ethnic groups. So community media can contribute positively to peace and nationalism, but they can also be misused to de-stabilize the country by fuelling ethnic conflicts. It would thus be a misconception to view ethnicity negatively as a cause for conflicts always.

From their study on Uganda, where Weinstein et al (2008) investigated the relationship between ethnicity and conflict, they recommend that rather than separating groups as a strategy for mitigating the corrosive effects of ethnic divisions, it would be far more important to invest in creating impartial and credible state institutions that facilitate cooperation across ethnic lines. With such institutions in place, citizens would no longer need to rely disproportionately on ethnic networks in the marketplace and in politics (Weinstein et.al 2008).

The Public Service Broadcaster (PSB) can be categorized as such a state/public institution where all ethnic groups would benefit if reform is made for it to function as a true public media that caters for the public good.

Is Public Service Broadcasting in Uganda still of relevance?

UBC Radio and UBC TV are Uganda's public broadcast stations or national broadcasters. Like in other developing countries, these have largely been used as uni-directional communication channels from government to the masses. The *National Electronic Media Performance Study* (2004:58) found that these stations had become mouth-pieces of government instead of playing the role of public broadcaster. With the existing media pluralism in Uganda, the private/commercial media is now dominating the media industry and people have more media outlets (local and global) to choose from. The national broadcasters no longer have a monopoly of the national audience they had before the liberalization, so they have to compete with other media. The government deregulation and increased concentration of ownership have created a powerful economic incentive to ignore local programming needs (Jonson & Menichelli: undated).

In his discussion on democracy and belonging in Africa, Nyamnjoh (2009:74) submits that inclusion, not exclusion is the best insurance policy under the global consumer capitalism that individuals are subjected to. He challenges the media to capture the spirit of tolerance and negotiation beneath differences as the way forward in an increasingly interconnected world of individuals and groups who long for recognition and representation. His observation is very much applicable to the PSB in Uganda that should work towards inclusion of the interests of the various ethnic groups.

Within the context of changed utility of PSB, critics have argued that it is no longer reasonable to require people to pay PSB licensing fee. They argue that this curbs the individual consumer's choice and allege that through such financing, PSB is given unfair advantage over other media. Moreover, they further argue, these systems that were created in an age of spectrum scarcity have been rendered redundant by the increased abundant channels. However, others like Murdock have countered these arguments contending that such pessimism is misplaced and submit that PSB is a project whose time has finally come. He argues that rethinking PSB is essential given the centrality of broadcasting to contemporary cultural life. The core rationale for PSB lies in its commitment to providing the cultural resources required for full citizenship (Murdock 2005:213). PSB is also viewed as a solution to counteract the negative forces resulting from market-driven media and globalization forces (Wurff 2007:110).

Conclusion

Although several ethnic communities have established their own media, these media do not serve or cater for all individuals, so national media still has a role to fulfill. As Stewart Hall (cited in Waisbord 2004:384) observes "the national" remains a primary form through which cultural identity and difference are maintained in the contemporary world, adding that nations have a future as long as human groups require a basis to establish unity and difference from others, and as far as group identity is based on aspects of inclusion and exclusion. Thus Uganda cannot afford to relegate the national media to the backseat. There is need to revamp the UBC Radio and UBC TV as tools for enhancing the national identification process. The ethnic-based community media should also be utilized for facilitating peaceful ethnic co-existence premised on the principle of respect for ethnic diversity as well as freedom of cultural expression. Ultimately, the national media and community media will succeed in creating the sense of national identity that fosters a conducive environment for overall national development.

References

Ake, C. (1993). "What is the Problem of Ethnicity in Africa?" *Transformation* 22 (1993). Accessed 21 October 2009
http://www.transformation.und.ac.za/archive/tran022/tran022002.pdf

AMARC, (2003 June 2). "Draft Declaration and Draft Action Plan," Document WSIS/PC-3/CONTR/107-E. Accessed 10 August 2009
www.itu.int/dms_pub/itu-s/md/03/wsispc3/c/S03-WSISPC3-C-0107!!PDF-E.pdf

Braman, S. (2003). "From the Modern to the Post-modern: The Future of Global Communications Theory and Research in a Pandemonic age," In Mody, B. (ed) *International Development Communication. A 21st Perspective.* Thousand Oaks: Sage, pp 109-125.

Dennis E.E. (1991). "The Media are Quite Powerful" in Denis E.E. & Merril, C.J. *Media Debates: Issues in Mass Communication.* New York: Longman.

Downing, J. (2007). Grassroots Media: Establishing Priorities for the Years Ahead (Electronic version). *Global Media Journal – Australian Edition*, 1(1), 1-16.

Golding, P. & Murdock, G. (1997). "Ideology and the Mass Media: The Question of Determination" In Peter Golding & Graham Murdock (eds) *The Political Economy of the Media* Vol.I. Cheltenham: Edward Elgar Publishers, pp. 465-475.

Gumucio-Dagron, A. (2001). *Making Waves: Stories of Participatory Communication for Social Change* (Electronic version), New York: Rockefeller Foundation.

Gumucio-Dagron, A. (2004). "The Long and Winding Road of Alternative Media" In Downing, J., McQuail, D., Schlesinger, P. & Wartella, E. (eds) *Sage Handbook of Media Studies.* Thousand Oaks: Sage, pp. 41-65.

Hoijer, B. (2007). "A Socio-cognitive Perspective on Ideological Horizons in Meaning-making" In Hoijer, B. *Ideological Horizons in Media and Citizen Discourses. Theoretical and Methodological Approaches.* Gottenberg: NORDICOM, pp 33-57.

Interview of the Week: Anyone Torturing Ugandans will be Punished Severely, *Sunday Vision* 18 October 2009.

Johnson, F. & Menichelli, K. *(undated).* "What is Going on in Community Media" University of Massachusetts, Boston. Accessed on 14 August 2009 http://www.benton.org/benton_files/CMReport.pdf.

Kurian, S. & Thomas, G. (1992). *Encyclopedia of the Third World,* fourth edition, volume III, Facts on File: New York, pp. 2009-2010.

Lewis, P. (2009). "Council of Europe Report on Promoting social cohesion. The role of community media." Accessed 10 August 2009. http://www.coe.int/t/dghl/standardsetting/media/MC-S-MD/H-Inf(2008)013_en.pdf

McQuail, D. (1997). *Audience Analysis,* California: Sage.

Megwa, E. R. (2007). "Community Radio Stations as Community Technology Centres: An Evaluation of the Development Impact of Technological Hybridization on Stakeholder Communities in South Africa." *Journal of Radio Studies* 14(1), pp. 49-66.

Murdock, G. (2005). "Building the Digital Commons: Public Service Broadcasting in the Age of the Internet" In Lowe, F.G. & Jauert, P. (eds)

Cultural Dilemmas in Public Service Broadcasting, Gotenborg: NORDICOM, pp. 213-230.

National Electronic Media Performance Study (2004). Uganda Broadcasting Council: Kampala.

Nyamnjoh, F.B. (2009). "Africa's Media: Democracy and Belonging" In Njogu, K. & Middleton, J. (eds) *Media and Identity in Africa*, Edinburgh: Edinburgh University Press, pp. 62-75.

Olausson, U. (2007). "The Ideological Horizons of Citizenship, National Media as Discursive Bridge" In Hoijer, B. (ed) *Ideological Horizons in Media and Citizen Discourses: Theoretical and Methodological Approaches.* Gottenborg: NORDICOM, pp. 51-74.

Okuku, J. (2002). *Ethnicity, State Power and the Democratisation Process in Uganda.* Uppsala: Nordic African Institute..

Plant, S. (2004). "On the Matrix: Cyberfeminist Simulations" In P. Marris & S. Thornham (Eds.) *Media studies: A reader.* Edinburgh: Edinburgh University Press, pp. 835-849.

Sinclair, J.: (2004). "Globalization, Supranational Institutions and Media" In Downing, J., McQuail, D., Schlesinger, P. & Wartella, E. (eds) *Sage Handbook of Media Studies.* Thousand Oaks, Sage, pp. 65-83.

Thurlow, C., Lengel, L. & Tomic, A (2004). *Computer Mediated Communication, Social Interaction and the Internet.* London: Sage.

Tomlinson, J. (1999). *Globalisation and Culture.* Chicago: University of Chicago Press.

Uganda Communications Commission http://www.ucc.co.ug/spectrum/RadioTVStationsInUganda28Feb2009.pdf, Accessed 14 August 2009.

Uganda Ethnic Groups, *Encyclopedia of the Nations*, Accessed 14 August 2009 http://www.nationsencyclopedia.com/Africa/Uganda-ETHNIC-GROUPS.html

Waisbord, S. (2004). "Media and the Reinvention of the Nation" In Downing, J. McQuail, D. Schlesinger, P. & Wartella, E. (eds) *Sage Handbook of Media Studies.* Thousand Oaks: Sage, pp. 375-393.

Weinstein, J.M., Habyarimana, A., Humphreys, M. & Posner, D. (2008). "Is Ethnic Conflict Inevitable? Parting Ways over Nationalism and Separatism." CISAC Publications. http://cisac.stanford.edu/publications/is_ethnic_conflict_inevitable_parting_ways_over_nationalism_and_separatism/ accessed 14 August 2009.

Wilkins, K.G. (2003). "International Development Communication: Proposing a Research Agenda for a New Era" In Mody, B. (ed) *International Development Communication. A 21ˢᵗ Perspective.* Thousand Oaks: Sage, pp. 245-260.

World Internet Usage Statistics. (2009). Internet Usage and Population Statistics. www.internetworldstats.com, Accessed 14 August 2009.

Wurff, R.V. (2007). "Focus on Audiences: Public Service Media in the Market Place" In Lowe, F. & Bardoel, J. (eds) *From Public Service Broadcasting to Public Service Media.* Gotenborg: NORDICOM, pp. 105-118.

Ethnic Diversity Background and Issues: The Case of Rwanda

James Vuningoma

Introduction

It is impossible to deal with the ethnic diversity issues after genocide in Rwanda in 1994 without considering historical flash backs that could shed some light and indicate what characterised the country at its different stages of state formation. It is in that history that one sees the social, political and economic developments and the evolution of social diversity which Rwanda still enjoys today.

Social scientists have, among others, carried out extensive research on the origins of people and their final settlements in areas they call home. The ultimate findings indicate the birth of nations and nation-states. They have raised questions of the origins, migration trends, affinities, attitudes of the people as they move to settle and these have later informed future researchers and readers. It is on the basis of this experience that scientists, archaeologists, anthropologists, travellers and early missionaries have used now and then the vocabulary and familiar terms of race, ethnicity, ethnic group, tribe and clan to describe societies they "discovered". But societies had their own names and their own organisations. A case in point is ancient Rwanda which for centuries used the term "Ubgoko" and its plural form "Amoko" to describe the people who constituted Rwandan society.

With the scramble and partitioning of Africa at the 1884 Berlin Conference, the "newly found lands" were reshaped and people were described differently, given the time and its context. For example, new terms and labels were coined to describe communities. When new seeds emphasising the differences are planted and watered, they produce a new society different from the one people knew. The terms would carry emotive charges and bear aspects of rejection of another and generally hide anger and hate of the person seen as different. These newly imported terms were used, interiorized and even accepted as the new way of seeing oneself. It was the beginning of the politics of divide and rule. Rwanda has not been an exception to this imposed colonial reality.

As a country, Rwanda has had a history of migrations over several centuries. It has had a history of peopling Rwanda and eventual expansion of the Kingdom of Rwanda. It has also known the official history of being explored and being ushered in the colonial history as the newly "found land" by travellers, missionaries and subsequent colonial masters. The history of contact with Germany first and Belgium second tells it all.[1]

This chapter seeks to present an overview of the political and social construction of Rwanda before the country met the West. It will further present the experience of contact and cultural clash the contact provoked while the colonial system became busy deconstructing and destroying values on which Rwanda was built. The consequences of divisionism and promotion of ethnic ideology will explain the divisiveness between Abahutu, Abatutsi, and Abatwa. Later the chapter will highlight the current efforts Rwanda has undertaken to reconstruct the nation by trying to heal the wounds of divisionism as a direct consequence of the past bad political leadership of colonial and post independence periods but above all deal with the pressing issues as a result of the genocide of Batutsi in 1994.

The construction of a nation: an overview of Rwanda before colonization

> ".... Rwanda, like Buganda, Burundi and other kingdoms is the result of the political and cultural construction both of which allow us to reaffirm the existence of an old "people's nation" (…) The paradox of the Rwandan society is not surely the existence of some sort of pluriethnic unity but the continued hereditary cleavage, which is felt for centuries despite a remarkable cultural unity." [2]

For too long a culture of oral tradition has been a powerful tool of communication relating to the myths of origin and how Rwanda was peopled. In the recent past such myths as they are told, are taken as historical truths. In Rwanda's myths of existence, we learn that the origin of Rwandans emanates around two persons: Kigwa and Gihanga. According to the recent research we can distinguish through the following tales:

> The birth of Kigwa in the world beyond marks the beginning of the tale (the founding myth). On Kigwa's arrival on earth with his companions, the Bimanuka, they introduced seeds, fire wood-carving, tanning and hunting. Kigwa and his group are at the root of various clans in Rwanda.[3]

We are also told of the birth and life of Gihanga, the Kingdom's founder. The story goes further to show Gihanga with many faces: He reflects his father

Kigwa as a civilising hero, son of a blacksmith and a blacksmith himself. He is known to be skilful in wood-carving and tanning.

In Benjamin Sehene (1999) we are told:

> "I was born in Kigali in 1959 from Batutsi parents. My father, son of Ruhezamihigo from Nyabugogo village belonged to the Singa clan. According to the oral tradition he was related to the Renge predecessors of Bahutu and Batutsi linked to Gihanga, mythical founder of Rwanda's dynasty (…). According to the legend, Gihanga is the father of the three ancestors of Banyarwanda: Gatwa is the ancestor of Twas, Gahutu is the ancestor of Hutus and Gatutsi is the ancestor of Tutsi.[4]

References of this nature are common to many Banyarwanda be they Batutsi, Bahutu, or Batwa. However, this is not limited to Banyarwanda. Take the case of the founding myth of the Baganda who refer to their origin from Kintu who also descended from heaven. Early ethnological studies ignored such founding myths from which the king could legitimate the will to rule and encourage people to participate in different activities under his leadership. The observation closer to reality is captured in the words of Sehene when he says:

> "The ancient Kingdom of Rwanda, had social structures built on three classes which fulfilled functions based on different roles in terms of principal economic activities, namely animal husbandry and agriculture. Cattle stood as the baseline and reference to wealth. The notables and most cattle keepers were recruited among the Batutsi. Some Chiefs and a majority of the peasants were Bahutu whereas the Batwa kept the role of hunters and *cueilleurs*. The social mobility, however, remained open and intermarriages wiped out class distinctions. From what is known as "*kwihutura*" a Hutu who had several cows and got married to a Mututsi woman became a Mututsi. Likewise, a poor Mututsi who did not have cows and became a cultivator and got married to a Muhutu woman, he became a Muhutu."[5]

Sehene's observations describe pre-colonial Rwanda and he goes on to say, "if the notion of ethnicity already existed, there wasn't any rigid racial divisions as they would appear later in Rwandan society."[6] To that socio-economic reality there was a political reality where the king considered Banyarwanda as his people and in who he recognised competencies and skills and was called to serve the kingdom without discrimination. The king had direct deputies who served as the Council for consultative purposes. He delegated powers to Umutware w'Ingabo, the head of the Army, Umutware w'Ubutaka, the Chief of the Land and Umutware w'Umukenke, the Chief of Pastures. There were other norms and values which were identified as ingredients of unity, a cement that strongly connected and built Banyarwanda to live together by looking at what they did rather than what they were; cherished what held them together rather than what divided them. Among them we note the spiritual belief of protection of *Imana y'I Rwanda yirirwa ahandi igataha I Rwanda* (God spends the rest of the day elsewhere but comes back to Rwanda at the sun set). Banyarwanda speak one language, Kinyarwanda and share the same culture. They live together yesterday like today; there is no land for Batutsi, no separate land for Abahutu and no land which is separate for Abatwa. There is land for Abanyarwanda.

Briefly, all the tales of myths of origin indicate the essence of social-political organization of the Kingdom of Rwanda. They legitimate the basis of an organized monarchy and highlight the social-economic and political order of things. The same cultural values and will to live together despite the Banyarwanda's diversity indicate the power behind the construction of Rwanda. The meanings and lessons learnt from such tales indicate a country of Banyarwanda with a sense of belonging to one monarchy. They refer to the construction and reinforcement of the organized kingdom and the unity of one people.

Deconstructing of monarchical order as colonialism takes over

Rwanda had a double fold colonial experience. First came the German colonial era (1885-1919)[7] followed later by the prolonged Belgian Trusteeship over Rwanda, (1916-1962).[8] The colonial experience was dominated by the interpretation and reinterpretation of monarchical history of Rwanda as the country was turned into a new image as colonial masters understood it. Both colonial masters maintained the pre-colonial monarchy each trying to make do with it. Germans found a strong organized monarchy. The sense of unity in diversity existed and people lived harmoniously. The sense of self protection, defence of the monarchy and rising as one when life was in danger were all signs that led the Germans to prefer working closely with the King. The Belgians came after the First World War which saw Germans out of the colonial business in Rwanda.

The experience of contact with colonial masters like elsewhere in Africa demonstrates that indigenous people were relegated to lower citizenship and the entire power lay in the hands of the master. It is him who picked anyone he wanted among the colonized peoples to execute his will and colonial interests were paramount. After realizing that the Kingdom of Rwanda was well organized in structure, the colonial master could only build his own power by getting the King, and the rest would follow. King Musinga was not allowed to retain strong powers as any other Kings used to have before the colonial era. From 1917, King Musinga had his prerogatives and powers curtailed.

The down fall of King Musinga is seen from the progressive dismantling of the monarchy: from a real monarchy to a nominal monarchy (1917-1931),"[9] especially under Belgian military occupation (1919-1926). In 1917 "one of the first measures undertaken by the Royal Commissioner, in agreement with the Belgian Government, was to strip the indigenous sovereigns from their unconditional right over the life and the goods of their subjects. This *"ius gladii"* (sword right) was reserved for the King of Belgium. The King remained an honorary title only. Other measures taken were the declaration of religious freedom in favour of the catholic church (1917). Traditionally, the King had the highest integrity; his decisions were always right and beneficial and his judgement was without appeal. In 1922, the undermining of the King's legal power was executed. It was decided that the King would be assisted in his legal prerogatives by the delegate of the Resident at Nyanza. Then came the limitation on the nomination of political appointees (1923) where King Musinga was notified of the prohibition to appoint or revoke chiefs, notables and heads of provinces without prior consultations with the Resident. Lastly, came the abolition of *ubwiru* and *umuganura* (first harvest festival) institutions in 1925. King Musinga was a king without a kingdom and any form of resistance to what was said and done would be interpreted as a rebellious attitude against the too powerful colonial rule. His dethronement and subsequent exile to Kamembe in 1931 was a strong message to warn the traditional ruling elite.

Reading Rwanda's attitudes and mentality and having carefully observed the traditions of the Kingdom, Belgians chose to enthrone King Mutara III Rudahigwa who was thought to be responsive. The coming of King Mutara Rudahigwa showed how much colonial masters feared going it alone but preferred to work closely with the institution of the monarchy. By this time it became easy for the colonial power to envision Ruanda-Urundi as part of an administrative structure attached to the Congo, a Belgian colony. In line with this evolution, we note the introduction and reinforcement of christian culture to the detriment of the cultural identity. According to Rev. Brard, "Missionaries had nothing good to expect from a Rwandese. That is why they did everything to abolish his practices and beliefs and to create another religious identity."[10] Then came education with church schools. It is from this early breed that was born the new class known as *evolue*. On the economic front, money was introduced as an economic yardstick to transact business. All these influenced the indigenous colonized peoples and obliged them to operate with the new changes. They had to consider the new order as a reality. There was no visible resistance to this power of occupation.

The reading and interpretation of socio-political landscape of Rwanda went hand in hand with the undermining and sapping of the King's power. The introduction of the identity cards, labelled Hutu, Tutsi and Twa, marked the beginning of seeing Banyarwanda in terms of social groups which came to be labelled as three distinct ethnic groups. The establishment of identity cards formalized the division of Banyarwanda, thus paralysing the once unified society.

The theories of Bahutu being of Bantu origin, Batutsi being of Hamitic origin and the Batwa as pygmoid, led to the perpetuation of ethnic stereotyping. With time people went to schools and joined churches and learned they were Bahutu, Batutsi and Batwa. The notion of being Munyarwanda had started dying slowly. The people's consciousness was attacked and Rwandans started adopting the colonial reading of themselves. They became the victims of that early divisionism. The identity of being one, the dignity of being Munyarwanda died slowly leaving space for the evolution of a colonial mentality among Banyarwanda.

The second colonial reading of Rwanda was the interpretation of monarchical institutions of Rwanda. The distortion lay in the reinterpretation of the words *ubuhake, ubukode, ubudehe,* which used to determine social relationships among Banyarwanda but were described during the colonial era as symbols and forms of exploitation by one group against another. The effect of this divide and rule strategy was to split a one united people. Furthermore, the colonial power by using Batutsi elite as colonial officials to reinforce unpopular colonial measures such as taxation, forced labour, and exertion of pressure to grow cash crops led the Batutsi elite to be seen as collaborators in colonial crime. By giving them preference and access to education and other colonial benefits such as posts, the consciousness of injustice increased and further widened the gap between Bahutu and Batutsi. Later, as we shall see, the Bahutu elite used the divide as an argument to pinpoint at Batutsi as the source of their troubles. This situation gave the impression that Batutsi and Bahutu were different peoples. The Batwa remained aside of the majority society; marginalised.

As the erosion of traditional power continued, the colonial power gained political momentum, thanks to the establishment of colonial institutions. Until 1950, the Belgian rule had assembled a highly authoritarian rule and a centralized administrative structure which touched all sectors of life. The dual colonial enterprise between the Catholic Church and colonial politics worked unhampered. The consecration of Rwanda to Christ—*Christu Umwami Ingoma yawe yogere hose*—by the King indicated a new mentality among Banyarwanda who became Catholics. Later other religions and denominations opened their doors. We should remember that in this context the undermining of traditional power from the King went on until the abolition of the monarchy in 1959 and the establishment of the republic in 1962.

Disconnecting with the past

> "From now on words did not have the same meaning and relations became simply and purely those of class, taking over slowly ancient feudal relationships. The specificity of this is that it was based on racial differences".[11]

To begin with, people who in the past called themselves Banyarwanda, began seeing themselves as Batutsi; the privileged Bahutu; the underprivileged; the exploited but numerically many. This was the beginning of the words "majority -vs- minority". The ethnic identity as a term became rampant in colonial language and Batutsi, Bahutu, Batwa meant simply and purely three ethnic groups who peopled Rwanda at different times. In other words people who shared by nature everything: culture, spiritual beliefs, a common language Kinyarwanda and taboos, became "ethnic groups" now institutionalised as different.

One observable experience of the time was for Rwandans to slowly get used to the new order of things. This is the logic of a conquered people subjected to the erosion of the traditional way of life and are powerless. They were unable to resist hence the acceptance of the colonial reality leading to the development of a colonial mentality and the erosion of national pride. The power of occupation was double fold: political power in the hands of Belgium while spiritual power was exclusively entrusted to the catholic church. Rwandans participated at both levels at different times. The colonial power used Tutsi Chiefs and Clerks for colonial administration who diligently fulfilled colonial objectives even when, to the indigenous, these were questionable. Rwandans knew that they were like any other colonized

Africans. Colonial power was paramount and one had to be with it or not with it and bear the consequences. Those who worked and became closer climbed on the colonial bandwagon and shared work and the responsibility and certainly some benefited from whatever was offered by the new order including employment, education, and welfare.

The Batutsi who were in power during the Kingdom era came to be preferred and were retained by the new power; they were enrolled and carried on. The execution of the colonial will by the Batutsi elite became, at a later stage, a charge against them by Bahutu elite who put them in the collaborative role by accusing them of being the root cause of their problems. Strangely, the same elite did not seem to see anything wrong in the detestful colonial rule. Poor Banyarwanda remained onlookers and watched the game of the colonised elite quarrelling over the remains of the colonial cake. Hence the slow growth of the culture of resignation and the mentality of non-commitment mentality often referred to as *ntibindeba or ntibinturukeho*. This *laisser faire* mentality was a terrible development leading to the alienation of Rwandans.

The continued choice of identifying oneself with colonial images through benefits of work, education, health, and christianity led to the forging of a new Rwandan divorced with the past and obliged to navigate in a colonial ship whose destination was unknown.

The triumph and trap of ethnic ideology

For political reasons and a strong need to plan ahead and take power at the advent of a weakened colonialism, Batutsi, Bahutu and Batwa came to be organized in political parties and started the race to Independence. That political struggle for power was characterized by the urgency of self determination against a background of a poisoned history of existence packed with wrong interpretation of Rwanda's history, and a distorted cultural identity.

> "At (sic) the eve of independence, the Rwandan elite (elites and counter elites) had re-interpreted the founding myths of the country and its history as transmitted through the deforming prism of Hamitic and Bantu myths. The Hutu leaders opposed the nationalist movement that requested the departure of the Belgians and insisted on "the end of the black Hamitic colonizers yoke", the emancipation of the majority Hutu; while the extremists were calling for the Tutsi to go back to Abyssinia. The publication of this racial theory was carried out by colonizers and

missionaries before independence. It was taught in schools and disseminated through political speeches."[12]

During the 1950's four developments characterized the period which saw the rising of radicalism in the country. The first was the King's realization that things were going wrong and his people had been divided and, worse, the claims of rights were now high on the agenda.

King Mutara III Rudahigwa participated in the administration of the country with the help of the *Conseil Supérieur du Pays* which had limited powers. Through this remaining voice, despite the limitations and cracks in the already weak traditional power, the King was awakened by the increasing demands. He knew the division between Batutsi and Bahutu; he knew the exploitation of the card of ethnicity that drew apart the two social categories symbolising the cheater and the cheated, the exploiter and the exploited. This reading of the social-political history continued and in 1959 it reached a transformative stage. The King had tried to reduce the level of inequality through a system called *ukugabana ubutaka* or sharing the land. He had seen that he could use colonial power and its loopholes to introduce changes and lead the country to relative peace. This move was not in the interest of colonialists and that is how the King could not be allowed to realise his objectives. The unresolved question surrounding his death left the country in disarray.

Second, new associations around economic, social, cultural and religious initiatives were mushrooming. Many of them were organized around ethnic lines predicting the rise of further claims and possibly widening the gap even further between Abatutsi and Abahutu. Third, this is the period when most of the colonized countries were getting organized following the rise of Pan-African aspirations for self-determination and eventual independence. Rwanda was part of this process.

Fourth, the colonial power and the Catholic Church were aware of this evolution. They were ready to change the guard:

> "When the struggle for independence started in Africa, Rwandan leaders in power also started thinking about independence, which provoked a change of alliance by the colonizers. The latter decided to work with the Hutu. The Hutu were then sensitised on the oppression they underwent during the Tutsi rule. Around 1957, the Hutu elite with the support of their new allies exploited this theory and rallied many Hutus to the recurring massacres against Tutsis who were considered as invaders

and oppressors. The Rwandan politicians who took over after independence used this distorted history to divide, manipulate and mislead Rwandans in a series of conflicts that culminated in the 1994 genocide that saw the death of over a million Rwandans.[13]

The pro King political party, *Union Nationale Rwandaise* (UNAR), which claimed the pursuit of self determination to the point of antagonizing the colonial might led the colonial power and the powerful Catholic Church to change the alliance in the hope that they will have more time to continue with their colonial agenda. By shifting from the Tutsi elite to Hutu elite spearheaded by Grégoire Kayibanda the game of ethnicity was now full swing and the widening gap between Abatutsi and Abahutu was irreversible. The Abatwa surfaced through *Association pour le Relèvement des BATWA* (AREDETWA) but they never influenced the new political environment.

Any analyst of the Rwandan socio-political history would see that all Rwandans operated under colonial rule and all suffered differently the effects of the politics of divide and rule. Whether one was used to serving colonial interests or one suffered the yoke of it, the common denominator of that suffering was that all Rwandans were colonized and their being, together with their values, were diluted and replaced slowly by others.

Between 1959 and 1962, Rwanda embarked on a new unprepared democratic experience. Political parties were born. These major developments of the time showed ethnic divisions, rivalries and conflicts. Civil society associations were formed; they became politicized and highly partisan. Rwanda was now divided into two camps, the first camp was composed of *Parti du Mouvement pour l' Emancipation Hutu* (PARMEHUTU) and *Association pour le Progres Social de la Masse* (APROSOMA) exclusively for Hutu political elite ready to claim rights for all Bahutu, even for those who didn't know what was happening. This camp had the blessing of the colonial administration and the weight of the Catholic Church was assured. The second camp was comprised of UNAR with the major component of the Tutsi political elite and Bahutu who for a long time had served and remained loyal to the King. Many Batwa were in this camp. The political picture was clear. Society was paralysed by the ensuing power struggle *but* underneath divisionism and sectarian ideology progressively took over.

The camp of Mbonyumutwa-Grégoire Kayibanda took upon itself the political claim of being social revolutionalists rejecting the monarchy and all the associates. Fights and massacres broke out in 1959 and peace was no more in Rwanda. In his book *L'Afrique Aux Africains,* Pierre Biarnes describes

Rwanda as "the Republic of the Bahutu"[14] while thousands of Batutsi, Bahutu and Batwa went into exile.

The first and second Republics in Rwanda (1962-1994)

The First Republic led Rwanda to independence celebrated on 1/7/1962 under close supervision of Guy Logiest and Mgr. Andre Perraudin. Rwanda had had a disastrous turn of events with the Bahutu being referred to as "*Rubandanyamwinshi*" to legitimate and hammer in Rwanda the politics of hate, divisionism and exclusion. The section of Banyarwanda who at different stages fled the country were labelled as minority, *inyangarwanda* (those who hate their mother land), *inyenzi* (cockroaches), *inzoka* (snakes). The politics of hate, divisionism and exclusion, continued hand in hand with the political discourse of exclusion and dehumanization with extreme virulent dose of hate to the others. Conflict is natural but when violence is allowed and explodes, then the worst can be expected. That is what happened in Rwanda. Killing, violations of all forms of human rights were allowed and backed by in-coming powers. Worse, anyone who remained in Rwanda and was suspected of connivance with refugees was exposed to inhuman treatment. Civil rights to the non "*rubandanyamwinshi*" camp were denied; more so when the identity card read Tutsi.

President Mbonyumutwa became the first to lead the "Bahutu Republic" but for a short period. President Gregoire Kayibanda who took over after him is renown for his radicalism and his reign of power is remembered for having left behind a culture of hatred, fear, suspicion and segregation.

Gregoire Kayibanda became the first republican dictator in Rwanda. Under him all Batutsi, even those suspected to resemble them, lost rights. When he had silenced the Batutsi, he became suspicious of the Bahutu from the North (Abashiru and Abagoyi). The politics of exclusion was no longer limited to Batutsi but included sections of the Bahutu too. The question of ethnicity as a factor for political alliance did not count any more. Kayibanda's suspicion that the Bahutu from the north wanted to take power from him led to their slow expulsion from close centers of power. The fear of the northerners led to political tension and he forgot Batutsi who were no longer a menace. In this political atmosphere there was no room for dialogue and debate on crucial issues of national concern. The list of those excluded kept rising and anything could happen.

In 1973 the mass killings indicated that society hid a violent conflict because of intolerance, greed and hatred. The same year a military coup d'etat led by the incoming President Juvenal Habyarimana marked the end of that Hutu north-south divide and tension among the Bahutu, between Abanyenduga vs Abashiru and Abagoyi.

The Second Republic was characterized by temporary peace and hope. This did not totally address all the issues which for a long time paralysed Rwandan society. The military coup d'etat led by the *Camarade du 5 Juillet* had some Banyarwanda killed, others thrown into prison; few managed to escape and joined several other Rwandese in exile.

Like his predecessor, President Habyarimana remained highly ethnic in his thinking and deeds. Furthermore, he did what Kayibanda had not managed to do: he cultivated the politics of regionalism (another form of exclusion) and established a quota system in education (the famous *"iringaniza"*). He reinforced "the Hutu ideology of *rubandanyamwinshi* by cultivating the culture of obedience and the cult of work said to be inherent to Bahutu."[15] Divisionism among the Bahutu of the north against those of the south widened the gap of the people once thought to be the same. Regionalism camouflaged a hatred of Batutsi since it hid aspects of discrimination and exclusion.

Impunity became rampant in the totalitarian rule of President Juvenal Habyarimana. Opposition political parties were not allowed and if any of such voices came up they were considered as traitors. Mr. Habyarimana was in good books with donors and at one time in 1990 at a Francophone Summit in La Baule, President Francois Mitterand of France described President Habyarimana and Rwanda as a good democratic example for others to emulate. What the Rwanda of Habyarimana hid to many was the development of a system of ethnic-military dictatorship which had never been there before. Speeches and political language of the time indicate the irreversible system of hate against Batutsi and the hidden determination to divide the Bahutu for political gains limited to Abashiru and Abagoyi.

Internal struggles for more political space and the pressure exerted by Rwanda Patriotic Front (RPF), a political front for Rwandese in exile, obliged President Juvenal Habyarimana to reconsider his hard-line position and admit to accommodate other political persuasions and expressions. It is against this background that the President ushered in political liberalization in the country by allowing the formation of political parties during the period (1990-1994). This period also saw the coming of the first human rights organizations.

The process of searching for solutions to end the ills in Rwandan society had now come to address issues related to the return of all Rwandan refugees and abolish all the causes of statelessness and insecurity. The aim was to pave the way for rebuilding the nation.

Genocide and challenges of rebuilding Rwanda: No easy walk to the reconstruction

"There are some who think that the Tutsi genocide ideology rose during a period of political crisis, when all Africans were claiming their right to independence from the colonizers and when Rwanda's Hutus, long excluded from the management of their country, found defensive means to get rid of their "old oppressors". Stereotypes that had been taught to Rwandans had created a "superiority complex" among Tutsis and an "inferiority complex" among Hutus, which persist in some quarters to this day. The systematic misrepresentation and exploitation of historic events by successive leaders certainly contributed to the intensification of hatred between the two main ethnic groups ultimately leading to genocide"[16]

The quotation above captures the content of what characterized the long standing issues of divisionism among Banyarwanda, the deliberate choice of anti-values accepted as new Rwandan values leading to the exacerbation of hatred and greed for power. This invariably led to a widening of the gap between communities and entrenchment of incomprehension and intolerance. As a consequence, social injustice became rampant and many Rwandans went into exile, while many others were killed by other Rwandans between 1959, 1962-63 and 1973. April 1994, was the height of the genocide in Rwanda.

Behind this culture of violence developed over several years back, there was bad governance. People were instructed to kill and they killed. They followed blindly all the directives without questioning the effects of their actions.

The interests of political and church leaders weighed high; thus downplaying national priorities which could have put Rwandans first. The preference of exclusion and hate of the other destroyed the country. Hutuism as the ideology of "*rubanda nyamwinshi*" destroyed nationalism in Rwanda. As a result of the leadership in both 1st and 2nd Republics and the cultivation of the politics of hate, sowing seeds of divisionism and segregation from which the detestful values became part of Rwandan norms, the worst was done and Rwanda reached a point of no return. While colonialism divided and disorganised Rwandan society and obliged them to live a completely different life, the post independence period divided and deconstructed society further and led Rwanda towards a path of *"democracie assistée"*. Many African countries at independence believed in Western democracy as a good alternative to govern the newly liberated countries. It is now known that Western experiences are not necessarily good for plural-ethnic societies in Africa. The climax of the unjust society led sons and daughters to take up arms with the political and military determination to influence the positive change with the hope of recovering peace and security. This was the beginning of the war of liberation led by Rwanda Patriotic Front and Rwandans inside the country tired of prolonged denial of citizenry rights.

The struggle to liberate Rwanda was driven by the determination to deal with several evils. How does one deal with the reconstruction of a country with disunited people full of hate, mistrust and above all suspicion of each other? Genocide had widened the gap between Abatutsi and Abahutu. The former see themselves as victims while the latter as the killers. The leadership after four months of genocide, which deprived Rwanda of over one million souls of Abatutsi, had a tough task to make choices that treated all Rwandans as one despite what had befallen the country. The aftermath of the 1994 genocide of Batutsi still shows seeds of suspicion of "the other". For example, when people are discussing it is not unusual to stop the conversation because an intruder has joined the group. The healing is slow but steady because of the will to overcome evil.

The Government of National Unity which gained power in July 1994 had first to take stock of the weaknesses and strengths that still existed. A destroyed society, torn apart and reduced to ashes, that was the heritage of the new Government. The challenges were many. President Pasteur Bizimungu backed by RPF liberators and other Rwandans embarked on what looked like an impossible task to put Rwanda on the map again. The issue of security and protection of those who could be saved featured high on the post genocide agenda. Putting together the different pieces of a torn and a devastated society was a difficult task to undertake. Several questions led to self examination; an exercise which took a whole year. What could explain the destruction of the society? Is it the divide between Bahutu and Batutsi? Is the struggle for political power an explanation to the loss of lives and property? Can the many years of division, conflict, service to colonial and church interests continue to serve as an explanation to what happed to the Rwandese? Has there been a long standing history of violence and exploitation that could explain the atrocities that happened to Batutsi? What happened in the minds of the destroyers of the nation?

Rwanda's social groups (Bahutu, Batutsi and Batwa) are part of that nation's diversity. They exist and it is a reality. To claim that genocide was possible because of the divide between the two major groups of Bahutu and Batutsi is not true. Genocide was possible because of continued bad leadership which lured people into the crime.

Social diversity is the wealth of the nation

"Amoko" were used as catalysts to commit the abominable crime. More than ever before, Rwanda recognizes that its social diversity is the wealth of the nation. What it lacks is self confidence; the rediscovery in itself of the lost dignity of a Munyarwanda. The long colonial and neo-colonial beliefs in post independence Rwanda have built attitudes to the point of believing that Rwanda's social groups are foreign to each other. Rwandans after genocide are faced with the imperative duty of working together and learning to live in peace and security because all have a common destiny. However, all is not well. Disturbingly, despite the 1994 genocide, some Rwandans still have the deadly ideology, the genocide ideology. The international community bound by the Geneva conventions related to this crime and which pronounced the historical words of NEVER AGAIN still continue to support negative forces.

Rwanda today is not a society where killings justify the affirmation of one's identity. Those days are gone. The challenges remain on how to deal with poverty and ignorance. For years now, Rwanda is counted among the developing countries. The country's trends of development show it, yet the mentality and attitudes send the picture of a society still struggling with itself. The level of education is low. The pyramid of education indicates the enrolment rate in primary schools to be over two million pupils while secondary schools enrolment stands at 288,000 students and only 44,000 in high education institutions. According to educationists, if the level of education is low, the few educated ones tend to be pulled down by the many who are not educated. Poverty complicates matters even further. These are among the challenges the government has to address. It has the political will to move Rwanda to prosperity and Rwandans are ready to move together in the pursuit and determination to realise a better future.

In Rwanda's Vision 2020, the guideline document on the Economic Development and Poverty Reduction Strategy 2008-2012 (EDPRS), fighting poverty, putting emphasis on quality education, making Rwanda an Information Communication Technology (ICT) hub and laying the ground to make Rwanda a knowledge based economy are some of the priorities to enhance development in Rwanda.

Evidently, the Government of Rwanda led by Paul Kagame, the President of the Republic of Rwanda since 2003, realizes that everything went wrong in the past because of bad leadership. The current leadership has encouraged the growth of democratic institutions to guide government business where all able and capable Rwandans participate. Laws have been put in place and the three levels of government, namely executive, legislature and judiciary, are functioning. Getting Rwandans to follow the law is an important stage towards the rule of law. People do not necessarily have to live together and accept each other but, their coexistence is facilitated by obedience to the laws which they respect. Previously, the rule of law has been missing in Rwanda's political culture. In the past, laws were imposed and people never took them seriously.

Currently, Rwanda is alive with political, economic and social debates. When a space for dialogue is created quite a lot is done in terms of sharing ideas. In a recent study conducted by the National Electoral Commission, Rwanda National Civic Education raised issues, for example, related to how Rwandans should be reflecting and referring to themselves through their own values. During the presentation of the book, proposed aspects of the Rwandan culture were shared. The new culture was to be characterized by such values of competition, courage, politeness, wisdom, telling the truth, sociability, patience, nationalism, good quality of work, to be reasonable and work with perseverance and reach the desired goal. These values were opened to discussion and debate. It was interesting to note that some participants were not ready to prescribe to the above mentioned values immediately because they had other values which they were following including religious ones.

Reflecting on their sad past, Rwandans are in the process of drawing positive cultural values in Rwandan tradition to help them distance themselves from negative colonial and modern values that tend to yield bad results in society. If we are looking at putting work first, and the tradition provides the example of "*Umuganda*", we adopt that. If we are looking for the expression of solidarity as a value, the tradition provides "*ubudehe*", we adopt that. To inculcate the spirit of supporting each other in good or bad times "*Girinka*" can be invoked and encouraged. This means that aspects of Rwanda's culture which were in the past denigrated and described as "negative, atavistic, backward, pagan" and indigenous practices not adaptable to modern life are now coming back because they have more potency to unite and reconcile Rwandans. Getting resources from Rwandan culture to unite people and reconcile them goes hand in hand with a whole range of proposed programmes for the development of the nation.

All the programmes call upon people to participate and own them. The politics of decentralization of political and economic power are aimed at making Rwandans participate in governance through decentralized structures. Power is given to the people through their elected council members. The National Electoral Commission is responsible for the electoral process in the country to ensure equity, transparency and discipline. To manage that important democratic activity, it conducts different levels of trainings, undertakes civic education and administers consultations and elections.

The Government of Rwanda has chosen the path of making Rwanda a human capital and a knowledge based economy relying first on its people: "*Akimuhana kaza imvura ihise*". Emphasizing improved education is one way of achieving future development plans which go hand in hand with training. The youth are very important and by putting emphasis on basic education the country looks at utilizing education as a way of combating ignorance. Lack of education played an important role in the genocide:

> "Because the genocide came as the culmination of a long process in which people were taught to hate one another and ultimately to commit this crime, we believe that through education we can also make sure that it never happens again."[17]

The current education process from basic education to higher education will certainly help Rwanda answer questions on how to reduce the high level of ignorance and eradicate poverty.

In 2003, Rwandans adopted a new constitution after three years of consultation and open debate. It guides the democratic experience of New Rwanda and remains the guarantor of security, peace, forward looking and fairness. The constitution gives all citizens an opportunity to set up political parties, enjoy freedom of expression and participate in the construction of the country. The national symbols of the new flag and the Court of Arms depict the current and new way of forging the new Nation out of the ashes of genocide. The making of the symbols attracted all Rwandans through an open competition not because there was money put on the good production but the pleasure one yields out of knowing that "I am a citizen and I am called upon and allowed to participate." This was important because it was inclusive; it was an antidote to the exclusion of the past.

Conclusion

> "Before, we had no conflicts here, people had cows; a Mututsi could be a Muhutu's cattle keeper, or vice versa... No illiterate Rwandan has ever caused these conflicts. Only the elite caused these problems. Why? Greed."[18]

The above words by a farmer summarises part of the problem but does not explain it all. In this chapter, we have tried to show the origin of the antagonism between the Bahutu and the Batutsi, the major social groups in Rwanda. We have brought to light their differences which are not based on ethnic antagonism as portrayed in the course of Rwanda's history but rather we have pointed at the entrenchment of the climate of suspicion between the two social groups as an outright consequence of the cultivation of ethnic ideology.

Since the late 1950's the cultivation of an ethnic virus which expanded and reached unimaginable proportions in 1959, 1963, 1973 drew two parallel paths: the set up of what Pierre Biarnes calls, in his book *L'Afrique aux Africains*, "La Republique des Hutus"[19] and Tutsis relegated to exile. That entertained ideology became, ever since, a part of life. It had people who believed in it, while others took it up because it served their immediate interests.

The manipulation of that ideology became possible in everyday life to the point where concepts of "Hutu majority" and "Tutsi minority" invaded the young democratic experience of the time. This is the origin of the Hutu slogan of "*rubandanyamwinshi*" a concept which some people still believe in as the basis of democracy in Rwanda. The ethnic ideology was sown, natured and allowed to grow unchecked until it became an instrument of division and destruction. Today all Rwandans have become victims of that ideology because at its zenith, it landed the whole nation into the abominable crime of genocide. Now that there is nothing else to wait for after having touched the depth of the evil, Rwandans are trying hard to overcome the nightmare caused by the genocide of Batutsi in 1994. The healing process will take a long time but the essential and quite encouraging episode of recovery is on. Rwandans have made an analysis of their past. It has taken time but all have finally come to accept the sad and dark history of the past.

Rwanda's diversity is accepted as a living example but what is illegal is to use one's "*ubwoko*" (clan) to get what one has no right to have. By putting in place new institutions, legislation against corruption and regulatory mechanisms to enable Rwandans to live in a secure and peaceful society the government is able to make strides. The fatal ideologies of ethnicity and genocide are still a threat to Rwanda. They are rampant in Great Lakes Region and beyond. Rwanda is busy reorganizing itself. By uprooting the seeds of the country's destruction and planting anew the seeds of unity and reconciliation, the country is walking towards being a united and reconciled society ready to face the challenges of rebuilding and reconstructing a bright future for the nation.

In order to reach these objectives the government of Rwanda has put in place the democratic institutions. It has forged the structures of economic and political governance to ensure that citizens own the process of recovery. To cement all this, Banyarwanda have rediscovered positive cultural values which had been denigrated by the detractors of the unity of Banyarwanda. With time, and given the political will embedded in the country's good governance, people's rejection of divisive ideologies is a continuous process. The current political, economic and social environment in Rwanda places the country in an era of peace and development guided by the national Vision 2020 and above all a clear minded leadership. In brief there is in Rwanda a determination to be one people in diversity searching for a common ground based on positive values that unite. Rwanda is looking ahead to recover its lost identity as a unified nation. This will be possible as citizens continue to strive to be part of the healing process and ready to engage in the development of the nation.

Notes

[1] Peres A. Pages, Louis de Lacger cited by Jean Pierre Chrétien in *Le Défi de l'Ethnisme*, Paris, Karthala, 1997, p.64.

[2] Chretien Jean Pierre, *ibid*, 1997, p.65 (translation by the author of the paper).

[3] "Myths of origin" in *History and conflicts in Rwanda*, IRDP, 2006, pp. 29-42.

[4] Sehene Benjamin, *Le Piège Ethnique*, Paris, Editions Dagorno, 1999, pp. 13.

[5] Sehene Benjamin, Ibid; p.16.

[6] Sehene Benjamin, Ibid; p.16.

[7] Gudrun Honke et al, *Au plus profound de l'Afrique, Lee Rwanda et la colonization allemande 1888- 1919*, 1990, p. 120.

[8] Rumiya Jean, *Le Rwanda Sous le Régime du Mandat Belge* 1916-1931, Paris, Harmattan, 1992, 249p. Read also, Jean Pierre Chrétien, *L'Afrique des Grands Lacs: Deux mille ans d'Histoire*, Paris, Aubier, 2000, p. 410.

[9] *History and Conflicts in Rwanda*, IRDP, 2006, pp. 144.

[10] *Ibid*; IRDP, 2006, p.156.

[11] Pierre Biarnes, *L'Afrique aux Africains* 1980. p. 430) Translation by the Author of this paper.

[12] IRDP, *History and conflict in Rwanda*, 2006, pp. 69-70.

[13] IRDP, *Ibid*; 2006, p. 16.

[14] Biarnes Pierre, op. cit; 1980, p. 426.

[15] Sehene Benjamin, Op. Cit; p. 22.

[16] *A Time for Peace*, A publication by IRDP, 2008, p. 73.

[17] *A time for Peace*, IRDP, 2008, p. 55.

[18] A Time for Peace, p. 35.

[19] Pierre Biarnes, l'Afrique aux Africains, 19, p. 426.

Glossary

Ubuhake	"....A clientele institution through which an individual, inferior in terms of prestige and wealth, offers his services to another who in turn provides him with the usufruct of one or more cows. "According to J.J. Maquet in *Le Système des relations dans le Rwanda ancien*, Turvern, 1954, p.154.
Ubukonde	The property of the person known as umukonde or one who cleared the land first.
Ubwoko	Clan, plural form Amoko.
Gacaca	Traditional court system. After Genocide, this system was readapted to introduce a system of justice whose aim will be to allow Rwandans to reconcile.

Imana	A polysemic word. It could mean God, Supreme Being, also to have good luck or chance (Kugira Imana).
Umutware w'Ubutaka	The Chief of the Land.
Umutware w'Umukenke	The Chief of Pastures.
Umutware w'Ingabo	The Chief of the Army.
Guterekera no Kuraguza	Forms of traditional ways of worshipping Lyangombe and Nyabingi.

References

Biarnes, P. *L'Afrique aux Africains, 20 ans d'indépendance en Afrique Noire, Francophone*. Paris: Armand Colin.

Chrétien, Jean-Pierre. (1997). *Le Défi de l'Ethnisme (Rwanda et Burundi: 1990-1996).* Paris: Karthara.

Erny, P. (1994). *Rwanda 1994- Cles pour comprendre le calvaire d'un peuple*. Paris: Editions L'Harmattan.

Prunier, G. (2006). *The Rwanda Crisis, History of a Genocide.* Kampala: Fountain Publishers.

Rumiya, J. (1992). *Le Rwanda Sous le Régime du Mandat Belge (1916-1931).* Paris: Editions L'Harmattan.

Rutazibwa, P. (1999). *Les crises des Grands Lacs et la Question Tutsi, Reflections sur l'Idéologie du génocide dans la sous-region.* Kigali: Editions du C.R.I.D.

Sehene, B. (1999). *Le Piège Ethniques.* Paris: Editions Dagorno.

Vallois, V. Henri. (1969). *Les Races Humaines,* Que Sais je, Paris: Presses Universitaires de France.

Vallois, V. Henri. (2006). *History and Conflicts in Rwanda,* A publication of the Institute of Research and Dialogue for Peace (IRDP). Kigali.

Vallois, V. Henri. (2005). *L'état de droit au Rwanda.* IRDP.

Vallois, V. Henri. (2003). Voices of the People, IRDP, *Building lasting Peace in Rwanda.*

Vallois, V. Henri. (2008). *A Time of Peace, Convassing the views of Rwanda's People in the Search for Lasting Peace,* a publication of IRDP. Kigali: Pallotti Press.

Vallois, V. Henri. (2007). *Rwanda National Civic Education Policy,* A publication of National Electoral Commission.

Vallois, V. Henri. (2007). *Rwanda Decentralisation Strategic Framework.* Minaloc.

Internet search

www.onlinedictionary.com/ethnicity.co

www.findarticles.com/ethnicity in africa.fr

www.sidamaconcern.com/eth.html, Issue of political ethnicity in Africa, The Journal of Third World Studies, Spring 2004.

The Challenges of Ethnicity, Multiparty Democracy and State Building in Multiethnic States in Africa: Experiences from Kenya

Paul N. Mbatia,
Kennedy Bikuri & Peter Nderitu

Introduction: Ethnicity and Multiparty Politics in Kenya

By 1990 when Kenya's movement towards democracy had intensified, the ruling party (KANU) decided to extract political mileage from ethnicity. Many Kenyans thought, perhaps wrongly, that under democracy, there should be competitive politics that parties would be free to take their messages to voters ... When Kenya moved from one party to multi-party democracy, ethnic patterns developed along party lines (Machira, 2001:123).

During the 1990s, a wave of change in the form of political reforms swept through the world and modified the political terrain of many states. In Kenya, the late 1980s and the 1990s marked a period of struggle for democratization and change including reverting to multiparty politics championed by groups and individuals in civil society. Indeed, this was the decade of democratization for Kenya because multiparty elections were successfully conducted in 1992 and 1997, albeit with minimal changes in the composition of the ruling political elite, as the incumbent ruling party KANU[1] won both the elections and remained in government. In the successive elections of 2002, KANU was trounced by a coalition of other parties under the banner of National Rainbow Coalition (NARC). However, former KANU diehards re-emerged in government in new party outfits.

Even with the adoption of multiparty democracy, practices of poor governance and corruption are still widespread. Furthermore, multiparty democracy appears to have heightened ethnic nationalism and has been associated with ethnic violence. In Kenya, for example, except for 2002, ethnic violence has been witnessed in all the general elections held after Kenya formally adopted multi party democracy in 1991. Indeed, Muigai (1995) and Ndegwa (1997:599) affirm that multiparty democracy has been a prelude to ethnic competition and have led to "protracted transitions or outright conflict" in Kenya. Drawing from these observations in various African countries, scholars have raised questions over the suitability of multiparty democracy in multi-ethnic states. How can multi ethnic African countries manage multi party democracy without provoking ethnic groups to engage in violence during and after elections? Such violence has become a characteristic of many fragile States – these are States that are too weak to hold different ethnic communities together as a nation state.

In general, the outbreak of ethnic nationalism the world over dilutes the anticipated benefits of democratization. Accordingly, as African scholars attend to the problem of democratization and multiparty politics, they should also address the escalating problem of ethnic nationalism and violence. The overriding question is this: how can multiparty democracy in multi-ethnic African states be managed?

This chapter attempts to address the challenges of multiparty democracy in multi-ethnic states using the Kenyan experience. The chapter examines the emerging dynamics of ethnic nationalism and their impact and consequences on the process of building democratic multi-ethnic states in Africa. Further, the chapter seeks to explore possible strategies for the management of democratic and multiparty transition in multi-ethnic societies using the Kenyan experience as the basis of reference.

Meaning and application of ethnicity

Various scholars have attempted to define the term ethnicity (see for example, Chapman et al, 1989: 15; Eriksen, 1993:4), but there is no consensus reached on its meaning (Hutchinson and Smith, 1996:5). Some have defined ethnicity as *"a consciousness among people with shared cultural and linguistic roots that get utilized for political affiliation and mobilization to compete with other groups for scarce resources"* (Mungai,1995). This definition captures both the *passive* and *active* nature of ethnicity.

In its passive nature, ethnicity provides community members with a sense of belonging (identity), language, and other cultural resources (e.g., values, beliefs, myths, ideology, tradition, heritage, etc.). On the other hand, in its active nature, ethnicity provides a forum for competition with "outsiders" for scarce resources. Further, ethnicity in its active form is used to provide security and advance the interests of its members. In Kenya, active ethnicity is exemplified by ethnic groups, which work aggressively; they assert their identity and interests, compete with other groups for scarce resources, fight other groups to enlarge their geographical and political space, mobilize their members to capture more political power and create/form new ethnic based social structures (associations and networks) to strengthen their bargaining power at the national level.

Scholars who perceive ethnicity in its passive form adopt the primordialist approach in which ethnicity is seen as aligned to primordial ties i.e., personal relations based on kinship bonds, blood, race, religion, language, and custom. For primordialists, ethnicity persists due to the durable nature of the primordial ties. In this approach, ethnicity can be viewed as a passive cultural consciousness and is considered as a given natural phenomenon. On the other hand, instrumentalists adopt an active view of ethnicity; they treat ethnicity as a social, political, and cultural resource for different interests and status groups (Hutchinson and Smith, 1996:8). Accordingly, political elites could mobilize their respective ethnic groups to achieve personal gains — such as wealth, power, status, privileges and security.

In an attempt to understand ethnicity, some scholars have conceptualized it as a product of contact and not of isolation, and by implication entailing commonalities and differences between categories of people in a process. Eriksen (1993) has referred to this process as complementarization and dichotomization. He argues that in spite of the very many contested notions of ethnicity, ethnic groups or categories tend to have notions of common ancestry, common culture, (in the Kenyan case we would argue common territory) justifying their unity. Most importantly, ethnicity is a relational aspect and not a cultural property for if a setting is wholly mono-ethnic then there would be no ethnicity (Ibid). In this context, we argue here that few studies have examined how ethnic communities have overtime developed mutual interdependencies through exchange of goods and services. Such interdependencies enhance unity of purpose and contribute to harmony as opposed to competition that eventually leads to conflict, and at worst, violence.

One can delineate several significant points about ethnicity drawn from the various interpretations of the concept. First, we argue that ethnicity is not a static but a dynamic concept that is socially constructed. We evoke its passive or active meanings depending on the obtaining circumstances i.e., situation. Second, and drawing from the first point, ethnicity is a situational concept – its meaning and interpretation is largely determined by where we are and who we are with for whatever purpose. In this context, ethnic differences are "invisible" (hidden) between people of different ethnic groups who have common business interests or who meet in a foreign country. However, the same people will make their differences "visible" (manifest) when they engage in politics and campaign for their ethnic-based political parties. Third, we further observe that ethnicity is an elastic concept – it can be interpreted rigidly to exclude others or interpreted generously to include them albeit in a different situation.

Critical viewpoints about ethnicity in Africa

Scholars focusing on the challenges of ethnicity in Africa – that largely include ethnic struggles and violence—are confronted with critical (and also controversial) viewpoints that we have found worth interrogating in this chapter. Our aim is to bring out the viewpoints and possibly ignite a debate that should inform the discourse of ethnicity in Africa. Clarification of these viewpoints is essential particularly in the formulation of strategies or interventions meant to address the challenges posed by ethnicity in Africa.

The chapter considers the following viewpoints (hypotheses) as critical and worth studying to establish their validity in the context of ethnicity discourse in Africa:

1. Is ethnicity in Africa a colonial creation?
2. Is ethnicity the root cause of violence in Africa?
3. Are ethnic conflicts the main cause of underdevelopment in Africa?
4. Is ethnicity rendering multiparty democracy irrelevant in multi-ethnic African States and is Africa not ready for multiparty democracy due to ethnicity?
5. Can ethnicity be utilized as a resource in Africa?

The chapter attempts to reflect on each one of these five issues in the following section.

Is ethnic conflict a colonial creation in Africa?

Scholars who uphold this viewpoint observe that historically, *"prior to independence, some colonial administrators manipulated ethnic rivalries amongst indigenous populations by employing a strategy of divide and rule. Colonialism amplified African ethnic identities and the ethnic sense of belonging through the establishment of ethnically pure residential enclaves for African populations and by ensuring little exchange if any, between the various different ethnic groups. Indeed, even nationalist movements in many African nations were founded on ethnic identities. Accordingly, what came to symbolize national political parties was indeed an amalgam of ethnically based civil society networks and organizations. The strategy created enmity and suspicion among African people and the situation has not significantly changed"* (see http://www.africaresource.com/). Colonialism as a cause of ethnic conflict in Africa is also underscored by Irobi (2005:1) whose study compares the challenges of ethnicity in Nigeria and South Africa and posits that:

> Politicized ethnicity has been detrimental to national unity and socio-economic well being. It is important to note that most of these ethnic conflicts were caused by colonialism which compounded inter-ethnic conflict by capitalizing on the isolation of ethnic groups. The divide-and conquer method was used to pit ethnicities against each other, thus keeping the people from rising against the colonizers.

However, this view is contradicted by those who hold that "African societies are characterized by deep ethnic cleavages that are ancient and permanent" (Githinji & Holmquist, forthcoming). Indeed, African politics have been traced to traditional and ethnic organization, norms and practices around age group systems, councils of elders, religious authorities and political leadership founded on ascribed status. Furthermore, to argue that ethnic conflict in Africa was a creation of the colonial regime would suggest that prior to colonization of Africa, indigenous communities lived in harmony. Yet, it is evident that ethnic violence in the form of civil strife of various magnitude predated the colonial state in Africa. The persistence of ethnic violence in Africa should therefore not be blamed exclusively on external factors. Internal factors should be critically examined to establish the extent to which they contribute to ethnic conflicts in many African states.

Is ethnicity the main cause of underdevelopment in Africa?

Smith affirms that "many researchers have sought to explain the relationship between underdevelopment and ethnic conflict." Overall, many scholars have rightly argued that political and social instability is a major cause of underdevelopment (see Paglia in www.africaeconomicanalysis.org).

Africa's underdevelopment is therefore associated with the persistence of ethnic conflicts and violence that undermine democracy. In recent times, the Darfur crisis exemplifies how extreme ethnicity can lead to poverty and human displacement – underdevelopment. As long as ethnicity leads to political instability, chaos and bloodshed (see http://www.africaresource.com), it contributes to the continued state of underdevelopment.

In most African countries, modern services and democratic institutions have also been identified to be held captive by ethnic networks of those in power; the ethnic cabals are seen as incapable of dispensing their mandate using scientific or bureaucratic rationality. As such, modern institutions including democratic institutions appear to be held captive by ethnic interests among leaders and as such fulfilling their constitutional mandates becomes secondary (Leftwich 2000). But, is ethnicity a sufficient cause of Africa's underdevelopment? Besides ethnic conflicts, there are many external factors that contribute to poverty and human sufferings in Africa.

A more challenging view to this school of thought is that there are many African countries that have never experienced ethnic conflict, yet they remain poor. A good example is Tanzania. In our view, underdevelopment is not a logical outcome of ethnic conflicts and violence. Africa's underdevelopment has been explained based on other factors including historical marginalization and exploitation of the continent through technology and trade, disadvantages resulting from colonialism, weak competitive edge within the world system caused by existing global inequalities, hostile climatic and poor ecological endowment, weak human and technical capacities and poor endowment with capitalist entrepreneurial classes.

In addition, the weak African state has failed to channel development for the population it controls. More specifically, the weak African States have failed to regulate social relations (including ethnic relations) and to appropriate public resources in determined ways so as to avoid exclusion (Migdal, 1988). Such States have not achieved legitimate supremacy over the numerous other social forces within their societies that stand out against them and which resist the State's drive for social control (Leftwich, 2000).

Can ethnicity be used as a resource in Africa?

Most studies on ethnicity present it as a negative force; but under what conditions can ethnicity become a resource that could be used to improve the quality of life of African people? Ethnic diversity could be appreciated if it is well managed to create interdependencies and forge unity of purpose in a nation state. Ethnic differences in so far as they carry different cultural and material artifacts and values can enrich investments in tourism and other related economic ventures. There are several other ways in which diverse ethnic communities could be functional.

First, ethnic communities are a source of psychological relief for its members when they are faced with trauma. Two, ethnic communities provide a solid base upon which its members build social capital in the form of social networks. Third, ethnic communities are the repositories and carriers of

African heritage in the form of culture – values, customs, beliefs, myths, proverbs, vernacular languages, folk songs and dances, lifestyles, etc. Overall, ethnic groups could be mobilized to undertake development projects without provoking undue competition that could lead to conflict or violence. Unfortunately, there is limited evidence in Africa to demonstrate the potentiality of ethnicity as a promising resource.

We argue in this chapter that a strong state would be a prerequisite for transforming ethnicity from being a negative force to a resource. Turning ethnicity into a resource requires an acceptance of the challenges that result from negative ethnicity and institutionalization of mechanisms aimed at promoting complimentarity among the different ethnic groups as well as encouraging rationality as opposed to favoritism and cronyism within public service organizations. In addition, building functional institutions is essential – to protect the rights of citizens and provide them with the required security all the time within the state's jurisdiction. One step towards making ethnicity a resource is taming extreme ethnicity through enactment and enforcement of appropriate laws and regulations. Another strategy would be to discourage negative stereotyping among competing tribes through civic education.

Is ethnicity the root cause of violence in Africa?

Ethnic conflicts have been presented by scholars as a common feature of Africa. Proponents of this school can cite many cases to include the Rwanda genocide, the on-going crisis in Darfur in Sudan, the civil wars in Nigeria, the civil strive in South Africa before the dismantling of apartheid and the continued conflict between the whites and blacks in Zimbabwe. But to what extent are ethnic conflicts the root cause of violence in Africa? We underscore the observation that multi-ethnicity by itself should not be taken as the bases of ethnic conflict and violence in Africa. As correctly stated by Browen in Machira (2001:116),

> Some of the world's most ethnically diverse States, such as Indonesia, Malaysia and Pakistan, though not without internal conflict and political repression, have suffered little inter-ethnic violence, while countries with very slight differences in language or culture, such as Somalia and Rwanda, have had the bloodiest of all conflicts.

This provides some evidence suggesting that multi-ethnicity should not of necessity be a source of conflict or violence.

Pamela Paglia (see www.africaeconomicanalysis.org) observes that "in Darfur conflict, the ethnic division between the Arab militias and African tribes has been described as the primary cause for conflict. However, she cautions that:

> Concentrating on ethnicity as the primary cause for conflict underestimates the complexity of African societies and politics, and deviates policymakers' attention from the real causes of conflict. Ethnicity is a means through which conflicts in many African countries are conducted and a powerful tool for political mass mobilization.

If ethnicity is but a secondary cause of conflicts and violence in Africa, scholars should cast their nets wider to establish the real triggers of conflict in Africa. As suggested here, ethnicity could only be a symptom. In our view, a set of more convincing causes of conflict would include poverty, exclusion and biased distributive systems that breed glaring inequality in the distribution of key resources like income and land (see Machira, 2001:115). Resource-based conflicts have been rife within the African continent and many of them particularly those national ones have been fueled by international interests.

An invisible critical cause of ethnic violence in Africa is weak states— "Weak states have low capacity to penetrate society, regulate social relationships, extract resources and use resources in certain predetermined ways (Migdal, 1988: 5 and Leftwich 2000). Their lack of capabilities and sometime goodwill to control other actors (e.g., ethnic groups rising against other) create opportunities for ethnic violence.

Ethnicity is rendering multiparty democracy irrelevant in multi-ethnic African states and due to ethnicity. Is Africa not ready for multiparty democracy?

The capability of the African state particularly in purveying democracy has been questioned by many scholars. The African states democratic institutions are seen as held captive by the variety of social forces and as such not able to be subjected to necessary reforms to make them work effectively. Accordingly, institutional reforms in many of these countries are not possible because ethnic and other networks obstruct change which is seen as not benefitting the networks of ruling elites.

In the 1990s, a wind of change swept through Africa that significantly changed the political terrain. Many countries embraced multiparty democracy (Machira, 2001). However, in a number of countries (including

Kenya), the adoption of multiparty democracy heightened ethnic consciousness; through elite mobilization, multiparty elections eventually precipitated ethnic conflict and violence. This has been precisely so because party politics have been based on ethnic identities of party strong men/women and many of the parties have lacked ideological leanings and democratic practices opting to follow the whims of their strong men/women who are often political chiefs of certain ethnic coalitions or tribes.

Evidently, party strong men/women have amplified ethnic differences by often appealing to ethnic sensibilities during political campaigns and electioneering. In the absence of well defined class differentiation as well as class interests in many of the African societies, ethnic identities have been pushed to the center stage of political organization and mobilization for votes during election periods. With the emerging challenges associated with multiparty democracy, Ndegwa (1997: 599) aptly observes that a debate has been provoked over which institutions are appropriate to govern a multiethnic democracy. While multiparty democracy has enlarged democratic space, protected human rights and freedoms, the rising cases of ethnic violence, particularly during and after elections, tend to dilute the anticipated benefits of the new political system of governance. Multiparty democracy has in some countries threatened the national cohesion of African states—as has been the case in Kenya, Zimbabwe, Zambia, Sierra Leone, Cote d'Ivoire, and Nigeria, among others.

While multiparty democracy is appreciated and even celebrated in Africa, it has also posed new challenges in multi-ethnic States. In the latter, ethnic nationalism threatens national patriotism as political elites increasingly mobilize citizens to participate in the political and electoral processes along ethnic lines. Citizens are now more conscious of their ethnic identity as opposed to their national identity as citizens of their nation.

Interestingly, in the 1950s and early 1960s, Kenyans united to fight for independence (uhuru)— they had a common enemy; the white rulers. In the same way, in the 1990s, they united to fight for the second liberation— restoration of democracy. During the latter period, Kenyans were fighting a dictatorial regime sustained by KANU. The two critical periods suggest that unity of purpose can be forged even among multiethnic states like Kenya. Scholars should therefore reflect on the emerging challenges of multiparty democracy and establish conditions that a State and other actors must satisfy for a successful adoption of multiparty democracy in multi-ethnic states.

Important too is the need for legal and institutional frameworks to manage ethnic differences particularly in multi-ethnic societies so that any mobilization that threatens national identity and undermines national consciousness and cohesion is curtailed. A legal framework should be formulated to guide leaders against perpetuation of political campaigns that are ethnically provocative and retrogressive. Along the same framework, political parties would be checked and regulated based on how: a) they appeal to wider multiethnic constituencies; b) how they institutionalize democratic and competitive management selection structures within them and c) how their bureaucratic structures and memberships are entrenched and spread within society so that they do not remain the property of just a few powerful and wealthy individuals in society.

If multiparty democracy in multi-ethnic states is a prelude for ethnic conflicts and violence, what is its future in Africa? Should countries revert to single party mode of governance? In Kenya, when advocates of multiparty democracy were fighting for it in 1990s, its critics (including Moi, the incumbent president) argued that "the country was not cohesive enough." To date, faced with persistent waves of election-based violence (in 1992, 1997 and 2007), one is forced to ask: could Moi have been right in the case of Kenya?

On a positive note, Sola Akinrinade (2008:1) in www.africaeconomicanalysis.org correctly observes that immediately after independence, in many Africa countries, single party mode of governance was "seen as remedy to social divisions." More specifically, he avers that "in a number of states notably Nyerere's Tanzania, the adoption of a single party system was indeed an honest attempt to address a potentially dangerous situation." It is however notable that even the era of single party rule in many of the African countries did not safeguard prolonged peace and stability in many of the countries where it was practiced. Single party strongmen in many of these countries turned out to be dictatorial, promoted rent seeking behavior among the ruling elite and in the absence of dissenting opinion, institutionalized privatization of the states through corrupt methods. Kenya during Moi rule serves as a good example of the outcome of single party rule in a developing country. Emerging evidence suggests that while it is unthinkable to revert to one party rule, due to the escalating waves of violence, multiparty democracy is increasingly weakening African States—reducing them to fragile states. Scholars and policy makers are therefore tasked to establish the necessary and sufficient conditions that multiethnic African States should satisfy to adopt multiparty democracy successfully. Africa should learn lessons from the few multiethnic states (Tanzania, Ghana, Indonesia, Malaysia and Pakistan) which have successfully adopted multiparty democracy without weakening their respective States or threatening their national unity.

Ethnic conflicts and the nature and role of African states

In all the countries of the world that have different economic and political systems (capitalist, socialist or communist), State remains the most critical development actor. Unless the State is functional, all other institutions of a society are rendered ineffective. In this regard, scholars (Migdal, 1988, Migdal et al., 1994 and Ghani & Lockhart, 2008) have paid prime attention to the theme of nature and role of States in current development discourses. These scholars have correctly argued that a nation's development is largely a function of the capability status of its State—whether "Weak" or "Strong." Most important, compared to other States, these scholars have presented Third World States as weak. States vary in their capabilities to execute their determined mandates. Migdal (1988) notes that Third World States are particularly weak in their abilities to regulate social relations and use resources in determined ways. How true is this analysis in Africa? To what extent are ethnic conflicts and violence a function of weak states in Africa? As we have argued earlier, ethnic conflicts and violence are widespread in Africa largely because of the weak States. Indeed, some states are incapable of even controlling the excesses of individual rogue political elites. To be a developmental state, any state should gain control of all its subjects – including the political class.

The way forward: How to make multiparty democracy work in multi-ethnic African states

How can we make multiparty democracy a suitable political model in multiethnic African states? Most states lack the apparatus required to enforce existing laws and regulations. For example, in Kenya, most law-enforcing institutions are riddled with corruption rendering them ineffective. In addition, the State lacks the required resources to fund law-enforcing institutions adequately – this reduces effectiveness of their operations. For example, during the 2007 post election violence, the State law-enforcing organs were overwhelmed by the massive numbers of those who engaged in the violence. Furthermore, the law enforcers took sides and supported (or sympathized with) participants in the violence who spoke their ethnic language. In general, the law enforcing agents were politicized. It has also been documented that the Kenyan state has not shown strong political goodwill to contain periodic waves of ethnic violence that have occurred periodically since the adoption of multiparty democracy in 1990. In an ideal situation, a capable state should be able to extract adequate resources from its subjects and deploy them prudently to insure security of all citizens.

In our view, a strong State is a prerequisite for restoration of social order in any nation. Accordingly, state building should be taken up as a priority task in Africa. This should incorporate all planned initiatives that are executed to boost capabilities of African States. Such initiatives could include building infrastructures that facilitate operations of state institutions, allocation of adequate funds to state institutions e.g., police, army, courts, prisons and rehabilitation centres, professionalization of police and judiciary

In many parts of Africa, given the atrocities associated with single party rule, it is unthinkable to revert to the latter. And in the absence of an alternative model, multiparty democracy still remains the only option. Our challenge therefore is to devise strategies of domesticating and to make it work. This will require interrogation of past experiences, undertaking comparative analysis and drawing lessons from Africa and beyond where multiparty democracy has worked.

In this section we suggest the following strategies to make multiparty democracy work in Africa:

1. *Understand the nature of African States*: It is imperative to assess the nature of each African State in terms of their capabilities and establish whether they are weak or strong. Of importance, African States should have the capacity to control all other factors – internal as well as external. Internally, the State should dismantle any form of networks or associations that threaten national unity. As has been aptly observed, in Africa, "for the nation to live, the tribe must die." Citizens should elect leaders with determination and proven track record; they should support the state dismantle all tribal-based networks and political associations that undermine national interests and security.

2. *Fixing the weak African States*: In this chapter, we argue that to develop, Africa requires strong not weak States. Unfortunately, during the 1980s and 1990s, African States were dented through the Structural Adjustment Programmes (SAPs) that advocated for leaner and weak States. As succinctly put by Ghani & Lockhart (2001:4),

> The ground reality is that many states have collapsed and are unable to provide even the most basic services for their citizens. The failure to maintain basic order not only makes fear a constant of daily life but also

provides a breeding ground for a small minority to perpetuate criminality and terror.

To date, African nations should therefore invest in state strengthening and building. As recommended by Ghani & Lockhart (ibid), "…solutions to our current problems of insecurity, poverty, and lack of growth converge on the need for state-building project… Only the State can organize power so as to harness flows of information, people, money, force, and decisions necessary to regulate human behavior."

3. *Dismantle the bases of ethnic-based politics*: Part of state building should entail dismantling all networks and associations that promote and perpetuate negative ethnicity. For example, States should enact laws and regulations that discourage or undermine flourishing of political parties formed along ethnic lines. In addition, ethnic auditing should be conducted regularly to identify and penalize those who engage in practices that enforce ethnic exclusion in hiring or distribution of public resources. Importantly, mechanisms aimed at promoting rationality, equity and equality should be inbuilt through policy and legislation to ensure that no particular community gets favored in the distribution and allocation of national resources and opportunities.

4. *Transformation of the inherent repressive and undemocratic State structure*: There is a popular view shared by scholars that multiparty democracy has not transformed African states as was expected (Newbury, 1994, and Nyang'oro 1994). To make multiparty democracy work, structural transformation of the African State is inevitable. There is evidence suggesting that even after the adoption of multiparty rule, African political elites continued to protect their powers and privileges at the expense of public interests. The popular structural reforms associated with multiparty democracy have aborted in many African countries—Kenya included. For example, since 1991, Kenya has not managed to draft a new constitution. Structural transformation should entail, inter alia, public sector reforms to improve delivery of goods and services, constitutional reforms to devolve and decentralize power and strengthening civil society institutions that should help control excesses of the State. Most importantly, structural transformation should promote political emancipation of citizens.

5. *Promote national unity and increase State legitimacy:* While national unity is critical in State formation and building, there are few interventions undertaken in Africa to promote this noble agenda. In Kenya,

"Harambee" was a national rallying call for national unity. However, after NARC[2] took over from KANU in 2002, the State has relegated it to a micro-level initiative. In Kenya, promotion of national unity will require revival and nurturing of symbolic activities that unite people. For example, there is need to expand space or forum where Kenyans can share the national anthem, share national festivities including theatre and music. Most importantly, there is need to promote a national culture and language. Promotion of national unity ultimately enhances state legitimacy – citizens develop a sense of belonging to their nation and comply with the State's laws without the use of force. Land and related settlement patterns are at the center of strengthening ethnic identities and therefore, dismantling the ethnic orientations requires de-ethnification of land and settlement by giving premium to holding land for productive purposes as opposed to social capital reasons. This requires a land policy that taxes idle land, encourages community members to lease out land not being used by respective families and broadly promotes urban settlement for larger sections of the population.

6. *Strengthening institutions that nurture and safeguard democracy*: State building in Africa will entail strengthening state organs or institutions particularly those that enhance democracy. They include police force, electoral commission, judiciary etc. Beyond these state-owned institutions, efforts should be made to re-awaken and mainstream Civil Society Organizations (CSOs). In 2002 elections, many leaders of CSOs in Kenya joined politics and became part of the political elites. This weakened the civil society movement that was instrumental in pushing for multiparty democracy. To date, the civil society movement is weak and disjointed. In general, non-state actors should reclaim their space – part of which has been usurped by the State (and external forces).

7. *Craft appealing ideologies for mobilizing citizens*: One missing variable in mobilizing masses in Africa is a popular ideology. In the Kenyan history, MAU MAU[3] is recognized as an appealing unifying force that empowered Africans to fight the colonists. However, after independence, nationalist movement lost its appeal. In Tanzania, President Nyerere used *Ujamaa* as an ideology to unite and mobilize his followers. To date, there are few nations in Africa with popular ideologies. In the absence of the latter, politicians appeal to ethnic identity as a basis for mobilizing the masses. A nation without a popular ideology has weak pillars on which to build its unity and legacy. President Kenyatta struggled with *Harambee* while President Moi tried to adopt the slogan of "Peace, Love and Unity" (*Nyayo*)

as his political philosophy. The incumbent President is yet to make an attempt.

8. *Address the weakness of liberal democracy* (see Attafuah and Chege): A critical review of liberal (Western) democracy suggests that its major weakness is the tyranny of the majority. Practically, in liberal democracy – exemplified by multiparty democracy – the winner (majority) takes it all. This practice spells doom for smaller tribes in multiethnic states dominated by one or a few large ethnic groups. In essence, unless liberal democracy is "moderated" by homegrown laws and regulations, it is despised by the minority groups in any country. In Kenya, for example, a presidential candidate is required by the electoral laws to have majority votes in five out of the eight provinces in order to win in a presidential contest. This is but an attempt to make the votes of the minority tribes significant in determining the president of the country. To mitigate against the tyranny of the majority in liberal democracy, Kenya needs to appreciate the diversity of its people in terms of ethnic and regional representation and cater for this reality in not only elective political representation but also in public appointments. Kenya needs to appreciate that democracy can only thrive where all sections of the population and the nation are participant in it otherwise it will turn into a dictatorship of the majority and basically remain an ethnic struggle of the minority against the majority.

   As a referee, the State must ensure checks and controls to prevent tyranny of the majority – by taming competing interests, limit the rise of ethnic nationalism and reduce the escalating problem of exclusion in the distribution of national resources. Unless it is tamed, liberal democracy could increase inequality as dominant ethnic groups largely use their numeric strength to influence (at worst control!) political processes and resource allocation – endlessly.

9. *Promote new mindset among Kenyans*: The new mindset should help dismantle the patron-client networks and unrealistic expectations. Would like to see a Kenya where *wananchi* (citizens) raise funds (like it was with Obama supporters) to support their leaders politically. Indeed, that is how it was traditionally—Kenyan communities would welcome their kings and queens without expecting kickbacks or wanting to manipulate them. On the other hand, leaders need to support Kenyans in the process of claiming their dignity and in discarding pathological dependency on them (leaders). Unfortunately such dependency as exists between the leaders and the subjects in Kenya has now been institutionalized in policy

through such programs like the Constituency Development Fund (CDF), among others.

Notes

[1] KANU stands for Kenya African National Union. This was the main political party that took over from the colonial government. Shortly after independence (1963), Kenya operated as a one-party state and KANU was the only party in existence until 1991.

[2] NARC was initially viewed as a party of change. Its proponents had radical ideas on how to bring about socio-economic and political transformations in Kenya after the fall of KANU. However, this was not to be.

[3] MAU MAU is a catchword used to refer to the freedom fighters especially from the central region of Kenya who spearheaded a rebellion against the colonial rule. It is a symbolic catchword that signifies solidarity of peasants from Central Kenya against the white rule. MAU MAU therefore envisioned a movement against the colonial rule in Kenya.

References

Azar, P. (1998). "Understanding the Contemporary Conflicts" in Azar P. (eds.) *Conceptual Framework for Analyzing Contemporary Conflicts*.

Akinyemi, B. (2008). "The way Forward for Africa" *www.africaeconomicanalysis.org*.

Chapman, N. 1996. "History and ethnicity" in Hutchinson F. and Smith D.A. (eds.) *Ethnicity*. London: Oxford University Press.

Ericksen, T. Hylland. (1993). *Ethnicity and nationalism: Anthropological perspectives*. London: Photophers.

Githinji, M. & F. Holmquist (2008).*The Default Politics of Ethnicity in Kenya*. Forthcoming.

Ghani, A. and L. Clare. (2001). *Fixing Failed States: A Framework for Rebuilding a Fractured World*. New York: Oxford University Press.

Glickman, H. (1995). "From ethnic conflicts to ethnic competition" in Glickman H. (eds.) *Ethnic conflict and democratization in Africa*. Atlanta, Georgia: The African Studies Association Press.

Glickman, H. (1995). *Ethnic conflict and democratization process in Africa today.* Atlanta, Georgia: The African Studies Association Press.

Hutchinson, F. and D.A. Smith. (1996). *Ethnicity.* London: Oxford University Press.

Kenya Thabiti Taskforce. (2009). *Root Causes and Implications of the Post Election Violence of 2007.* Commissioned by the Inter Religious Forum. Nairobi: Kijabe Printing Press.

Leftwich, A. (2000). *States of Development: On the Primacy of Politics in Development.* Malden: Polity Press.

Machira, A. (2001)."Ethnicity, Violence and Democracy" in *Africa Development,* Vol xxvi, Nos 1&2.

Migdal, S. Joel. (1988). *Strong Societies and Weak States: State-Society Relations and State Capabilities in Third World.* New Jersey: Princeton University Press.

Migdal, S. Joel; K. Atul and S. Vivienne (eds.) (1994). *State Power and Social Forces: Domination and Transformation in the Third World.* Cambridge: Cambridge University Press.

Muigai, G. (1995). "Ethnicity and the renewal of competing politics in Kenya" in Glickman H. (eds.) *Ethnic conflicts and democratization in Africa.* Atlanta, Georgia: The African Studies Association Press.

Ndegwa, S. (1997). "Citizens and ethnicity: An examination of two transition moments in Kenyan politics." In *African Political Science Review,* 91 (3) pp.1-18.

Newburry, C. (1994). "Introduction: Paradoxes of Democratization in Africa." In *African Studies Review* Vol 37, No. 1 (African Studies Association).

Nnoli, O. I. (1989). "Ethnic conflicts in Africa." A Working paper presented at the Council for the Development of Economic and Social Research in Africa (Codesria), Dakar, Senegal.

Nyang'oro, E. J. (1994). "Reform Politics and Democratization Process in Africa. In *African Studies Review,* Vol 37, No. 1. (African Studies Association).

Omolo, K. (1998). "The politics of ethnicity in Kenya." A paper presented to the Centre for Law and research International in a conference on Ethnic Relations in Kenya held between 12th and 13th March 1998 at The Stanley Hotel, Nairobi.

Omolo, K. (1999). "Causes and dynamics of conflicts in greater horn of Africa." A paper presented to the seminar on Peace Building and Conflict Resolution Mechanisms, with Special Reference to Mine Action by Kenya Coalition Against Land Mines & Jaramogi Foundation on 3rd and 4th August 1999 at The Stanley Hotel, Nairobi.

Republic of Kenya. (2008a). *Report of the Independent Review Commission on the General Elections held in Kenya on 27th December 2007* (Chaired by Johann Kriegler). Nairobi: Government Printer.

Republic of Kenya. (2008b). *Report of the Commission of Inquiry into Post Election Violence (CIPEV)* (Chaired by Philip Waki). Nairobi: Government Printers.

Rawlinson, A. (2003). "The Political manipulation of ethnicity in Africa." *www.insolens.org.*

Rosenberg and Bennet. (1961). *The Kenyatta election: Kenya 1960-1961.* Institute of Commonwealth Studies. London: Oxford University Press.

Seligson M.& J. Smith (1993).(ed) *Development and Underdevelopment: The Political Economy of inequality.* Boulder and London: Lynne Rienner Publishers.

Schermerhorn, Richard (1996). "Ethnicity and Minority Groups" In John Hutchinson and Anthony D. Smith (eds.) *Ethnicity.* Oxford: Oxford University Press.

Shiroya, Okate J.E. 1975. "The evolution of territorial nationalism in Kenya." A paper presented at the Annual Conference of Historical Association of Kenya held in August, Nairobi, Kenya.

Stewart, Frances. 2008. *Horizontal Inequalities and Conflict: Understanding Group Violence in Multiethnic Societies.* New York: Palgrave Macmillan.

Smith, Garret Brian. 2008. "The Nature of Ethnicity in Africa; A test of political Relevance." Paper presented at the 17th Midwest Political Science Undergraduate Research Conference.

A Political Economy of Land Reform in Kenya: the Limits and Possibilities of Resolving Persistent Ethnic Conflicts

Nicholas O. Odoyo

Introduction

A high economic growth rate of 7 per cent per annum in the 1960s and the consequent social investments by the post-independence state in Kenya were underpinned by agrarian and land reform programmes that sought to redress historical injustices and consequently to restructure agrarian relations. Its limited success was due to the conjuncture of both external and internal factors. Internally, a nationalist consensus provided the glue of legitimacy to the state and facilitated the land reforms. This was reinforced by the international consensus on the necessity of state involvement in the economy as a vanguard of modernization.

Recent events have however, shattered this legacy. In the context of a deepening agrarian crisis characterized by high unemployment and poverty rates, food shortages and persistent ethnic conflicts, questions have emerged as to the extent of success of the previous land reform program and the possibilities of inaugurating a new set of "second generation" land reform programmes. Underlying these calls is the recognition that land is still not only a critical source of livelihood for a large majority of Kenyans but is also a basis for ethnic identification and hence the multiple conflicts over access to and ownership of land.

Pivotal events which have necessitated these questions include the 2008 post-election violence in Kenya and the increasing pervasiveness of a militia culture in both the rural and urban centres. This paper will seek to examine the political economy of land reform and describe the shifting priorities of the state in response to new global market opportunities. In other words, what does the present configuration of socio-political forces portend for the possibilities of resolving ethnic conflicts over land as a basis for revitalizing economic growth, creating jobs and new livelihood opportunities through land reform?

Land policy in Kenya: A short history

British imperial ambitions engendered a process of violent enclosures beginning in the 1890s in which large swathes of highly fertile land covering 8 million acres were carved out from the native land. On December 13 1899, the British Crown, under its Foreign Jurisdiction Act 1890 declared all "waste and unoccupied land in the protectorate where there was no settled form of government and where land had not been appropriated to the local sovereign or to local individuals" free for its disposal. These were henceforth declared Crown lands under the Crown Land Ordinances in 1902 and 1915. The designation 'Crown land' referred to all public lands in the East African protectorate.

The consequences of these legal enactments were threefold. One, the relocation of ultimate ownership of land to the imperial Crown. All land allocations would be done at the behest of the state and the natives would assume the role of tenants at the will of the Crown. Two, the establishment and evolution of an agrarian capitalist economy spawned a series of labor laws, tenancy laws, vagrancy laws and identification mechanisms (*kipande*, ethnic stereotyping) to facilitate the exploitation of labour and hence guarantee the profitability and viability of the agrarian capitalist economy. Lastly, the emergence of a white settler class controlling both 8 million acres of fertile land and relevant state institutions.

Meanwhile, the native reserves were developing increased land pressure. By the 1920s, out-migration was a marked feature of the Kikuyu reserves. Some of the complaints included decreased soil fertility, low food production, sub-economic parcelization and inheritance disputes. Political agitations had begun. By the 1940s about 100,000 Kikuyu were already settled in the Rift Valley. These were either farm labourers or squatters awaiting the possibility of more land resettlements. By the 1950s, the Mau Mau rebellion had crystallized into an agrarian movement which precipitated the Lancaster House independence talks. In the course of these talks, it was agreed among both the colonial administration and the smallholder Kikuyu agrarian middle classes that enjoyed colonial state privileges that land would be set aside for the resettlement of all landless people in order to assuage the land hunger that was capable of threatening the post-independence economy.

Post-independence land reform

The "Land Question" was a central factor in the negotiations for independence in Kenya. This is because of the uneven development experiences of different ethnic communities in the colonial agrarian capitalist economy. This situation crystallized two dominant political formations – a conglomeration of different ethnic groups and their patrons – which were the main drivers of the nationalist movement, viz. KANU and KADU. KADU drew its support predominantly from the less mobilized ethnic communities of the Kalenjin (a conglomeration of ethnic groups from the Rift Valley), the Luhya and Arab and Mijikenda Coastal ethnic communities while KANU's support base revolved around the most politically and economically mobilized ethnic communities largely constituted by the Kikuyu, Luo and to some extent the Akamba.[1] In this context dissimilar interests emerged on the land question and ethnicity would be a critical factor on the forms that emergent conflicts over land would take.

Indeed, in post-colonial Kenya, the land re-settlement process was ethnicized *ab initio.* Modern ethnicity is a convenient colonial construction. It emerged from the imperatives of colonial political stability and was enacted through the policy of 'indirect rule'.[2] The latter consisted of appropriating invented traditional authorities as mediators between the indigenous population and the colonial state in the allocation of political and economic resources especially land. In the post-colonial context ethnicity took (and continues to) the form of an exclusivist identity instrumentalized by political elites who represent themselves as guardians of a mythical common ethnic interest in the competition for limited political and economic resources vis-à-vis other ethnic communities. As Colin Leys rightly argues:

> The foundations for modern 'tribalism' were laid when the various tribal modes and relations of production began to be displaced by capitalist ones, giving rise to new forms of insecurity, and obliging people to compete with each other on a national plane for work, land , and ultimately for education and other social services seen as necessary for security.[3]

However, while ethnic-based competition for resources increasingly permeated all spheres of society, its most violent consequences came to revolve around the land re-settlement process. The land is a critical resource in agrarian societies with multiple political, economic, social and cultural meanings. Hence in Kenya land is a critical substantive issue on which the discourse about ethnicity and citizenship in Kenya converges. Who belongs and who does not belong and the bundle of rights and obligations one is entitled to in the ethnic political community and the elusive nation-state hinges on a persons claims to ancestral land. However, according to Ndegwa[4], in Kenya ethnic citizenship competes with the liberal citizenship traditionally sanctioned by the nation-state in Western Europe. The liberal vision holds that rights inhere in individuals, exist prior to community, and are guaranteed with minimal obligation to the community. The civic-republican [akin to ethnic citizenship] vision considers rights not as inherent but as acquired through civic practice that upholds obligations to the community. Thus, he continues, liberal citizenship *qualifies* one to participate in the inclusive national community, while in the ethnic community republican citizenship *requires* members to participate in the group's preservation, especially in competition against other communities and against the national community – unless the state is controlled by fellow community members.[5]

Very briefly, on the eve of independence a coalition of white settlers and Kenya African Democratic Union (KADU) nationalist leaders successfully campaigned to have their suggestions for a regionalist constitution (also known as *majimbo*) – recognizing individual political and economic rights – was accepted by the British colonial government. The purpose of this constitution was to ensure that at independence it would safeguard them from the centralist ambitions of the KANU nationalists who they feared would resettle the majority of landless Kikuyu in the Rift Valley and therefore deny them what they regarded as their ancestral land.

A confluence of both internal and external factors ensured these demands were met. Internally, drawn out ideological differences between 'radical' sections of Kenya African National Union (KANU) members and an alliance of 'conservative' members from both KADU and KANU revolved over the nature of the political-economic system to be created out of land reform. The 'radical' wing of KANU (Jaramogi Oginga Odinga, Bildad Kaggia *et al.*) was able to tap onto the deep frustrations of a land hungry militant peasant constituency who felt that the independence promise of free land and social justice was being delayed and, in fact, was beginning to be betrayed by the insistence by Jomo Kenyatta on the need to forgive and forget and that nothing would be free in the new political dispensation.

On the other hand, the external factors revolved around the bilateral and multilateral assistance programs of the World Bank, the British government and other Western countries on the efficiency of the willing-buyer-willing-seller model of land redistribution which would serve the twin purpose of promoting the emergence of a small conservative Kikuyu agrarian middle class and to avert the breakdown of socio-political order[6]. Two divergent opinions on the land issue emerged from both KADU and KANU. KADU's campaign for a regionalist system was meant to secure land in their ethnic strongholds from what they perceived as the ambitions of larger ethnic groups to resettle in their lands. Notable is that KANU had pledged to uphold land reform as a central plank of its manifesto in order to fulfill its objective of nation-building. The target was to cement the process of land consolidation and registration, resettle squatters, ensure just compensation for expropriated land and facilitate the provision of land stabilization loans from the British government.

In this regard, it was envisaged that about one million acres would be set aside from the white highlands to resettle 35,000 families who had suffered the brunt of colonial oppression and exploitation. Preceding this was the Land Development and Settlement Board (LDSB) schemes which initially sought to resettle 1,800 large scale farmers and 6,000 peasants on 73,000 ha by September 1963. Indeed, policy prescriptions by the World Bank, which informed the schemes, were guided by the assumption that at an interest rate of 6 $\frac{1}{2}$ per cent per annum for both development and land, loans were to be repaid in 10 and 30 years respectively.[7]

Land reform by the post-independence government was therefore seen as a way of redressing colonial injustices and engendering rural development. These would be achieved by land resettlement facilitated by the provision of extension services, establishment of cooperatives and various loan schemes. Furthermore, secure land rights to private property would be guaranteed by the promotion of land consolidation and registration in all parts of the country. In short, the Africanization of the economy through land tenure reform which would integrate peasants into the expanding agrarian sector.[8]

Undergirding post-independence land reform policies was the Sywnnerton Plan of 1954 which was geared toward the creation of a smallholder conservative Kikuyu agrarian middle class capable of stemming the wave of Mau Mau rebellion and hence the evolution of conditions of political stability favourable to the evolution of a neo-colonial economy.[9]

The shifting priorities of land reform

From the early 1960s to 1969, the post-independence government was committed to a market-led approach to land reform through the establishment of settlement schemes plus loans/grants to poor landless Kenyans to enable them to purchase land. However, because eligible buyers had to make a down payment of 1,000 and 10 000 shillings for small- and large-scale farmers respectively, by around the mid- to late 1960s, settlement schemes began to unravel. Evaluations by critics of the resettlement programme had shown that the real income of a squatter at the time came to about 60 shillings per month, way below the requirements for loan eligibility.

Moreover, as a project that was meant to be self-financing, the government was forced to adhere to the strict guidelines as to its implementation by the Bank. In recognition of this, the 1970s were marked by consistent policy reviews in which the economic viability of the settlement schemes was a basis of questioning the whole programme vis-à-vis the opportunity costs of investing in other sectors of the economy in which rapid returns would be guaranteed. In response, in the context of an increasingly close relationship between an emergent bureaucratic elite and foreign capital, the state's role in development began to be re-oriented toward serving the latter through various largely urban-based investment programmes. The failure of various rural development programmes (Special Rural Development Programme, etc) has been attributed to the fact that such programmes were antithetical to the logic of urban biased development. This is because rural development had the potential to redistribute resources, in the context of a regime that relied for its accumulation on the exploitation of the peasantry, from the urban to rural sector and therefore benefit the masses at the expense of the urban-based political classes (ibid, 1975).

In sum, while the government had earlier announced a freeze on further settlements in the 1966/70 Development Plan, the persistent threat of land invasions forced a renewed allocation of 2.5 million pounds (of British aid) by 1969 to set aside 150,000 acres for new settlements. This is despite the fact that over 1.6 million acres were still left intact for the large scale farm sector.[10]

Due to the sensitivity of the Land Question in Kenya, it is not possible to make confident conclusions about the current structure of land ownership in terms of land sizes and who owns what. Land sizes and land use patterns vary according to provinces and districts, and within those districts, according to agro-ecological zones. In Nakuru District, for instance, 235 large farms cover about 214, 298 hectares of the total land area of 724,230 hectares. This represents 30% of the whole district. In Uasin Gishu district large farms control a similar amount of land.[11] Figures obtained for Trans Nzoia district also show that close to 3,500 large farms exists covering 30% of the total land area of 2487.3 km². On the other hand, Central province exhibits a markedly different picture. In Nyandarua and Nyeri districts, for example, the average large farm sizes range between 10 to 20 acres while in Kiambu the same figure for large farms goes up to a high of 20 acres[12].

Most of the owners of these farms are male, former and current senior civil servants, cabinet ministers, and MPs and military officials. Through their close connection to the incumbent regimes, illegal/irregular allocations have ensured such powerful individuals control the best prime land in the country. The geography of settlement in Kenya speaks to the crucial role that control of state power affords to processes of personal accumulation of wealth on the holders. Indeed it shows that while the post-independence land reforms realized some limited benefits, the rich and poor continue to compete for limited resources.

The competition for limited resources revolves around the problems of the availability of land for sale at reasonable prices in areas of high demand and in parcels appropriate to the needs of applicants; financial and practical obstacles to the poor accessing the programme; and limited post-transfer support in the form of extension services, training, infrastructure development and access to credit and markets. Limited land reform processes initiated by post–independence governments in the context of highly repressive measures meant to deter popular dissent has formed the background to the state–instigated clashes that has rocked the country ever since the restoration of multiparty politics.

Thus politically-charged rallies were to be a marked feature of the early 1990s in which Kalenjin politicians allied to the Moi regime urged their supporters through inflammable speeches to evict those communities ('strangers'/ madoadoa/ outsiders, etc) perceived to be sympathetic to the opposition. The impact of these conflicts has been huge population displacements, loss of lives, and property. Between 1991 and 1996, over 1500 people were killed and over 300,000 people displaced in Rift Valley and Western Provinces. A second wave of violence in the run-up to the 1997 general election witnessed renewed violence especially in the Coast claiming over 100 lives and displacing over 100,000 people.[13]

Underlying these conflicts are the differentiated access to and ownership of land based on class, ethnic, and gender and generational hierarchies. The consequence of a skewed land distribution is the large population of squatters and landless people all over the country. Squatters can be defined as those who have access to at least some parcel of land although the state has never recognized ownership claims through the provision of secure title deeds, yet to such people (i.e., the squatters) land is still a critical basis of their livelihoods. This phenomenon is more common in the Coast province. On the other hand, landless people are those who possess no land at all largely due to gradual displacement as a result of population pressure in the context of unequal land distribution. For instance, Coast province leads in the country in terms of the highest number of squatters while landlessness is a phenomenon predominantly of the rest of the country. The highest proportion of land-based poverty is Central (15.8%) while the lowest is Western with 6%. Indeed across all the provinces over 60 % of the population hold less than 4 hectares of land. Most notable is also that a large percentage (68.8%) of these households are engaged in crop farming with mean holding sizes of 1.7 acres, with various regional variations.[14] Clearly Kenya is still an agrarian economy par excellence. How has the state responded to these violent processes? A Commission of Inquiry into the violence, first, in 1992[15], immediately after the first multiparty elections and, in 1998[16], and in 2008[17] underscores the salience of the land question in persistent conflicts between and among ethnic communities and classes in Kenya.

The common findings by these commissions are the deep seated grievances over historical injustices meted by the colonial state and papered over by the subsequent post-independence regimes. These grievances were instrumentalized by political elites and the Provincial Administration 'based on the misconception that some ethnic communities could chase away other ethnic communities in order to acquire their land'.[18] The commissions made various recommendations for prosecution, re-settlement of internally displaced persons, amendments to the Land Laws, but none of these recommendations have been implemented. Not all of those originally displaced remain homeless. A large number went back to their farms without outside material assistance. Others were assisted with resettlement materials by the Catholic Church, National Christian Council of Kenya (NCCK) and NGOs such as Action Aid, Oxfam, and World Vision. Yet resettlement of Internally Displaced Persons (IDPs) has never been a systematic policy of government but has been *ad hoc* in response to internal and external pressures.

The government has provided some material assistance which is, however, inadequate given the magnitude of the problem. Relief food has also been provided, but more to alleviate the consequences of drought and floods than to feed displaced persons. The relief and resettlement project by the churches has been scaled down because many of the displaced have returned to their homes. Many have not, and still live in settlement camps. Out of government neglect, IDPs thus continue to complain of insecurity, poverty, land ownership disputes, and finding sources of alternative settlement. Acceptance by relatives living elsewhere has been difficult due to weakened social ties. Landowners have been unwelcoming also due to the threat of adverse possession. On the other hand, the long term decline of the cash crop economy (coffee, tea, pyrethrum, etc), largely dominated by men has meant increased levels of unemployment. Those fortunate to hold even small tracts of land continue to face tenure insecurity and limited market opportunities for their products.

It remains to be seen how the state will confront the contradiction between the pervasive sub-economic parcellation of land, rising unemployment and poverty levels and the existence of an under-utilized, externally oriented large farm sector. These questions emerge in the context of wider changes in the agrarian sector driven by emerging opportunities in global markets for tourism, energy and high value horticultural crops. In consequence, current trends point to the possibility of job losses by farm labourers, evictions of squatters/landless in a bid to tap into the lucrative globalized market niches of conservancies, horticultural crops, energy, cereals and port facilities. Hence an accelerated process of semi- proletarianisation/ proletarianisation. This seems to be accelerating the completion of long trajectories of dispossession by separating rural workers from access to land. A comprehensive land policy has been presented and discussed in cabinet and finally adopted. It was then adopted by parliament as a Sessional Paper. However, prospects for its implementation, especially since continues to draw controversy given the far reaching land reforms proposed therein.

The policy seeks to vest control of land in a National Administrative Committee away from the state and combine all the disparate land laws into a few statutes through the categorization of land into the simpler categories of private, public and community land.[19] It stipulates that land reform will be guided by the principles of restitution, resettlement and redistribution. The focus of popular grievances, through various NGOs and militarized forms, have fallen on the large farms in order to ease the population pressures and loss of livelihoods. Ultimately the question of land reform revolves around the equalization of stark class differences in Kenya today.

Macro-economic policy and the land question

The current policy approach to revitalizing the Kenyan economy contains certain objectives which are questionable in light of the inherited dual structure of the colonial economy. The reasons behind this lie in the class character of policy prescriptions which are geared toward maintaining and reinforcing the dual structure of the economy with disproportionate benefits to the large farm sector. Neo-liberal reforms anchored on the triadic goals of privatization, liberalization and deregulation have consistently informed development policy ever since the 1980s in Kenya. Within this market-led paradigm, the state has consistently withdrawn from public funding of social projects and has assumed the role of a 'watchman'[20] over private property rights in order to create an enabling environment for private foreign investment.

Yet how the state seeks to comprehensively reform land is not clear. This is in the context of a limited resource base. In the 2005/2006 financial year, the Ministry of Lands envisaged that Land Sector Reforms would cost an estimated Kshs. 9.6 billion (approx.). A good proportion of the estimated costs, it argued, will be met from the various revenue sources available to the Ministry, while the rest will be sourced from development partners. With effective implementation of the proposed land sector reforms, the revenue collection in the Ministry of Lands will more than double the current annual estimate of Kshs.2.0 billion.[21] According to budgetary allocations for the financial year 2009/10 a total of only 29.5% was allocated for development expenditure, while recurrent expenditure accounted for the rest (62.2%). This does not represent a significant change from the 2005/06 and 2008/09 year.

During this period, the budget for land reform has remained at or below 0.5% of the national budget.[22] At the same time land prices have gone up substantially over the past few years especially in agriculturally productive areas due to speculation, influx of foreign investors (Western, Arabian), and real estate boom. The cost of land has thus gone out of reach for many poor, landless households. If past experience is anything to go by, then land redistribution through the market may cost billions of Kenya shillings; a prospect that a shrinking state fiscal base would not be able to support. Estimates for carrying out such an enormous project are not clear. But the Draft Land Policy projects around Kshs.9 billion. Hence the option of sourcing the shortage from 'development partners' and the establishment of a Land Bank for the implementation of the core principles of redistribution, restitution and resettlement of the landless.

Reinforcing the already narrow fiscal base of the state is the proportion of recurrent expenditure that goes to run the bureaucracy of land administration. This should be taken into account because if land reform acquires the political will it deserves for implementation, substantial outlays will have to be made for post-land reform support infrastructure like extension services, irrigation, social amenities (water, health, education, etc) and marketing. Indeed the success of land reform is hinged on the post–transfer phase which is capable of socially and economically transforming the rural areas. The question is: Is this possible with the current neo-liberal consensus that privileges a shrinking state in place of an expanded role for (usually) foreign private capital?

A detailed study of the governments *Poverty Reduction Strategy Papers* (PRSP), political party manifestos and the *Economic Recovery Strategy for Wealth and Employment Creation* (2003-2007) and *Vision 2030* reveals the silence on the explosive land issues yet it is not clear how land can be overlooked as it is critical to the modernization of agriculture and self-sufficiency in food.[23] For instance an end term review of the Economic Recovery Strategy, 2003-2007 is still proof of the government's commitment to a balanced budget and the reliance on external private capital flows. Furthermore Vision 2030 envisages the same. Government spending is regulated to avoid accumulating unsustainable debt and even seeks to promote public/private partnerships so as to secure external financial resources. Entrepreneurship is also promoted as a way of creating jobs together with infrastructural projects (roads, ICTs, energy) geared toward establishing enabling environments for local and foreign business investments.

The purpose is to mop up the high levels of unemployment. The restructuring currently taking place in the agrarian sector in Kenya is primarily being driven by new global market opportunities. The prelude to this involved the removal of farm subsidies, the collapse of state-run cooperatives and state marketing boards and the dismantling of tariff barriers in order to open up the Kenyan economy to external competition. One of the effects of deregulation and liberalization processes has been a growing re-concentration of land due to collapse of traditional markets for coffee, tea, pyrethrum, etc. and the emergence of new income earning opportunities in the financial markets, high value crops, tourism and real estate and speculation.[24] Deepening inequalities have thus characterized the Kenyan polity. Kenya's top 10% households now control 42% of the total income while the bottom 10% control less than 1%.

The attractiveness of new foreign investments by both Western and Arabian capital for their investment in oil exploration, energy and food crop plantations and port facilities has engendered a hostile reaction from local inhabitants faced with the prospect of evictions by the state. Indeed the potential lucrative opportunities for such markets has also led to a frenzy in land speculation which in turn has pushed land prices up as to make ownership by the average farmer difficult. On the other hand, the large scale commercial farm sector vis-à-vis the small farm sector accounts for a marginal proportion of the total gross marketed production. In the period 2002/2007 the small farms consistently accounted for over 70% of this output representing more than 50% of agricultural GDP against the large farm proportion of less than 4%. Agriculture is still a major source of livelihoods for over 60% of the lower strata of the Kenyan population and employs nearly 70% of the labour force, thereby (by extension) supporting numerous dependents and supplying a large part of the urban and rural countryside with food and raw materials for agro-industrial establishments.[25]

The possibility for an industrialization take off is found in the potential forward and backward linkages in agriculture which would go along way in raising rural incomes. However the implementation of a host of neo-liberal reform programmes since the 1980s has steadily eroded the income generating opportunities of the small farm sector thus leading to the loss of farm sector jobs. Economic growth policies being pushed by government are anchored on the assumption that land reform can be short circuited by the investment in Information Communication Technology (ICT) and the increased capitalization of the large farms sector through encouragement of foreign investment. From PRSPs to Vision 2030 the recurring theme is the need to abide by the macro-economic imperatives of the bilateral and multilateral financial agencies as conditionality for further donor aid. They thus tend to give priority to large farm commercial agriculture reinforced by emerging global market opportunities at the expense of the poor and marginalized.

An entrenched view among the state bureaucracy for the preference of large farms seems to reinforce government policy. In the course of land reform in the 1960/70s, debates revolved around the relative efficiency of large farm versus the small farms. The bilateral and multilateral donors led by the World Bank had argued for the superiority of small holders in terms of overall efficiency and total production which would at the same time avert the prospects for political instability wrought by the militant mobilization of radical nationalists and the Mau Mau. However, the 'higher bureaucracy' has instead seen itself as charged with providing an enabling environment to meet the investment needs of foreign investors. The evidence for this lies in the ideologically driven choice of land for resettlement of the poor landless, where such have been done, and the lack of post-settlement support services which include extension services and social infrastructure. Moreover, the market-led approach ignores the fundamental role that the existing structure of demand has on the viability of small plot holders in the absence of such support. For instance, criteria that have been used to determine the eligibility of applicants were a record of farming, educational level and ability to make a down payment.

Yet the literature has shown that despite the policy bias for large farms, within a few years of settlement it was the large farmers who were experiencing debt obligation problems. In fact, a good number of them were absentee farmers with other sources of income. This meant that large parts of their farms were underutilized. On the other hand small holders have registered increased gross output despite the lack of support and favourable marketing opportunities.

Popular demands for land reform

Land is dear to many Kenyans as shown by the emotion it elicits and the struggles that continue to revolve around its access and ownership. Therefore, calls for land reform are not misplaced given the fact that alternative off-farm employment in the small industrial sector is not able to absorb the growing labour force. Apart from the rural –urban migration, a trend is emerging whereby rural slums are mushrooming due to the lack of job opportunities in the urban centres. A government study shows that on average small holders use 40% of their available crop land for nonagricultural activities, which amount to an annual loss of Kshs. 87 billion. It adds that only 7.25 million acres of agricultural land is exploited out of a total acreage of 144 million acres.[26]

The demand for land has increased through land occupations in urban and rural areas. These include government and private land. In parts of Rift Valley (Trans Nzoia, Nakuru, etc) encroachment on what were large farms have created in their place rural slums without proper access to social infrastructure. The famous encroachment on Mau forest has shown the extent of unregulated settlement and lack of proper land policy with the result that poor peasants have gone ahead to establish homes and engage in agricultural production. In extreme cases land deprivations have engendered militarized groups, such as Mungiki, who are frustrated out of false promises of land by politicians and lack of employment opportunities. In Laikipia, conflicts between pastoralists and agriculturalists revolve around the incompatible land tenure systems which privilege settled farming at the expense of pastoralist livelihood strategies.

The most evident example of the close relationship between land and livelihood opportunities is the persistent ethnic conflicts especially around electoral cycles.[27] These trends have seen the deepening of inequalities between the rich and poor with a consequent change in the structure of households due also to the decline of the cash crop economy. For instance, with the loss of cash crop income by men, women have been forced to assume the role of economic managers by the intensification food crop production, involvement in petty trade while the increased prevalence of HIV and AIDS, malaria and tuberculosis has meant that in their already overburdened domestic chores (cooking, collecting firewood, etc) has been added extra home-based care for the sick household members especially those returning from urban-based wage labour.

The 2007/2008 post-election violence was a violent reminder of the urgency of the land reform in Kenya. Yet there has been no organizational outlet to voice the concerns of a large number of poor Kenyans to force a rethink of the government policies. What organizations such as Kenya Land Alliance (KLA) and Kenya Human Rights Commission (KHRC) have done or limit themselves to concerns about land-based conflicts and their attendant human rights violations or in other cases to electoral and governance related issues within a neo-liberal framework. They have thus articulated their concerns through the language of donor research agendas and have not yet resonated with the demands of the poor majority.

Accumulation from above

Since the agrarian sector has deteriorated steadily with the liberalization of the economy, small holder opportunities have been limited while large capital interests have found new lucrative opportunities offered by globalization. A key organization that has come out to defend the status quo and even rejected the draft land policy is the Kenya Landowners Association, which enjoys privileged access to the highest levels of executive authority. A spokesman of the group revealed to journalists that several ministers have contacted them over some aspects of the proposed land policy. He went on to assert that cabinet ministers were divided over the proposed Land Policy and that a big number of ministers oppose some of the proposals.

In alliance with the Kenya Landowners Association is a group of Western countries whose citizens hold extensive land interests in sections of the Rift Valley, Central, Eastern and Coast provinces.[28] Indeed the Kenya Landowners Association spelt out its views on land policy in a 19-point document, in October 2008, to the Lands Ministry, critiquing a number of recommendations contained in the policy. The recommendations that have drawn the most fire include those that would see thousands of acres of land held under leases in excess of 99 years revert to the State. Formed in 2007, the Association brings together tea farmers, coffee and maize growers, as well as the ranching community. Most of its members are large-scale farmers from the Rift Valley and Central Province.

Though as yet not a clear-cut powerful class known to all, it represents an emerging vocal agrarian class on the land reform agenda. Counterpoised against it is a coalition (Non-State Actors on the Land Sector) of various private and public professionals and Civil Society Organizations (CSOs) calling for the full implementation the Draft Land Policy. The class position of these groups is still not yet clear. However, there seems to be an evolving antagonism on land policy between external Western interests, local middle and upper agrarian middle classes and fractions of the state on the one hand and a middle class situated within the leadership of the CSOs. Among the key concerns the Non-State Actors Association raised were that the policy removes security of tenure for millions of domestic, commercial, agricultural and pastoral land users; limits the rights of registered title holders to deal freely with their land; stifles investment confidence in Kenya; increases the government's powers of compulsory acquisition and removes the constitutional requirement of compensation; and reduces all freeholds and all 999-year leases to 99-year leases or less.

There are also concerns about proposals to terminate group ranches, increase rights of squatters and trespassers, introduce capital gains tax, inheritance tax and land taxation. They are further concerned with what they call a "disproportionate" focus on historical injustices.[29] Its interests therefore seem to be to preserve the existing structure of land ownership, stable land market and the growth of large scale commercial agriculture with the attendant political power that these will entail. The future configuration of these classes is, however, dependent on the response of the landless and poor to increased marginalization and the options the state will evolve in order to avert such an eventuality. Current indifferences to such a looming threat perhaps also explains the procrastination over the Draft Land Policy.

In the event that a competent leadership will gather the popular legitimacy and other resources to institute land reforms, such a leadership is likely to come up against three broad constraints. First, the simultaneous long term decline in both the rural and urban economy and the consequent rise in demand for land all over the country due to migrations into both rural and urban areas by various classes and ethnic groups. Second, state institutional weaknesses, materially and politically, and, third, the contestations between ethnic group and individual rights to land on the one hand and historical claims to territory on the other. A short examination of these factors will illuminate their importance.

Land is still closely related to ethnic identities in Kenya. While this was part of the repertoire of divide and rule policies of colonial administration, no radical attempts were made to overcome it. Instead an expansion of so-called native reserves was undertaken in the context of state-led resettlement efforts.[30] Over time, however, the dynamism of the post-independence economy challenged this by encouraging migrations to various parts of the country predominantly by emerging upper and middles classes with the financial capability to buy and invest in different parts of the country. Exemplary in this regard is the tremendous growth of Eldoret, Uasin Gishu district, as an emerging agro-industrial hub in the North Rift valley. The emergence of land-based conflicts has, however, tended to freeze out-migrations to certain parts of the country.

Hence, while the economy dynamized migrations; the state punished these trends through violent ethnicized evictions in the context of power struggles.[31] This has formed the basis of contestations over the relative merits of ethnic group versus individual rights to land. The former is usually framed in the discourse of 'historical injustices' while the latter is couched in the language of constitutional rights. And the potential of further conflict exists in other parts of the country as the demand for land continues to be driven by both new market opportunities and lack of employment elsewhere.

Secondly, the issue of land administration. Kenya's land administration system is highly centralized and bureaucratic. Its evolution from the colonial period to date has been characterized by the steady dysfuntionality of its structures. This is due both to the complex tenure regimes as a result of imposed law and subsequent political interference by post- colonial elites. And because its control was recognized as a gateway to accumulation of wealth, it has over time developed an entrenched class and ethnic bias which has greatly contributed to the current land reform problems. Any new settlements that have been created are small scale private lands with no impact on landlessness and agricultural productivity generally.

Ultimately, land reform with the potential to resolve conflicts and set the foundation for economic development will lie squarely in the re-organization of state power and its corresponding institutional manifestations. At the core of reform is not just the formulation and implementation of new land laws/ constitutions but also of the re-activation of social movements capable of putting pressure on an entrenched political class whose only motivation for holding state power is the accumulation of private wealth.

Conclusion

The limited performance of post independence resettlement has recently been questioned by statistics showing increasing unemployment and poverty levels, class, generational, gender and intra- and inter-ethnic violence. The failure was due to a combination of class prejudice revolving around the changing configuration of internal and external socio-political forces. Indeed, land tenure reform has been emphasized at the expense of redistribution with post-transfer state support. The presence of a dual agrarian structure, however, points to the unfinished decolonization process. The market-led approach to land reform is costly, slow, fraught with legal injunctions and is largely unsustainable in the light of unequal income and resource access opportunities hence the persistence of exclusion, poverty, and land-based conflicts. The challenge of the state remains to radically reorganize agrarian relations in order to set the basis for economic revitalization and democratic development.

Notes

[1] Ajulu, R,"Thinking through Kenya's Crisis of Democratization in Kenya: A Response to Adar and Murunga", *African Sociological Review*, 4,(2)2002.

[2] See Mamdani, M. *Citizen and Subject: Contemporary Africa and the Legacy of Late Colonialism*. Princeton, N.J.: Princeton University Press, 1996.

[3] Leys, Colin. Underdevelopment in Kenya: The Political Economy of Neo-Colonialism, 1964-1971. Nairobi: Heinemann, 1975.p.199

[4] Ndegwa, Stephen. 1997. "Citizenship and Ethnicity: An Examination of Two Transition Moments in Kenyan Politics." *American Political Science Review* 91 (3): p.4.

[5] Loc.cit.

[6] Leo, C. *Land and Class in Kenya*. Toronto: University of Toronto Press, 1984.

[7] See also Leo, 1978; 1981.

[8] Republic of Kenya, 1965.

[9] Leys,1975.

[10] Ibid, p.84.

[11] District Development Plan, 1989/1993.

[12] District Development Plan, 2002/2008.

[13] Kenya Human Rights Commission. *Killing the Vote: State Sponsored Violence and Flawed Elections in Kenya*. KHRC, 1998.

[14] Republic of Kenya. *Kenya Integrated Household Budget Survey. Basic Report, 2005/2006*. Nairobi: Government Printers.

[15] Republic of Kenya. *Report of the Parliamentary Select Committee to Investigate the Ethnic Clashes in Western and Other Parts of Kenya, 1992*. Nairobi: Government Printers, September, 1992.

[16] Republic of Kenya. 1999.

[17] Republic of Kenya. *Report of the Commission of Inquiry into Post Election Violence*. .Nairobi: Government Printers, October, 2008.

[18] Op.Cit,p.82

[19] See Draft National Land Policy.

[20] Musambayi, K, "A City Under Siege & Modes of Production in Nairobi, 1991-2004", *Review of African Political Economy*, Vol. 32, No. 106, Dec., 2005.

[21] Draft National land Policy, 2005

[22] Budget Financial Estimates, 2009/10.

[23] "Vision 2030 Silent on Land", Business Daily (Nairobi), 11 June 2008.

[24] DPMF Report, forthcoming.

[25] See Statistical Abstract, 2008; Republic of Kenya, 2007.

[26] Republic of Kenya, 2007.

[27] Oyugi, W O, *Politicized Ethnic Conflict in Kenya: A Periodic Phenomenon*. Addis Ababa, 2000, http://unpan1.un.org/intradoc/groups/public/documents/CAFRAD/UNPAN010963.pdf

[28] "How powerful forces have blocked land reforms", Sunday Nation, September 20, 2009.

[29] Francis Ayieko, 'Land barons in high-level lobbying over Kenya's 999-year leases', The East African, Saturday, February 7, 2009.

[30] See Regional Boundaries Commis sion Report, 1962.

[31] See Mamdani, M. *Citizen and Subject: Contemporary Africa and the Legacy of Late Colonialism*. Princeton, N.J.: Princeton University Press, 1996.

References

Daily Nation, various editions.

Harbeson, J.W. (1973). *Nation-Building in Kenya: The Role of Land Reform.* Evanston: Northwestern University Press.

Kenya Human Rights Commission. (1998). *Killing the Vote: State Sponsored Violence and Flawed Elections in Kenya.* KHRC.

Leo, C. (1981). "Who Benefited from the Million-Acre Scheme? Toward a Class Analysis of Kenya's Transition to Independence", *Canadian Journal of African Studies*, Vol. 15, No. 2, pp. 201-222.

Leo, C. (1984). *Land and Class in Kenya.* Toronto: University of Toronto Press.

Leys, C. (1975). *Underdevelopment in Kenya: The Political Economy of Neo-Colonialism, 1964-1971.*Nairobi: Heinemann.

Mamdani, M. (1996). *Citizen and Subject: Contemporary Africa and the Legacy of Late Colonialism.* Princeton, N.J.: Princeton University Press.

Musambayi, K. (2005). "A City under Siege: Banditry and Modes of Production in Nairobi, 1990-2004", *Review of African Political Economy.*

Nakuru District Development Plan, 2002/2008.

Ndegwa, Stephen. 1997. "Citizenship and Ethnicity: An Examination of Two Transition Moments in Kenyan Politics." *American Political Science Review* 91 (3): 1-18.

Oyugi, W.O. (2000). "Politicized Ethnic Conflict in Kenya: A Periodic Phenomenon", Addis Ababa, http://unpan1.un.org/intradoc/groups/public/documents/CAFRAD/UNPAN010963.pdf

Regional Boundaries Commission Report, 1962.

Republic of Kenya, 2007.

Republic of Kenya. (1965). African Socialism and Its Application to Planning in Kenya. Nairobi: Government Printers.

Republic of Kenya. National Land Policy (Sessional Paper No. 3, 2009). Nairobi: Government Printers, 2009.

Uasin Gishu District Development Plan, 1989/1993.

Epilogue — Emerging Issues in Managing the Challenges and Opportunities of Ethnic Diversity in East Africa: Is Good Governance the Destiny?

Ngeta Kabiri

Introduction

The essays in this volume raise pertinent issues on the question of ethnicity in Africa, East Africa and Kenya in particular. They address the question of the challenges and opportunities of ethnic diversity in Eastern Africa, with a view to understanding, supposedly, a malice that afflicts Africa with adverse consequences. The essays cover a wide range of themes, from the nature of ethnicity in Africa, including how it is a socio-political construct, to how it can be harnessed for socio-economic and political development in an attempt to build a harmonious multi-ethnic society. A number of issues emerge that are significant to an understanding of, and formulation of responses to, the question of ethnicity in Africa. There are issues on how to conceptualize ethnicity (including how it is to be investigated), the question of whether ethnicity is a project of the political elites or the elites are merely responding from pressures from below; the conditions under which ethnic tranquility can be secured; the incentive structures that can be put in place to alter the calculus of those who use ethnicity from employing ethnic mobilization as a tool of negotiating for status, power and resource allocation; the extent to which ethnicity can be deployed for positive economic outcomes, and whether the bulk of the above can largely be reduced to a question of governance. Each of the foregoing issues is highlighted below in light of what the chapters in this volume suggest, plus some insights from the wider literature in this field.

On conceptualizing, and problems of investigating, ethnicity in Africa

There seems to be a dominant view that ethnicity is a fluid phenomenon and that it is not always easy to define what it is. Moreover, there is a view that presets ethnicity as something not given (with the meaning that it can be constructed and deconstructed) (Mbatia et al, Munene, in this Volume— henceforth Vol.). Within this frame, there also emerges the point that there is a lot of shared characteristics amidst differences (see, for example, Schipper,

Vol.). The question posed then is that of how the phenomenon of ethnicity can be studied and policy responses proposed if it is as ephemeral as the investigators purport it to be. Of interest from this perspective is the question whether those analyzing what they refer to as ethnic problems are actually referring to the same thing. In other words the question is how we can know ethnicity when we see it. Are we, for example, confronted by the same problem of investigation as when we are dealing with religious problems (where religious interests, beliefs and doctrines are cited as informing the behavior in question)?

In the discussion on ethnicity in Kenya, many analysts and popular opinion refer to the disturbances of the 1990s and more recently, the 2008 upheaval as ethnic. Yet, as some in these papers indicate, there is also an attempt to refuse to read these events as ethnic. Odoyo (Vol.), for example, refers to them as state sponsored violence thereby representing a clear attempt to refuse to call them, unlike many other commentators, ethnic violence. Thus Odoyo suggests a way of conceptualizing ethnicity in a manner that is very similar to that enunciated by Ake (1993:4) who contends that:

> If ethnicity is manufactured at will and manipulated to serve any number of selfish purposes, then it is only an 'object', the case for calling it a cause of the numerous problems regularly attributed to it would not be sustainable. Conflicts arising from the construction of ethnicity to conceal exploitation by building solidarity across class lines, conflicts arising from appeal to ethnic support in the face of vanishing political legitimacy and from the manipulation of ethnicity to divide colonized people, are not ethnic problems but problems of a particular political dynamics which just happens to be pinned on ethnicity.

(see also Keefer (2010) on the possibility of ethnicity effects being a by-product of other functions of the political environment.)

This suggests, therefore, a need to conceptualize what is called the ethnic problem in Africa politically rather than simply in terms of what is visibly observable. To this extent then, some like Ngugi (2009) have suggested a materialistic conception of tribalism that issues only two tribes: the halves and the have-nots. This conceptualization is more resourceful in terms of a policy response to the so-called ethnic problem than the conventional measure of ethnicity based on ethno-linguistic fractionalization (ELF), namely, the possibility that two people picked at random will belong to different ethnic groups. It is nearer to Posner's measure of ethnicity in terms of politically

Relevant Ethnic Groups (PREG) in that it speaks to the idea of (political) competition that groups are involved in (Posner, 2004a).

Is political ethnicity an initiation of the political elites, or are they just responding to pressures from below?

The dominant view both in this volume and in popular opinion is that ethnicity as a problem emanates not from anything intrinsic to ethnicity itself, but rather when manipulated by opportunistic ethnic political elites to further their insecure political careers (Vol.: Aseka, Attafuah, Vuningoma and Odoyo; Posner, 2004b). The theme of manipulation may be a fruitful way of looking at the ethnicity problem because it can show that what is at stake is nothing essentially ethnic, but the interests of the rational political elites. As Vuningoma demonstrates, the elites look for differences that they can capitalize on so that ethnicity just happens to be one such readily available difference. Once the diversity provided by ethnicity is no longer an available resource, the elites look for another diversity such as geographical one as was the case with Kayibanda who after manipulating inter-ethnic differences provided by Hutu and Tutsi, turned to intra-ethnic diversity provided by the North-South Hutu divide.

This view of elite manipulation of their ethnic rank and file can, however, be problematic. It raises basic questions about the image of ethnic masses that the view of manipulation intends to portray. Increasingly, some commentators are beginning to ask whether it could be the case that ethnics give politicians an incentive to behave in the ethno-centric ways that they do[1]. In Kenya, the demise of politicians who fail to align themselves with the dominant party of their region, which in most cases is assumed to be the guarantor of ethnic interests at the national level, could be cited to be representative of what Rawlinson (2003) has called the pressure from below by politicians' ethnic base or client networks that compels leaders to abandon cooperative strategies at the national level[2]. In such cases then, it would be erroneous to model the ethnics as just subject to manipulation by political leaders. Obbo-Onyango (2008) has rightly problematized this situation thus,

> Is it that the masses are really so dumb, they join protests and get killed in civil wars because they are blindly following some opportunistic politician and have nothing to gain from it? Is it true that the people are "pure" souls, who are misled by their cynical leaders?

Obbo-Onyango's contention is that the ethnics make rational calculations when they support politicians' ethnic appeals, thereby concurring with Fanon that the people can make their own calculations and, therefore, we should not assume that they are just frog-marched around. Fanon contends that

> It is true that if care is taken to use only a language that is understood by graduates in law and economics, you can easily prove that the masses have to be managed from above. But if you speak the language of everyday, if you are not obsessed by the perverse desire to spread confusion and to rid yourself of the people, then you will realize that the masses are quick to seize every shade of meaning and to learn all the tricks of the trade (Fanon, 1963: 188-89).

The question of political ethnicity being a result of manipulation by ethnic elites should not be stated with abandon, and may even be disqualified altogether for, as Mutua (2010) has rightly stated, "You can only be captive to ethnic demagogues if you allow them." If we depart from a manipulation perspective of ethnicity, it is, therefore, imperative that in dissecting the ethnic question in Africa's development, attention be paid to how the incentive structures in place bear on the intersection of the interests of both the leaders and the rank and file.

Under what conditions does ethnic tranquility/cooperation obtain?

For the political elites, political competition is central. The problem in Africa is that this competition ends up being conflictual, yet this does not have to be the case. The reason why this conflictual outcome obtains, we suggest, is because political competition is constructed as a zero-sum game (as has been the case, for example, in Kenya and post-Boigny's Côte d'Ivoire, among others). The question then is: why this kind of zero-sum construction? The answer has to do with the distributional regime of state largesse that is in place. It is, therefore, a question of governance. Thus, we can now dispute at least two variables associated with the negation of ethnic tranquility, namely culture (and especially the question of a common language) and the media.

The question of language remains contentious for as we have seen in these chapters, it is credited with the ethnic tranquility that obtains in Tanzania (Huruma, Vol.). At the same time, however, other policies in similar situations have not benefited much from having a lingua franca (as is the case of Rwanda (Vuningoma, Vol.) and Somalia. Thus a question can, therefore, be raised as to whether even though Kenya is not as advanced in the use of Kiswahili as

Tanzania, can it be said that there is really a lingua franca deficit serious enough to account for Kenya's ethnic problem? This issue language and its import on ethnic tranquility is even more problematic when juxtaposed with the role of media, especially in the context of vernacular radio. Though some commentators claim that the use of diverse indigenous languages can unite a country or divide a country along ethnic lines (Standard 1, 2010), it is the latter view that seems to dominate popular opinion. Both Vuningoma and Linda (Vol.) point to the potential dangers and raise the question of whether there is a tension between national and vernacular media (Linda, Vol.). Linda (Vol.) nevertheless tends to subscribe to the view that local media can be used as an engine for local development (and thus shares Ake's (1993), contention that ethnicity has been used to spur rural development(see also MuneneVol.)). The key issue here then seems to be that of how to negotiate the intersection of the local and the national. In this regard, how the question of language and media is handled is thus central.[3]

The key question on language and media as agents of socialization then is that since the national broadcast should be expected to inculcate a national ideal, is this to be understood as being in contradistinction to local ideals? In other words, to what extent can focus on the national taste be simultaneous with, rather than at the expense of, the local or regional preference leading to what Munene and Mbatia et al (Vol.) call being Kenyan and Borana, at the same time? Consider, for example, the criticism of a related aspect of this local-national divide. There are some observers who contend that because Kenya's educational curricula does not begin to teach Kenya as a nation until grade 5, the focus on provincial geography and history in grades 1-4 probably serves to exacerbate regional and ethnic divisions, especially among those who drop out before grade 5 (when Kenya as a nation starts to be taught). In this case, it is argued, Kenya unlike Tanzania has, therefore, not been able to forge a national linguistic and ideological identity (Miguel, 2004:336). Others would, however, contend that this need not be a problem if Kenya's institutional architecture was designed to discourage divisive regional identities.

An institutional argument can also be advanced as a variable impacting on ethnic tranquility. It can be claimed that ethnic relations, in part, depend on expectations of what will happen in the event of infractions in inter-ethnic relations. Where states are able to police these relations, then conflicts are largely contained (Fearon and Laitin, 1996: 730-1), but where the state is either weak (Mbatia et. al. Vol.) or complicit, then maintaining inter-ethnic cooperation is likely to be compromised. The configuration of the state can also aid in maintaining ethnic tranquility if the public service dynamics are structured to be professional/competent and representative of the face of the polity (see, for example, Caroll and Caroll, 2000). This means that where the state impresses on society that its policy is premised on pursuit of careers open to talent, then individuals are more likely to be state-centric other than ethno-centric (Vuningoma, Vol., with respect to pre-colonial Rwanda). In the event of a contrary socialization, separatist tendencies, as Fanon observed, ensue. Fanon cautioned that

> ...This tribalizing of the central authority, it is certain, encourages regionalist ideas and separatism. All the decentralizing tendencies spring up again and triumph, and the nation falls to pieces, broken in bits. The leader, ...wakes up one day to find himself saddled with five tribes, who also want to have their own ambassadors and ministers; ... (Fanon, 1963: 183-84).

What this implies is that political leadership, as Aseka (Vol.) argues, is critical for effective management of ethnic diversity and hence, ethnic tranquility. In light of the argument on manipulation, political leadership is then a double-edged sword. Logically, if tribalism is an artificial construct, it can also be contained through responsible conduct by political elites (Rawlinson, 2003). Mboya, for example, contends that some

> ...people refuse to accept the challenge of tribalism and, instead of fighting it, have given in and are actually promoting it. ...Kanu concedes that tribal feelings exist but says they can be eliminated by wise leadership and positive action; Kadu is exaggerating these feelings to entrench tribalism... (Nation, 2010).

Mboya's contention was proved right by the careers of, among others, Nyerere, on one hand, and Moi and Mobutu on the other. In Cote de Voire, Boigny's rule (1960-93) was one of ethnic balancing acts that saw a reign of ethnic tranquility but which, thereafter, imploded when his successor departed from this tradition. In Kenya, unlike Tanzania, for example, commentators see Kenyatta and Moi as having played ethnic groups against each other to avoid the emergence of a group identity that could present a broad-based opposition (Collier, 2009; Rawlinson, 2003). The question of how to deal with the situation of those leaders whose orientation breeds ethnic conflicts has been raised, including in this volume, but the answers have been given in terms of a catalogue of what is desirable, other than how it can be produced, which is actually the key issue.

What incentive structures can alter the calculus of political leaders or pressures from below from employing ethnic mobilization as a tool of negotiating for status, power and resource allocation?

As argued above, a clear conceptualization of ethnicity is central to specifying the solution(s) on how to combat it. Thus the antidote should be pegged to what is diagnosed as the cause of ethnic problem (see, for example, Habyariamana et al, 2008). The incentive structures that can be specified if operating on ethnicity as product of manipulation are different from those of an approach that conceives ethnicity as (partly) fed by pressures from below.

a) On manipulation:

If, as Odoyo, Munene, and Attafuah (Vol.) argued, this aspect of ethnicity is fed by coupling of property rights with wielding of political power, then enforcement strategies governing the distributional regime should be addressed. Although some, even in this volume, have called for reforms in land and access to resources, for example, it is questionable whether the real problem lay here. It can be argued that even if the institutions in place are not perfect, they are not so weak as to explain the conflictual outcome characterizing access to land and other resources that has been the face of the ethnic conflict in countries like Kenya. The problem is largely at the level of political will to enforce the property rights in place. This is the aspect to address, not more specification of rights, which if still not enforced would not impact on the situation in any different way as it is now. How then, is political will to be generated to counter the extant political to appropriate ethnic diversity for nefarious purposes?

b) On pressures from below:

To a large extent, solutions to the problem of ethnic tension have been proffered in terms of what can be done to constrain political actors since they have been assumed to be the problem. A conceptualization of the ethnic problem that sees it in terms of pressures from below would imply different sets of strategies to combat it. The incentive structures should be such that those exacting pressures from below will not see the need for ethnic networks to navigate the Byzantine system or market place (Habyariamana et al, 2008) in their access to resources distributed by the state. For quite some time, the popular opinion has been that people benefit from state largesse depending on their political clout at the center, leading to what Chege (Vol.) alluded to as "our time to eat". Such a mind set was not without foundation. Barkan and Chege (1989), for example, showed that the budgetary allocation to roads in Kenya during the eras of both Kenyatta and Moi was heavily skewed in favor of the President's homeland.[4] Within such a context, ethnicity obviously becomes a currency for transacting business with the state.

Without credible institutions to inspire confidence that ethnicity is not a tool of accessing state benefits, then it would be difficult for political actors to ignore pressures to behave in the interests of their groups as opposed to the national interest (unless the same is compatible with the local interests). A number of contributors to this volume (for example, Aseka, Chege and Munene) points to the need for such institutions. The question that arises here, however, is that of why these credible institutions are absent. These institutions are not absent because their versatility in governance is disputed; to the contrary, they are absent by design. As Fanon argued,

> The people of Africa have ...decided, in the name of the whole continent, to weigh in strongly against the colonial regime. Now the nationalist bourgeoisies, who ... hasten to make their own fortunes and to set up a national system of exploitation, do their utmost to put obstacles in the path of this "Utopia." The national bourgeoisies, who are quite clear as to what their objectives are, have decided to bar the way to that unity, to that coordinated effort ... to triumph over stupidity, hunger, and inhumanity at one and the same time. ... African unity can only be achieved through the upward thrust of the people, and under the leadership of the people, that is to say, in defiance of the interests of the bourgeoisie (Fanon, 1963: 164).

The question of practice is how to generate this defiance so that the pressures from below will be for a trans-ethnic unity rather than ethnic solidarity as a weapon of competition with other groups. This question has not been addressed concretely. The furthest we have gone is exhort nationalism, even as imbalanced access to the state stare the people starkly to their faces. Such exhortations remain empty if the reality experienced by the people tells a different story. In this case, what Nnyago (2008), following Fanon (Fanon, 1963: 169)[5] has stated is instructive,

> In Uganda, when only graduates for a particular tribal group get jobs faster than the rest of the others with similar qualification, can lectures on "nationalism" prevent the simmering tensions? Only justice and equity can ensure a peaceful political future.

Thus it is more productive to invest in institutions and civic networks that ease access to justice for the citizens, and expose and hold to account within the existing infrastructures malpractices that make it difficult for people to honor the state. Such investments will provide an alternative focal point to the ethnic group and lead to the emergence of a broad based coalition that will undermine the salience of negative ethnic political solidarity.

If ethnicity has had negative political outcomes, how can it be harnessed into a resource for economic development?

What is self-evident in Africa is that ethnicity has been harnessed into a political resource by the political class. The question now is whether the same can be reproduced at the economic level.

So far, the dominant claim has been that ethnicity is a bane to Africa's economic growth (Easterly and Levine, 1997; Posner, 2004a; Miguel and Gugerty, 2005). In Kenya, for example, Miguel and Gugerty (2005) contend that ethnicity has had negative impact in the provision of public goods because of the difficulties it presents to imposing social sanctions across ethnic groups. (Social sanctions are considered vital for overcoming collective action problems, a prerequisite to provision of a public good under certain circumstances.)

On the other hand, some commentators, including political actors, postulate that ethnic diversity can be turned into an advantage for the common good (see, for example, Standard 2). Contributors to this volume address this issue. While Mbatia et al, claim ethnic diversity can be a resource for economic development, it is unclear how this can be so since they only outline prerequisites for such an outcome. Both Mboya and Kimonye, however, make the case that ethnic diversity is a valuable economic resource that can be exploited in more ways than it has so far been done. Nevertheless, the actual mechanics of how this can be effected need further attention, perhaps along the lines Mboya has suggested. How to convert the ethnic diversity variable into an economic asset is the issue here; it is a question of how an investment plan to make ethnic diversity an economic resource would look like. Moving along such a path would actually signal to development agencies as to what they may focus on so that their investments win in economic as well as socio-political fronts. If ethnic diversity can be shown to be a motor for economic development, that can provide a counter-narrative to the dominant one that portray ethnicity as a hinderance to Africa's economic growth.

Conclusion: On the need to invest in institutions of governance

The issues emerging from these papers on both the challenges and opportunities of ethnic diversity converge in underscoring the impact of governance in determining how ethnic diversity plays out in practice. The papers have demonstrated that there is nothing intrinsically conflictual about ethnic diversity. When conflicts do arise, mundane factors rather than primordial instincts, have causal significance. This means that the way ordinary facts of life are ordered is a central determinant of whether conflict or opportunities ensue from ethnic diversity. Contemporary experience tells us that this organization of mundane facts of life is largely what accounts for the variations in outcome between Rwanda and Somalia on one hand and Tanzania on the other, contrary to what received opinion about the dynamics of ethnic diversity would have us believe. The policy question then as to what to do with the tribe has to be answered not in terms of killing it as Mutua (2009)[6], following Samora Machel, contends, but rather in managing it as called for by Chege, Aseka, Attafuah, and Munene (Vol). Managing the tribe (ethnic diversity) implies undermining the appeal to ethnicity. This raises the question of how it is to be done.

Two variables of critical importance here are equity in resource distribution and the rule of law that operationalize the former into reality. Most of the contributors (for example, Chege, Munene, Attafuah, Vuningoma) who touched on this aspect suggested that the impetus to tensions is fed by a (perceived) sense of inequitable distribution of resources and fear of marginalization from power (see also, Rawlinson, 2003). As argued above, while provisions for equity in resource distribution are not wanting, the fact that some feel that even these provisions are honored more in breach is uppermost. Reversing this perception, therefore, would deprive ethnic political entrepreneurs of the lexicon they need to craft programs with an ethnic accent. As stated above, however, the question of instituting a credible rule of law is itself beset with the problem of extant vested interests. Kenya's recent experience has shown that the production of state institutions that are forwarded as capable of solving the ethnic problem is itself trapped in the ethnic interests these institutions are supposed to dissolve. Thus there is a cause-effect relationship here: ethnic interests generate an institutional environment that feed ethnic consciousness, and this consciousness in turn constrains the adoption of different institutions with a national ambience. The question then is how to break up the incentive structure of political ethnicity that society is already trapped in. It is a situation analogous to that confronting Plato (Plato, 380 B.C/ 1992) on how to mold a just city within the context of an environment that is already polluted.

Future attention on the question of ethnic diversity demands that inquiries be directed into making specific action plans on empirical issues such as those identified above. This is the imperative if we are to start addressing, rather than expressing wishful thinking on, the question of challenges and opportunities of ethnic diversity.

Notes

[1] Muller has rightly pointed out to Achebe's character in "No Longer At Ease" as a good example of how pressure from below can force otherwise nationally-minded actors to behave in parochial ways (see Habyariamana et al, 2008).

[2] No implication is intended here that such leaders necessarily represent a national mindset among politicians; they could themselves be using such cooperative strategies at the national level for their own self-advancement while cutting a figure of national outlook.

[3] In Tanzania, I have heard local development entrepreneurs I have worked with insist that during public gatherings, the language of communication has to be Kiswahili, irrespective of the linguistic homogeneity of the group; the content of the local language is limited to about 30%. Indeed, only this year (2010) is the Electoral Commission considering allowing candidates to use local languages while campaigning in rural areas.

[4] And then during Moi's era, the notion of security homeboys assumed dominance in common discussion. In another well publicized incidence in the 1980s, a Minister in charge of Teacher Training Colleges recruited a disproportionate number of admissions from his homeland; when there was an outcry, he countered that he just did what everybody else was doing (i.e. the mentality of a goat eats where it is tethered (see, for example, Bayart, 1993; and also Lindberg, 2003 on neopatrimonial tendencies).

[5] Fanon argued that lectures on nationalism are irrelevant if executed under conditions of poverty,

> The peasant who goes on scratching out a living from the soil, and the unemployed man who never finds employment do not manage, in spite of public holidays and flags, new and brightly colored though they may be, to convince themselves that anything has really changed in their lives (Fanon, 1963: 169).

[6] "We will not reform the country out of this mess unless we build it into a nation. *We must kill the tribe* (emphasis added). This is our path to the Promised Land."(Mutua, 2009); Mbatia et al (Vol.) seems to point to a similar approach.

References

Ake, C. (1993). What is the Problem of Ethnicity in Africa? In Transformation, 22.

Barkan, Joel D., and Chege, Michael, 1989. "Decentralising the state: district focus and the politics of reallocation in Kenya." *Journal of Modern African Studies* 27 (3), 431– 453.

Bayart, J.F. (1993). *The State in Africa: The Politics of the Belly.* London: Longman.

Carroll, B. Wake & Terrance Carroll. (2000). "Accommodating ethnic diversity in a modernizing democratic state: theory and practice in the case of Mauritius", *Ethnic and Racial Studies*, Vol. 23: 1, pp.120 – 142.

Collier, P. (2009). "The political economy of state failure", *Oxford Review of Economic Policy*, Volume 25, Number 2, pp. 219–240.

Easterly, W. and Ross Levine. (1997). "Africa's Growth Tragedy: Policies and Ethnic Divisions", in *The Quarterly Journal of Economics*, Vol. 112, No. 4, pp. 1203-1250.

Fearon, James D. & David D. Laitin. (1996). "Explaining Interethnic Cooperation", in *The American Political Science Review*, Vol. 90, No. 4, pp. 715-735.

Fanon, F. (1963). *The Wretched of the Earth.* New York: Grove Weidenfeld.

Habyariamana, Js, Macartan Humphreys, Daniel Posner, & Jeremy Weinstein. (2008). "Better Institutions, Not Partition", *Foreign Affairs*, July/August.

Keefer, P. (2010). "The Ethnicity Distraction? Political Credibility and Partisan Preferences in Africa", The World Bank, Development Research Group, Macroeconomics and Growth Team, March 2010: Policy Research Working Paper 5236.

Lindberg, Staffan I. (2003). "It's Our Time to 'Chop': Does Elections in Africa Feed Neopatrimonialism Rather Than Counter-Act It?" *Democratization* 10:2 (April 2003): 121-40.

Miguel, E. (2004). "Tribe Or Nation? Nation Building and Public Goods in Kenya versus Tanzania", in *World Politics* 56, 327–62.

Miguel, E. & Mary Kay Gugerty. (2005). "Ethnic diversity, social sanctions, and public goods in Kenya" in *Journal of Public Economics*, vol. 89, 2325–2368.

Mutua, M. (2009). "Why reforms have failed in Kenya" in *The Nation*, December, 29th. Nairobi: The Nation Group of Newspapers.

Mutua, M. (2010). "An open letter to the Kalenjin Nation", in *The Sunday Nation*, June 13th. Nairobi: The Nation Group of Newspapers.

Nation. (2010). "Unmasking Moi, the 'No' man of Kenya's politics", in *The Nation*, May 23rd Nairobi: The Nation Group of Newspapers.

Ngugi, wa Thiong'o. (2009). "The Myth of Tribe in African Politics", in Transition, December.

Nnyago, Omar Kalinge. (2008). "Africa's Problem Is Not Tribalism but Injustice and Inequality," *Monitor*, January, 25th, pp.1-2.

Obbo-Onyango, C. (2008). "Tribe and politics: Who is the joker in the pack?" *Monitor*, January, 16th.

Posner, Daniel N. (2004a). "Measuring Ethnic Fractionalization in Africa." *American Journal of Political Science*, Vol. 48 (October).

Posner, Daniel N. (2004b). "The Political Salience of Cultural Difference: Why Chewas and Tumbukas Are Allies in Zambia and Adversaries in Malawi", in *The American Political Science Review*, Vol. 98, No. 4 pp. 529-545.

Plato. 380 B.C/ 1992. *The Republic*. (Translated by G.M.A. Grube, 2nd Ed., revised by C.D.C Reeve) Indianapolis: Hackett Publishing Co.

Rawlinson, A. (2003). " The political manipulation of ethnicity in Africa", in www.insolens.org

Standard 1. (2010). "Vernacular broadcasts can foster unity, Chisano tells forum" in *The Standard*, March, 20th. Nairobi: The East African Standard Newspapers.

Standard 2. (2010). "Help end tribal tension, Kibaki and Raila ask elders" in *The Standard*, April 20th. Nairobi: The East African Standard Newspapers.

Notes on Contributors

Eric Aseka is a professor of political history in Department of History and Political Studies at Kenyatta University. / *Fr. Joseph Healey* is an American Maryknoll missionary priest who has lived in East Africa since 1968 and is presently based in Nairobi. / *Huruma L. Sigalla* teaches at the Department of Sociology and Anthropology, University of Dar es Salaam. / *James Vuningoma* is a Vice-Rector Academic, Kigali Institute of Education. / *Joy Mboya* is the Executive Director of The Performing & Visual Arts Centre Ltd, The Godown Arts Centre. / *Kabiri Ngeta* is a political scientist currently undertaking research on environment in Arusha, Tanzania. / *Karega Munene* is a professor of anthropology and history at the School of Arts and Sciences, United States International University, Nairobi. / *Ken Attafuah* teaches Governance and Leadership in the Graduate School of Public Management at the Ghana Institute of Management and Public Administration (GIMPA). He is also the Executive Director of the Justice & Human Rights Institute in Ghana. / *Kennedy Bikuri* is a sociologist and researches on conflict, land and ethnicity. / *Kimani Njogu* is a Director, Twaweza Communications and CEO, Africa Health and Development International (AHADI). / *Mary Kimonye* is a researcher in marketing and strategy development. She is the CEO of Brand Kenya Board. / *Michael Chege* is an Advisor to the Government of Kenya on International Development Partnerships. / *Mineke Schipper* is a professor of Intercultural Literary Studies at the University of Leiden in The Netherlands and attached to the Leiden Institute of Area Studies (LIAS). / *Nassanga Goretti Linda* is a Senior Lecturer/Coordinator Masters Programme and is in charge of Research & Publications at the Mass Communication Department, Makerere University. / *Nicholas Odoyo* is a researcher with the Development Policy Management Forum (DPMF). / *Paul Mbatia* is a Senior Lecturer and Chairman of the Department of Sociology & Social Work, University of Nairobi. / *Peter Nderitu* works with civil society and undertakes research on civic education and ethnicity.

www.ingramcontent.com/pod-product-compliance
Lightning Source LLC
Chambersburg PA
CBHW072102020426
42334CB00017B/1597